HORN BOOK REFLECTIONS

On children's books and reading

SELECTED FROM EIGHTEEN YEARS OF
THE HORN BOOK MAGAZINE — 1949-1966

EDITED BY
ELINOR WHITNEY FIELD

THE HORN BOOK • BOSTON

Copyright © 1969 by The Horn Book, Inc., Boston
Second printing 1971
Great Britain: B. F. Stevens & Brown, Ltd., Godalming
Printed in the United States of America

All rights reserved. No part of this book
may be reproduced in any form without
permission in writing from the publisher.

Library of Congress Catalog Card Number: 75-89793

To the Editors of The Horn Book

BERTHA E. MAHONY MILLER	1924-1951
JENNIE D. LINDQUIST	1951-1958
RUTH HILL VIGUERS	1958-1967
PAUL HEINS	1967-

PREFACE

A Horn Book Sampler, on Children's Books and Reading was edited by Norma R. Fryatt in 1959. The articles contained in it were selected from the first twenty-five years of *The Horn Book Magazine,* from 1924 through 1948. This collection continues from 1949 through 1966. The contributors are writers, illustrators, librarians, teachers, and parents, all deeply concerned about children and their books. They are aware of the importance that books can have in the development of the child, not only in widening his knowledge of the world around him but also in giving him an understanding of the essential values in human relationship and a consciousness of the deeper meaning of life. Their thoughts and experiences are valuable in supporting the belief that children's literature has a definite place in cultural life. If they were asked, "Do you believe in children's literature?" like the children in *Peter Pan* when asked if they believed in fairies, they would clap their hands.

The Horn Book Magazine over the years has pursued the search for the best in children's reading in varied fields and it has not become so involved with any educational objective that it has not kept in mind that a love of books in itself brings a great enrichment of life. Unfortunately the production of books for young people has increased to such an extent that many a fine book has been pushed off the publishers' lists by the onrush of much less worthy books. Mediocrity is fast overshadowing the whole field. Consequently it becomes more and more important that such articles as these be gathered together to stimulate discussion, encourage new concepts, and to remind everyone constantly of those great books of the past that form a child's literary heritage.

In the magazine the department called "The Hunt Breakfast" furnishes material of interest about the contributors which gives the reader assurance of his or her qualification and reliability. At the back of this book there is a similar section entitled "Notes and Comments".

Thanks are due to the contributors for their permission to reprint their articles. It is hoped that this book will give pleasure and enlightenment to all who are truly interested in children's books and have, or wish to acquire, a depth of understanding and appreciation. E. W. F.

INTRODUCTION

In 1949 *The Horn Book Magazine* celebrated its 25th anniversary. The September-October number of that year was the anniversary number and led off with a fine editorial by Lillian H. Smith, then Director of Work with Boys and Girls at the Toronto Public Library. She wrote:

> There is perhaps no more immediate help for a book's chance to survive than early recognition of its quality in the critical press. Here, it seems, is the great contribution of *The Horn Book*. Through a quarter of a century it has steadfastly adhered to the principle that fine writing for children is part of all literature and must be judged by the same standards: that children's books are not merely a simpler treatment of adult themes any more than that boys and girls are only diminutive adults.

Now *The Horn Book* has reached its forty-fourth year of publication and has held to that same principle. The first editor was Bertha E. Mahony, the originator of the magazine. She continued as editor until 1951 and had the vision and enthusiasm that made the magazine live and thrive. She brought to its pages contributions from the most enlightened and important critics and writers of children's books. A glance at *A Horn Book Sampler*, which brought together articles of those early years, will show that many wise and well-informed people helped to make the magazine authoritative and interesting — Anne Carroll Moore, Alice M. Jordan, Louise Seaman Bechtel, Frances Clarke Sayers, Anne Parrish, Robert Lawson, Ruth Sawyer, and Armstrong Sperry, to mention a few.

The later editors, Jennie D. Lindquist and Ruth Hill Viguers, have brought to the magazine further importance. Both had previously had wide experience in library work and in conducting classes in children's literature; furthermore they had excellent judgment and creative ability. This book has drawn articles from the magazine mostly during the years of their guidance, and shows the recognition of quality and the sincerity with which these editors have striven to keep up the standard set by the first editor and to extend the magazine's influence.

May *The Horn Book* long continue to carry on its good work!

April, 1968   E. W. F.

ACKNOWLEDGEMENTS

are made to the following publishers and authors for their kind permission to quote copyrighted material:

ALDUS BOOKS LIMITED for a short quotation from *Children's Illustrated Books* by Janet Adam Smith. Collis, London, 1948.

AMERICAN LIBRARY ASSOCIATION for a quotation from *The Unreluctant Years* by Lillian Smith. Copyright 1953 by American Library Association.

BASIC BOOKS, INC. for a quotation from "The Experience of Poetry in a Scientific Age" by May Swenson in *Poets on Poetry* by Howard Nemerov. Copyright © 1966 by Howard Nemerov. Basic Books, Inc., Publishers, New York.

THOMAS Y. CROWELL COMPANY for a short quotation from *... And Now Miguel* by Joseph Krumgold. Copyright 1953 by Thomas Y. Crowell Company.

THE DIAL PRESS, INC. for two short quotations from *George MacDonald and His Wife* by Greville MacDonald, one from G. K. Chesterton's Introduction to the book, and the other from a footnote to Chapter Seven in the same book.

DODD, MEAD & COMPANY for a quotation from "The Pobble Who Has No Toes" from *Complete Nonsense Book* by Edward Lear.

E. P. DUTTON & CO., INC. for a quotation from *The Dialogues of Archibald MacLeish and Mark Van Doren* edited by Warren V. Bush. Copyright © 1964 by Columbia Broadcasting System, Inc. Also for an excerpt from "Spring Morning" from *When We Were Very Young* by A. A. Milne. Copyright 1924 by E. P. Dutton & Co., Inc. Renewal 1952 by A. A. Milne. Permission also granted by METHUEN & COMPANY, LTD. and CURTIS BROWN, LTD.

NORMA MILLAY ELLIS for an excerpt from "Afternoon on a Hill" from *Collected Poems* by Edna St. Vincent Millay. Copyright 1917, 1945 by Edna St. Vincent Millay. Published by Harper & Row, Publishers.

HARCOURT, BRACE & WORLD, INC. for a quotation from *Surprised by Joy* by C. S. Lewis. Copyright © 1956 by Harcourt, Brace and World, Inc. And for a quotation of three lines from "For You" by Carl Sandburg in *Smoke and Steel*. Copyright 1920 by Harcourt, Brace and World, Inc., renewed 1948 by Carl Sandburg.

HARPER AND ROW, PUBLISHERS for a quotation from *Bronzeville Boys and Girls* by Gwendolyn Brooks. Copyright © 1956 by Gwendolyn Brooks Blakely.

HOLT, RINEHART AND WINSTON, INC. for three lines from "The Pasture" by Robert Frost from *Complete Poems of Robert Frost*. Copyright 1939, © 1967 by Holt, Rinehart and Winston, Inc.

HOUGHTON MIFFLIN COMPANY for brief excerpts from *Johnny Tremain* by Esther Forbes. Copyright 1943 by Esther Forbes Hoskins.

J. B. LIPPINCOTT COMPANY for five lines from "Poetry" from *Poems for Children* by Eleanor Farjeon. Copyright 1938 by Eleanor Farjeon, Copyright © renewed 1966 by Gervase Farjeon. Published in the United States by J. B. Lippincott Company. Permission also granted by DAVID HIGHAM ASSOCIATES, LTD. for use of the same five lines from their book, *The Children's Bells* by Eleanor Farjeon.

THE LITERARY TRUSTEES OF WALTER DE LA MARE and their representative, THE SOCIETY OF AUTHORS, for four lines from "The Hawthorn Hath a Deathly Smell" by Walter de la Mare in *Collected Poems 1901-1918*. Copyright 1920 by Henry Holt and Company. Copyright 1948 by Walter de la Mare.

LONGMANS GREEN & CO., LTD. for lines from *The Chilswell Book of English Poetry* by Robert Bridges.

THE MACMILLAN COMPANY for lines from "The Little Rose" from *Poems* by Rachel Field. Copyright 1924, 1930 by The Macmillan Company; also for "The Little Turtle" from *Collected Poems* by Vachel Lindsay. Copyright 1920 by The Macmillan Company, renewed 1948 by Elizabeth Lindsay; and for lines from "The Cat and the Moon" from *Collected Poems* by William Butler Yeats. Copyright 1919 by The Macmillan Company, renewed 1946 by Bertha Georgie Yeats. Permission for the latter also granted by M. B. YEATS and A. P. WATTS & SON, LTD.

NATIONAL GALLERY OF ART for a quotation from *Curiosités Esthétiques* by Charles Baudelaire translated in *Masterpieces of Painting from the National Gallery of Art* edited by Huntington Cairns and John Walker.

NEW DIRECTIONS PUBLISHING CORPORATION for "Flowers by the Sea" from *Collected Earlier Poems* by William Carlos Williams. Copyright 1938 by William Carlos Williams.

OXFORD UNIVERSITY PRESS for a quotation from *The Uses of the Past* by Herbert J. Muller. Copyright 1952 by Oxford University Press.

A. D. PETERS & CO. for a short extract from *One Thing and Another* by Hilaire Belloc. Copyright 1955 by Hollis & Carter, Ltd.

RANDOM HOUSE, INC. for lines from "The Unknown Citizen" from *Collected Shorter Poems of W. H. Auden*. Copyright 1940, renewed © 1968 by W. H. Auden.

FRANCES CLARKE SAYERS for a quotation from "The Books of Eleanor Estes," *The Horn Book Magazine*, August 1952.

SCOTT, FORESMAN AND COMPANY for a quotation from "Godfrey Gordon Gustavus Gore" by William Rand from *Time for Poetry* by May Hill Arbuthnot. Copyright 1951 by Scott, Foresman and Company.

CHARLES SCRIBNER'S SONS for several quotations from *Theodore Roosevelt's Letters to His Children* by Joseph Bucklin Bishop. Copyright 1919 by Charles Scribner's Sons.

And for short quotations from *Otto of the Silver Hand*, revised edition, by Howard Pyle. Copyright 1954 by Charles Scribner's Sons. And finally for the preface to "Illustrating The Wind in the Willows" by Ernest Shepard from the Willow Leaf Edition of *The Wind in the Willows* by Kenneth Grahame. Copyright 1954 by Charles Scribner's Sons.

UNIVERSITY OF CHICAGO PRESS for a quotation from *Boardman Robinson* by Albert Christ-Janer. Copyright 1946 by the University of Chicago.

HENRY Z. WALCK, INC. for two brief quotations from *The Eagle of the Ninth* by Rosemary Sutcliff. Copyright 1954 by Rosemary Sutcliff; a quotation from *The Shield Ring* by Rosemary Sutcliff. Copyright © 1957 by Rosemary Sutcliff; and a quotation from *Warrior Scarlet* by Rosemary Sutcliff. Copyright © 1958 by Rosemary Sutcliff. Permission to reprint also granted by OXFORD UNIVERSITY PRESS.

EUDORA WELTY for a quotation from *Place in Fiction*, a condensation of lectures for the Conference on American Studies, Cambridge, England, 1954. Published by House of Books, Ltd. Copyright © 1957 by Eudora Welty.

WESLEYAN UNIVERSITY PRESS for a quotation from *The Orb Weaver* by Robert Francis. Copyright 1948 by Robert Francis.

ANN WOLFE for "The Grey Squirrel" from *Kensington Gardens* by Humbert Wolfe. Published by Ernest Benn Limited.

THE WORLD PUBLISHING COMPANY for a quotation from *Caxton's Challenge* by Cynthia Harnett. Copyright © 1960 by World Publishing Company.

TABLE OF CONTENTS

PART		PAGE
	Preface	v
	Introduction	vii
	Acknowledgements	ix

I. INSPIRATION — HOW IT COMES

Yeast in the Mind	*Mabel Leigh Hunt*	3
Upon Writing for Children	*Elizabeth Coatsworth*	6
On Words, Singleness of Mind, and the Genius Loci	*Margot Benary-Isbert*	14
Gathering Honey	*Eleanor Estes*	23
Roots	*Marjorie Medary*	31
Where Did You Get *That* Idea?	*Elisabeth Hamilton Friermood*	38

II. GOALS AND GUIDELINES FOR WRITERS AND ILLUSTRATORS

The Writer's View of Childhood	*Philippa Pearce*	49
The Acid Test	*Marion Garthwaite*	54
Who'll Kill the Mockingbirds?	*David C. Davis*	59
The Common Ground	*Ann Petry*	67
Bench Marks for Illustrators of Children's Books	*Warren Chappell*	73
The Art of Illustration	*Henry C. Pitz*	78

An Illustrator's Viewpoint   *Barbara Cooney*   82

Story and Picture in Children's Books
   Bettina Ehrlich   86

III. RE-CREATING OTHER TIMES

From the Ground Upwards   *Cynthia Harnett*   97

Shakespeare of London   *Marchette Chute*   102

The Treegate Series   *Leonard Wibberley*   110

"Watch Your Language — You're Writing for Young People!"
   John and Patricia Beatty   114

Rosemary Sutcliff, Lantern Bearer
   Eileen H. Colwell   122

Biography: the Other Face of the Coin
   Rosemary Sprague   128

Dimensions in Time, a Critical View of Historical Fiction for Children
   Carolyn Horovitz   137

IV. THE MATTER OF POETRY

A New Garland for a Great Book
   Louise Seaman Bechtel   153

Poetry for the Youngest   *Leonard Clark*   156

Poetry for Children   *Harry Behn*   159

Speaking to the Imagination
   Samuel French Morse   168

"Not the Rose . . ."   *Myra Cohn Livingston*   174

Where Are We Going with Poetry for
    Children?   *Patrick J. Groff*   181

Flight Plan for the Winged Foal
                      Dorothy E. Ames   190

V. FANTASY, YESTERDAY AND TODAY

Dealings with the Fairies, an Appreciation
    of George MacDonald   *Jane Douglass*   203

Daily Magic   *Edward Eager*   211

Doctor Dolittle: His Life and Works
                      Helen Dean Fish   218

News from Narnia   *Lillian H. Smith*   225

A Letter from C. S. Lewis   *James E. Higgins*   230

Paul Fenimore Cooper and *Tal*
                        Louis C. Jones   238

The Flat-heeled Muse   *Lloyd Alexander*   242

"Out of the Abundance" (Editorial)
                      Ruth Hill Viguers   248

VI. PEOPLE AND PLACES

A Visit to Mrs. Tiggy-Winkle
                  Elizabeth H. Stevens   253

A Visit with Patricia Lynch
                    Hilda van Stockum   260

Walter de la Mare   *Pamela Bianco*   265

Perrin's Walk   *Harry Behn*   271

Illustrating "The Wind in the Willows"
Ernest H. Shepard 273

The River Severn Again   *Arthur S. Gregor* 276

Of a Peacock and a Wild Goose
Margery Evernden 282

A Present for Alice   *Margaret Reardon* 286

VII. FAMILY READING AND STORYTELLING

"The Peace of Great Books"   *Edith F. Hunter* 293

Reading with My Daughter   *Calvin T. Ryan* 301

Three Boys and Their World of Books
Ellen Wilson 307

Rhythm of the Night, Reflections on Reading Aloud to Children   *William Jay Smith* 315

Theodore Roosevelt and Children's Books
Peggy Sullivan 321

The Pleasant Land of Counterpane
Claudia Lewis 325

Storytelling in the Family   *Hilda van Stockum* 332

More Thoughts on Reading to Children (Editorial)   *Ruth Hill Viguers* 338

VIII. NOTES AND COMMENTS   343

I

INSPIRATION—HOW IT COMES

Like bees who by instinct go from flower to flower gathering honey, writers, merely by being alive, are constantly gathering ideas and impressions — their honey — which eventually will lodge somewhere in some book. To bees, some honey is sweeter than other, and some quite bitter. Yet, bitter or sweet, it is all gathered, and so it is with the born writer that all ideas and impressions are his potential nectar and must be gathered and stored by him, either to be used in a book, rejected, or held in reserve.

From "Gathering Honey" by Eleanor Estes

Articles

YEAST IN THE MIND *by Mabel Leigh Hunt*

UPON WRITING FOR CHILDREN *by Elizabeth Coatsworth*

ON WORDS, SINGLENESS OF MIND, AND THE GENIUS LOCI
by Margot Benary-Isbert

GATHERING HONEY *by Eleanor Estes*

ROOTS *by Marjorie Medary*

"WHERE DID YOU GET 'THAT' IDEA?"
by Elisabeth Hamilton Friermood

YEAST IN THE MIND

By Mabel Leigh Hunt

DO YOU wait for inspiration? This is a question frequently asked a writer. And how many of us, in the first stages of our professional years, respond by declaring enthusiastically that we "always feel inspired!"

Happily, such an answer often proves true. Sometimes inspiration is but aspiration. In the beginning it may be in part the elation of finding one's self the author of a book. But with experience, even the successful writer comes to realize that his work, inspired though he may have believed himself to be while creating it, too often falls woefully short of his own high ideals. Chaucer says of the springtime chorus of birds, "som of hem song lowe, som hye."

What is inspiration?

In its practical sense inspiration might be described as a kind of yeast in the mind, blended and working with that balance which the Friends, in spiritual matters, call "inreach" and "outreach." In its supernatural sense it is a power and a glory irradiating mind, spirit and body with magical influence, mysterious, exciting and lovely. We think of it as a thing of heaven, as indeed it is.

Are we "arty" or high-flown, then, in claiming intimate knowledge of inspiration in the creation of children's books? On the surface they seem such simple things. They are written so objectively, with such direct approach. And they are further simplified by the child's acceptance of them. Books may sometimes hold pure wonder for him, but they may also be as toys, as parks and swimming pools, as bread and jelly, as lamplight and sunshine and friends. If books are to be comprehensible to his understanding, can they be at the same time works of inspired art?

Most assuredly it is possible, for while inspiration may be a thing of heaven, it is also, blessedly, a thing of earth. It may amply serve the creators of children's books if we recognize its quality and its source. That source lies in the child himself, and in his world. Recognition is as simple as that. Moreover, it works. At once, without losing its spiritual quality, inspiration becomes usable. For we writers have no need of seeking painstakingly the true nature of our relationship with children. It is written in their young uplifted faces, bright with wonder, friendliness and expectation. To children we are first of all bringers of gifts. We are fairy godmother, entertainer, playmate, friend. Inspiration, therefore, springs from their faith in us, our affection for them. It comes to us readily if with hearts and minds and tongues we respect and understand them. It comes to us if we ourselves have never quite grown up, so that we share with children the May-morning of their youth. And it comes to us if we are artists, and artists more than a little unworldly. It is an irresponsible writer who does not pause occasionally to rededicate himself to children and children's literature.

The "juvenile" book so inspired, then, in the hands of the artist becomes a book of quality, however slight in form, however direct and simple of approach. It is a combination of graceful technique, good storytelling, and basic truths interpreted clearly through appealing forms. It is tasteful and disciplined. It has grass and earth and familiar things on a level with the child's eyes, but it has also treetops and wind and stars to draw his gaze upward. Whatever good qualities characterize the book, it must be of the child and for the child if it is to be his own. He will recognize it as his. He will carry it off into his world as a loved and necessary treasure. The delicate phrase, the wise and lovely interpretation he cannot name. Could he do so, it is quite likely he would be suspicious of it. Nevertheless, style and literary quality in a lively book make a definite sensory impression on him. The book becomes memorable.

There are pitfalls into which inspiration vanishes. They are created, unwittingly perhaps, by writers themselves. Haste is a pitfall, and overproduction. Anything to have a book on the market. It is true that ideas, characters and plots crowd the fertile mind. They clamor for expression. But the writer must listen for the still small voice, which chooses the one idea from among many, a conceit building up into something so stimulating to the writer that it eventually becomes a book to enrich children's literature.

Another pitfall yawns when the writer grows too greatly concerned with patterns of adult reaction. Does not each one of us crave intelligent adult praise? Do we not have real need of its stimulus and prize it highly when it comes our way? All the same, we dare not be aware of it during the act of creating our books, even of its finest and most coveted origins. It overshadows. We cannot see the children when adults loom too tall.

It is very salutary for the writing craft to keep in mind that a book is truly the fruit of its author. It not only bears his name, but his habits of thought, the turn of his speech, his temperament, the quality of his spirit. His book is himself.

> *. . . for som of hem song lowe,*
> *Som hye, and al of oon acorde.*
> . . . . . .
> *Was never y-herd so swete a steven,*
> *But hit had be a thing of heven.*

As some of our choir sing high, some low, our music does not always make "so swete a steven." But that which inspires us is flawless and pure. It is "a thing of heaven" and it is the best of earth — the eternal springtime of childhood.

From *The Horn Book* for May, 1951

UPON WRITING FOR CHILDREN

By Elizabeth Coatsworth

WHAT is the impulse behind starting a book for children? Probably nine times out of ten the author has been delighted by something, perhaps quite trivial, but a spark has shone inside him like the turning on of a light. Instantly he wishes to share that pleasure. He is like a man walking with his family who suddenly sees ahead of him an unexpected mountain, a monkey in the branches of a tree, or comes upon a house in the woods where a little while ago there was only a glade. His first impulse is to turn and say: "Look!"

And that impulse is the genesis of writing for children. Each book is merely an enlargement of that exclamation, "Look!"

The writer has come upon something in life which has amused or delighted or surprised him. "Look!" he exclaims; and, if he is lucky, the children look.

That unknown quantity which rouses an author is the most authentic thing in any book and the most indicative of the writer's own individuality. Like a catalyst it draws about it the rest of the story. Here an author's training enters. Given the start, a writer can usually manage the rest. There are three parts to any story: the people, the plot and the place. I say "plot" although today sometimes there is little plot. If a modern writer depends upon mood, it must be made to seem significant, and by its weight this mood takes the place of plot. One might be tempted to add a fourth ingredient to many stories for children, and that is the moral which may determine the evolution of the entire tale. It is better writing, perhaps, when this fourth element is so implicit as not to be recognizable or capable of being separated from the rest. So I shall hold to my original division of the story into people, plot and place.

With which shall the tale begin? That depends on the particular author. I might hazard a guess in the case of many books and perhaps guess wrongly. Only in the case of my own books have I a dossier relatively accurate.

Most often I begin with place. The sense of what the classical world called the *genius loci* is very strong with me, and again and again it has been a house or particular landscape or a village which has been the starting place for one of my books.

In *Away Goes Sally,* the impetus came partly from an old book about Salem, but also from a small house with a stove in it fastened on runners and used by the woodcutters in winter. We found this in the woods of our farm when we were first exploring our land and it made an instant impression on me.

Houseboat Summer was written because of ten days which my husband and I spent on the houseboat belonging to the artist, Maurice Day, and his wife. It was anchored in the cove of a Maine pond between two folds of wooded hills where the thrushes called through the long May twilights.

The Littlest House has for the real hero a tea-cup size cottage which was for two years my study in Hingham.

Trudy's Tree House was never built in the back of the cottage on Lake Erie where I spent my childhood summers, but it was promised to me. Our departure for California made the fulfillment of that promise impossible, but in the book *I* built it, rather more complete than it would have been in real life.

One summer a friend took us to Gott's Island near Mt. Desert. The motor boat was anchored offshore and we were rowed to the beach. There were empty fish houses by the water and from them we followed an unused path to the lane and the row of houses above us on the slope of the island hill. There they stood, fences, flowers, wells and outbuildings, but there was not a face at a window or a wisp of smoke blowing off from any of the chimneys. And several years later I got around to embodying the impression of that summer noonday in *Thief Island.*

Some books have begun with people, like that old ruffian Mulai Ismail in *The White Horse.* He was the Moroccan ruler who asked for the hand of one of Louis XIV's daughters and upon being refused rode forth on a black horse and vented his annoyance by killing every living being whom he met.

The Fair American had its beginnings in a very minor character, the old woman who terrified everyone by running backward at great speed. And there have been several others which would never have been written had not some particular character caught my fancy.

Once or twice the yeast for a tale has been its plot. Recently I wrote a short story deliberately on John Buchan's formula of a journey which for some reason must be accomplished to a given destination in a given time.

There are many formulas for plots but I am not good at remembering them, though probably they could be useful. I do remember reading that the Cinderella motif lay behind nearly half the stories ever written and that it never failed in its appeal. Let someone be neglected and overlooked and then let it be discovered that he or she is truly beautiful or remarkable and the reader is always moved. Probably most of us have memories of having sat at some time by a dying fire while others danced in their best bibs and tuckers without us.

Of course every beginner knows that a plot must have some suspense — and that it is wise to let some failure precede success and some false success sharpen the effects of failure. Occasionally I have found it useful to make references to the future of the "little-he-guessed-at-the-time-what-was-so-soon-to-happen" sort. But by and large I plan my plots very simply, mapping out titles for the chapters, and then the characters and I work it out as we go along.

That is the exhilaration of writing. Once the ball starts rolling many authors must feel as I do, that there is little to do except to jot down the story as it develops from its own beginnings. Even a little muse can dictate. What is it that happens? Are the conditions of writing such that the author reaches down to the subconscious and works from another level of experience than that of every day? One goes to one's desk after breakfast, feeling dull and listless. One can't remember where one's reading glasses are, or with whom one was to get in touch about something. Without much interest one picks up one's pencil — in our household we don't use the typewriter

— and suddenly the scene shifts. Ideas, words and motives fall into their proper places as though by magic and the joy of writing rules everything.

At least that is the way it is with me.

What should an author use for his theme? There are waves of fashion among the publishing houses; at one time the editors wish practical books on airplanes or city government; at another time historical stories are commended. Fairy tales are supposed to be out, yet when *The Little Prince* appeared the reviewers were vastly delighted; and Thurber's *Many Moons* was another triumph. Fantasy is out, but not when E. B. White makes the right mouse the hero. Series were out. Only my sister's insistence — she remembered her own pleasure in Laura E. Richards' "Margaret Mountfort" books — made me continue on the Sally stories. At that time the idea was discouraged by the publishers, but I insisted, although I tried to bring in new characters and situations with each new book so that the later ones would not be too dependent on the earlier ones. Yet since then the tide has turned and now publishers are getting out series: The Rivers of America, The Lakes, The Cities, The Readers for the States.

Various artists — Helen Sewell most recently — have experimented in making books that are intelligent comics, and why not? One has only to see the French tapestries, with their scenes from the lives of St. Stephen, or of the Virgin, or from the Apocalypse, to realize that telling a story by means of consecutive pictures is both an old and honored method. The question is one of attitude. It is vulgarity of mind of which one must beware, not any particular form. The most traditional type of story may be entirely cheap in outlook. Vulgarity and cruelty are the only two things of which I can think that are unsuitable in books for children. I don't mean that stories should always be happy or that they should avoid poverty, sickness and death, if these are necessary for the carrying on of the plot, but they should avoid sadism, or a lingering over the details. They should avoid the suggestion of dark things left to stir uneasily in the imagination. When dealing with the various forms of horror in children's books, I believe that the handling should be brief and matter-of-fact. The classic example of this method is that of the old penny dreadfuls: "Another Redskin bit the dust."

Cruelty and vulgarity aside, an author should write for children about the things which are of sharpest interest to his own imagination. His story then has an inner authenticity. He and his readers meet on common ground. I think of us all as of trees growing from the smallest saplings to full growth in rings with all the layers of experience still within us. This outer layer is adult surely, and handles adult affairs; within that is a less assured ring; and within that come youth and adolescence and childhood, all still complete and necessary but covered over and hidden from sight. A writer for children perhaps is a person who can more easily than others call upon those inner layers of his own growth, can remember them and return to them upon occasion.

Let an author enjoy his own book and it is probable that there will be children who will enjoy it too.

Perhaps you would be interested in a few details about a Maine book. My favorite is *Here I Stay*, a junior novel. That began with something I read in a book called *My Ancestors in Maine*, in which the author describes how entire communities emigrated to Ohio after 1816, often auctioning off the sick and old to the lowest bidder for their keep.

This seemed to me strange and dramatic. I immediately wanted to do a book laid in a time of such contending emotions. I like travel at all times. Should my hero or heroine go in the general exodus? No. He or she must stay behind. This must not be one more story of crossing the wilderness. Should my character be a boy or a girl? A girl seemed more touching. Why was she alone? Why did she stay? The two could be answered together. She was an orphan deeply attached to her dead father. He had chosen the land and built the house. She would not leave it.

Where was the house? That was easy. My husband a few years before had found what is now our Maine farm upon its pond, and we were still exploring its woods and rock ledges, its slides leading down to the water and its blue hills in the distance. As the plot worked out I had to place Horn Pond above what is now Portland on the route used by the Vermonters, but all the descriptions were of our own tenderly loved land. Henry was working on *Herbs and the Earth* and it was his herb garden which I brought in and his love of St. Theresa's mystical poetry and many of his opinions. I chose the name of Margaret Winslow both because I liked it and because it is a local name around Nobleboro. I made her of Tory stock so that there might be a slight barrier between her and her neighbors.

When does a story grow? Mostly at night before one goes to sleep. We had coming to help us at this time a neighbor, a woman who had been left with an old mother and two young children to bring up. She cut and hauled the winter firewood by herself, plowed and planted with the aid of a pair of oxen, milked and worked in the house.

My Margaret could not do all this, but I had before me the example of this modern woman who did, and who could find time to come to clean our house and the heart to whistle as she worked. Old Mr. and Mrs. Rollins, our dear neighbors, lived at this time next door to us and often I went down to sit with Mrs. Rollins in her kitchen to ask how much snow would have to be melted to water a horse, or how maple syrup is made over a fire.

Meantime in another book laid in Quincy called *Grandmother Brown's First Hundred Years* I came upon the account of a woman so genteel that she would eat only one pea at a time, and her I must bring to life. In a book of dull tracts found in a deserted house there was a little decoration of a sailor with a wooden leg, drawing behind him a handcart with the model of his ship on it. I had never heard of a disabled sailor doing such a thing, but I must have *him*. If Margaret was not to do all the work, who would help her? Her neighbors first — and here I must tuck in the phrase from an eighteenth century earthenware platter of which we were told by a potter in central New York:

"Earth I am, it is most true,
"Despise me not for so are you."

This platter would be given to her by a woman neighbor. A man would offer her love and protection, but she must refuse. Who would help her later? Having been brought up in a family deeply interested in Indians and Indian art, I introduce an Indian into any story when possible. Why should they help her? Ah, not for nothing have I already decided on an herb garden! Of course, Margaret or her father will heal someone who is sick — an Indian child probably.

I had been reading some town histories and had come across the name of Molly Molasses, an Indian woman who sometimes forecast the future. With a name like that, in she must go. Little did I guess that later I was to handle Molly's silver cross, now owned by a granddaughter, or have a letter from her white godchild to whom she had given the power to curse or to bless!

About this time we were having a picnic across the pond in wild pasture land. I was standing on a rock when an eagle began circling above me, coming nearer and nearer. The bird's action was very strange and impressive. When it at last veered away I felt that I had been in a very curious and elemental communion. Molly Molasses would understand the eagle better than I had.

A man who came to see us at the farm had been reading the inventory of his great-grandfather's general store at which the Vermonters traded. I listened to him and remembered. Elsewhere I read in one of the "Old Squire's" books of a wildcat's attack on oxen, and in the town histories there were accounts of Muster Day. Audubon, transfigured, was the prototype of my young botanist hero, French, gentle and courageous. Margaret must not be altogether alone — yet she must have no human companion — at one time my pity was so great that I let her take back an old lady from the auction, but I knew that this would spoil the story and in the end gave her an old dog and a lamb instead.

The animals seemed to give her the support of their need and affection, but they did not interfere with the essential solitude in which she found herself.

The Rollinses had a calf born that summer in the woods. The cow had gone to the edge of the cliff so that the newborn creature could be more easily protected, so I shaped the birth of Lady's colt in the same spot.

Thus out of the farm lands, out of my husband's interests,

out of the people and things about us, out of the accounts I read and the things that I imagined, I put the mosaic together, creating a character whom I respected. I saw her world with whatever tenderness and poetry I had at my command, catching a little of life for the time being into a book, as one fills for a moment the palms of one's hands with water from the stream which endlessly flows onward and out of sight.

From *The Horn Book* for September, 1948

ON WORDS, SINGLENESS OF MIND, AND THE GENIUS LOCI

By Margot Benary-Isbert

WORDS ARE a writer's material, his imperfect tool to transmit ideas, pictures, images. From beginning to end the writer's struggle is for the right word in the right place. It is a lifetime battle, a never-finished one, for there can be no truce between the vision of perfection and the limitations of ability.

To go on in spite of and against these limitations is what Charles Morgan, in the preface to his play, *The Flashing Stream,* called singleness of mind: doing what we have to do with all our heart, all our mind, and all our soul. Morgan tells of an old farm hand ploughing a field. When the squire came by and asked him, "What would you do if you owned my rents?" the man answered, "something useful," and after thinking, added, "A bit of ploughing." That is singleness of mind.

The peak of dedication, of singleness of mind, is reached by the saint; and every venture into the sphere of creative work, in any field, means following in the footsteps of the saint — at least to a certain degree and at certain periods. It does not matter whether you do a short essay about the eye of a spider, which will perhaps be read by a dozen scholars; or the great novel of the twentieth century, which will be read by millions; or simply — and not so very simply, either — a children's book. In each case you have to be dedicated to your work, to recognize it as what the saint would call a vocation, which necessarily excludes many other things you would like to do. It means renouncement of comforts, of hobbies, of joys; it can mean at times renouncement of your nearest and dearest. If your husband, your wife, your family and friends are able to accept, for a shorter or longer time, as the case may be, that they must leave you alone because you are concerned with your work, and with your work only — you are truly fortunate. If they love you enough to bear with you, the bond will be even stronger when one day you return to their world.

Another thing the writer has in common with the saint is his knowledge of what St. John of the Cross called the Dark Night of the Soul: the periods of inability to do your work, of utter despair, of the deep conviction that you will never write another worthwhile book. This is the crucial test of your existence as a writer. If you give up, you are lost. To struggle with your back to the wall; to hold onto your one weapon against despondency, your pen; to write even if you know that the day's work will end in the fireplace — that is singleness of mind.

Another battle, just as fierce and everlasting as the first, is the battle *against* words, against too many, too worn-out, too cheap words. Our language, all modern languages, have lost their innocence through too much and consequently too indifferent use. They have lost their power, their immediacy. There was a time when language was something sacred, when words were few, and precious, and potent. A word could give life and death; it could bless or curse, exorcise evil spirits, call the protective forces, make the sun rise and the rains come, the crops grow and the animals bear young. Words could lure the fish into the fisherman's net and the wild boar in the path of the hunter's arrow. The reverence for language, for words, has to be part of the writer's quest for truth, for clarity, for the pursuit — never quite accomplished — of the elusive unicorn.

Not long ago I read in the book of a German philosopher, "Every classical art of poetical expression consists in limitation. Compared to what is given, that which is omitted is infinite." Almost at the same time I found another quotation in a book by Freya Stark: "When we write, with the words we *use* we deal with all those which, unspoken, come to the reader's mind. It is not what we actually *say*; it is what we make him think that counts."

What we make him think! And I add, *that* we make him

think. To do so, we must rediscover the magical quality of words, must learn again to make words potent and few, as they were in the youth of humanity. We must do what a conjurer does in another way with another medium: make the reader see what is not there; make him create in his own mind what is beyond the words; let him find his own way and not even know that he has been led. This is especially important in writing for children, to counteract the pre-chewed food most television programs offer them; for the growing young mind needs challenge, needs the emptiness that asks to be filled.

The great masters of the Eastern world are the best examples of what I mean. Think of Lao-tse, who left only one tiny volume, the *Tao Te Ching*, truly a record for economy of words. But these words have survived more than two thousand years and have formed the way of thinking of millions of people. I am sure they will even survive communism, just as they survived another tyrannical rule in the second century. Here is what Lao-tse says (the translation from a German version is mine):

> Thirty spokes meet in a hub.
> The emptiness between them makes the usefulness of the wheel.
> We form vessels of clay;
> The void inside them makes the usefulness of the vessel.

(*Don't forget the emptiness!* I once wrote on a piece of paper and put it on the wall opposite my typewriter.)

There was a time in my life when I needed strict spiritual discipline because that seemed the only way to keep my mind from cracking under a strain I could otherwise not have survived. At that time I started translating Chinese poetry into German, the compact four-line verses that are scant in words and rich in meaning. The translating was a more-than-dubious venture, for I do not know Chinese. The only thing I could do was to collect all the German, English, and French translations I could get from university libraries and grope my way through the jungle of scholarly but unpoetic versions of the poems.

From these translations I wanted to get the essence of the matter. It was like trying to catch the almost indiscernible fragrance of a flower pressed between the pages of a book, the delicate ghost of a flower that might dissolve into dust at a touch of my inquisitive nose. At the same time it was like working under the implacable rule of a strict and relentless master, who pointed his finger at my paper over the span of centuries. But however imperfect the result may have been, working at it was a tremendously rewarding exercise.

Consequently, I got involved with the poets of the T'ang dynasty; and for many months, with the stubbornness of an explorer, I lived completely in the unbelievably productive period of Chinese art and poetry between the seventh and tenth centuries. This involvement led me to write a novel about Li T'ai-Po and his circle of friends — poets, mystics, painters, and calligraphers. And here again I found a hint of the perfection of Art. The friend of Li Po, Wang Wei, one of the great painters of his time and a poet besides, said: "The ultimate concern of the artist is not to paint mountains and clouds and trees but the air between them." The same concept again: Not what we say, not what we paint, but *the emptiness between the spokes of a wheel* is what counts.

Many years later, when a friend gave me a book of haiku, I met again the challenge of the art of few words, which reminded me of my work with Chinese poetry. I felt the irresistible urge to try my hand at expressing a hidden meaning in three short lines mentioning only seemingly small and irrelevant things: a floating petal on a muddy pond; the tiny melody of a cricket's song; raindrops on a gray stone. But the harder I tried, the more impossible it became to succeed. It was like unrequited love, absolutely and hopelessly one-sided. Not before I was in Japan did I find myself able to express my thoughts in a haiku with any degree of satisfaction. In the five weeks I spent in that beautiful country I wrote a dozen or so — and never another one after I had left.

This is only one incident of what I like to call the stimulus of the *genius loci*. It is indeed amazing what places can do and have done to my imagination; how often all at once a process of creativity started when I entered a strange house, walked through a strange city or a landscape I had never seen. Unprepared and unwarned I can get a feeling that this place has been waiting for me and will convey a message that has a very special meaning. It is what the Greeks meant when they said they felt in a certain locality "the God touching them." Such experience has an unrealistic, almost uncanny quality that cannot be described.

My home town, Frankfurt, Germany, is a very old city, saturated with history and so full of stories that you encounter them at every street corner. As a child I was fascinated by the web of crooked, narrow streets around the cathedral and the medieval town hall, called the Römer, in which the German-Roman emperors were elected. Whenever I found an excuse to escape the observant eyes of our succession of unimaginative governesses, I strolled among those old houses, which seemed to emanate tales of human fates, and tried to catch the voices that had long been silent. That must have been the time when I first started to do what disapproving adults called "making up stories."

There was one house that stood in a narrow lane inaccurately called Grosse Eschenheimer Gasse. I passed it often when I went back from school through the inner city instead of through the park, as we were supposed to do. The house had a stately entrance gate, and in my mind I saw footmen in *escarpins* and white wigs, torch lights in hand, directing coaches with glittering ladies and pigtailed gentlemen in them. Goethe's mother was once among the illustrious guests of the Prince of Turn-and-Taxis, who resided here. How I longed to pass through the wrought-iron gate and walk through the wide courtyard and into the magnificent house; how I wished to have lived in the gallant time when ladies wore crinolines and when the palace was the residence of one of the richest princes of the First German Reich. How could I have guessed that as a young girl I would belong to this house, work in it, and love it more every day. Here is how it happened:

I had registered for courses in journalism and German Literature at the University of Frankfurt. At that time a museum of ethnology and anthropology had been established in the old baroque palace in the Grosse Eschenheimer Gasse, of which I had not thought for some time. The man who had been the initiator and was now the director of the museum was a former physician who had worked for the Dutch government in the Malayan colonies and had lived for many years in inner Sumatra with one of the most primitive tribes known at that time. Somehow I had enrolled in one of his courses also and soon got so entangled with his way of teaching and with his alluring subject that I asked him one day where and how I could learn more about it. He advised me to visit the museum, study the collections, and use the small library to my heart's desire. I did; and instead of attending my other courses, I found myself a daily visitor of the house that had been a childhood love: now walking through the once-closed gate, ascending the stairs to the princely rooms with the precious stucco ceilings, and getting acquainted with the collections from strange countries, many of them specimens of Stone Age tribes.

After some time Dr. Hagen asked me to become his secretary. So, against all my intentions, a house and what I had found in it had drawn me into a career I had never planned. I found myself among fetishes and mummies, shrunken heads, tools of witchcraft and poisoned weapons; and I was the only female among a group of the oddest characters I have ever met.

All this held me in a magic circle for more than seven years with never a dull moment; and I might have been held for the rest of my life, had not a young scientist come to prepare himself for an expedition to the Stone Age tribes of New Guinea. Since I was at that time the librarian — probably the most outrageously unqualified librarian in human history — I had to advise this young doctor of philosophy about the use of our library and where he would find the books that were important for his purpose. However, instead of going to New Guinea, the poor fellow had to go into the First World War with the cavalry regiment of which he was a reserve officer. In 1917 he came home on leave, and we were married.

Certainly no other house has ever done quite as much for me as the Frankfurt Turn-and-Taxis palace! Thirty years later, I wrote a book about my slapdash career, *The Maid of All Work*, which one day I intend to rewrite for publication in the United States.

Later the old place of my husband's family in Erfurt had a

strong appeal to my imagination. This last home where we were happy and felt secure for many years lives in my books, though I may never visit it again. And there was Rowan Farm, where we found refuge when we fled from Thuringia as the Russians took over, and which became the background for two of my books.

Then there was the case of the Castle on the Border, which cast its spell even before I had seen it. I read about it in a newspaper in the fall of 1948, shortly after the currency reform, which left us all so poor that we did not know whether we would be able to buy a pair of warm stockings, let alone wood for our little iron stove for the next winter. The article in the paper said that a group of actors, swept from Berlin to Frankonia, had not been able to pay the rent for their lodgings in a town on the Main River; nor could they pay for the hall they had used for their performances after the city theater had been bombed in the last weeks of the war. They had found an old castle in a remote little place — where fox and hare say good night to each other, as we say in Germany — and after negotiations with the owner had started to fix up the inside of the castle. In the mornings after rehearsals, they did repairing jobs; in the afternoons and evenings they drove around the countryside to play to peasants and working people in little village inns or schoolrooms.

I remember putting down the paper and saying to my husband, "I must go to this castle." He asked, "Right away?" and I answered, "Yes." But when we inquired about connections, we learned I would have to change trains at least three times to get there; with the railway conditions being what they were after the war, it seemed more than doubtful that I could make it in one day. But Ben, experienced from more than thirty years of marriage, knew what it meant when I said, "I must." "I'll take you," he said.

Off we drove on a rainy October morning with only a faint idea about where we would arrive. The roads were very bad, but we got there after much inquiring from uncommunicative and vague country people. At a bending of the road I saw two towers and said, "Look, that is *It*."

It was. Ben had arranged to go on to Munich and was

reluctant to leave me in this strange place; but I knew that everything would be all right. So, he dropped me at the bridge that led over the former moat, intending to pick me up again on his way back from Munich. But I asked him not to bother about me. I might want to stay a little longer, and I would get home eventually.

I was received as one of them by the group of strange young people who had never seen me before. I stayed for a glorious, exhausting, exciting ten days, most of the time rather empty inside and chilled to the bone. I listened to their rehearsals, rode with them under the tarp of the rattling truck, helped to put up the scenery, and saw their excellent performances, and came back to the castle late at night, dead tired but happy.

One day, as I stood in the castle courtyard, almost at once the dim outline of a story began to dawn in my mind. It was not difficult to guess what my heroine would feel standing here for the first time in her life, a young girl with an obsession to become an actress. She would immediately be under the spell of the place, as I was now. Nobody needed to tell her that the little balcony hanging on one of the gray stone walls like a swallow's nest could only be Juliet's balcony; and moved by the enchantment Leni was sure to whisper: "Good night, good night! As sweet repose and rest come to thy heart as that within my breast."

Then and there Leni would know that against all odds she would fulfill the dream, would become an actress — just as I knew that I would write a book about this castle and about the young girl of whom I had never thought before.

The power of place was strong in the small German town on the river Lahn, where my father and his four brothers and one sister grew up one hundred years ago, when the Prussians took over the small dukedom of Nassau. My grandfather had been the *Amtmann* there, which at that time was judge and administrator in one person. Twice I started to write a book about that period and about the old courthouse in which the family lived above the offices and courtrooms on the ground floor. But somehow I could not find the right mood, and both times I destroyed the manuscript. Then, in the fall of 1961, I came to this old town with its narrow streets and its thousand-year-old cathedral to sniff around and try to get the scent of the place. I thought I did not know a living soul in the town, and in fact I didn't; but on the second day a chain reaction started. Without doing anything myself, I was handed from one person to the next, and information was poured out to me in the most unexpected way.

When I came home from the trip, I started the book for the third time. It took me another two years to finish it, and now the translator has it. When it comes back to me, I will have to fight the battle of words all over again. For the words of the translator, even with his best intentions, never seem to be *my* words; and I have to transform them back into my own style, often into my own intentions, which have not been completely understood. If you have trained yourself to leave things unsaid, the translator has indeed a hard time putting into words what is only hinted at. I know that I demand the almost impossible; but in the struggle for perfection and for the sake of my own singleness of mind, I deal as ruthlessly with the translator as with myself.

Despite the difficulties in all writing, help sometimes comes to us, undeserved and unrequested — small miracles gratefully accepted. What remains is the never-ending struggle of the writer, of everyone, to achieve not *the* best, for that will remain the ever-elusive goal, but *his* best, as humble as it may be. The furrow well ploughed, the seam properly stitched, the line clearly and truthfully written — let that be enough.

From *The Horn Book* for April 1964

GATHERING HONEY

By Eleanor Estes

TO MANY PEOPLE, including myself, it is provocative to try to unravel the threads that might throw light upon the mystery of the writing of a book. In the beginning there was nothing. How on the bare, blank, beguiling paper did words appear, join together in a right, harmonious, and sometimes beautiful fashion until, behold! the writer and the reader find themselves with a brand-new book, nonexistent a short time ago, and different from any other?

Like bees who by instinct go from flower to flower gathering honey, writers, merely by being alive, are constantly gathering ideas and impressions — their honey — which eventually will lodge somewhere in some book. To bees, some honey is sweeter than other, and some quite bitter. Yet, bitter or sweet, it is all gathered, and so it is with the born writer that all ideas and impressions are his potential nectar and must be gathered and stored by him, either to be used in a book, rejected, or held in reserve.

There are probably as many ways of writing a book as there are writers, and each individual has his own means, stemming from his own personality, of conveying ideas and impressions, so no two people could write the same book. Today I speak only for myself when I speak of how a book gets written. Sometimes I feel I am a blindfolded person and groping my way toward a book. Then I pick up the scent of the book and happily I am on my way, the trail of the book having become clear, direct, and straight. I am the sort of writer who would like to have plenty of time in which to do nothing. Time just to sit, or to stand at the window, or watch the ocean, or people, or to wander up the street or about the house, to pace. For often it is in these do-nothing times that the best honey is gathered. "How many hours a day does the writer write upon his book?" is a question often asked. "Twenty-four," the answer could be, for does not the writer call upon his dreams? And unlike the bee, who has to go and get his honey, the writer need never stir from one spot; his honey comes to him.

Sights, smells, sounds, and impressions often enter the mind in its most do-nothing time and take root. One may overhear a wonderful remark — "David's dog had expeditis" (for "hepatitis"), and, "There's a dragon in Gretchen's yard. It was in my yard, tomorrow" — remarks which etch themselves in the mind. A good sentence may simply hop into one's mind, a first sentence to a book or a chapter. "The way Mama could peel apples!" seemed a good way to begin a book and so it was I began *The Moffats*.

Do-nothing time must be coupled with do-something time, however, in which the real mechanics of writing must take over. Discipline, patience to go over one's work again and again, improving and refining, definite hours in which to write are all essential. Otherwise a writer might end up only with shelves of unwritten books. His books might be "air books" like the "air food" the family of shipwrecked dolls ate in Anne Parrish's famous classic, *Floating Island*:

> "Another cup of this delicious air, if you please, my dear," said Mr. Doll, passing his shell to Mrs. Doll.
> "But, my dear, you've had two already. I'm afraid you won't sleep a wink!"
> However, she poured him another shellful.
> "When do we start?" asked William.
> "Don't speak with your mouth full, my son."
> William swallowed the air.
> "Use your napkin, William," said Mrs. Doll.

Air food is all right for dolls and children at play, but people need more substance than air for nourishment, and happily writers have the need to turn their "air" books into real books, and have them savored, read, and cherished. A writer, lacking discipline, may spend more and more of his time in the do-nothing hours and may end up with not even as much of a book as our same Mr. Doll in *Floating Island* did. Let's see how Mr. Doll went about writing a book:

He took a swim every morning to clear his brain.
Then he took a sun bath.
Then a brisk walk along the beach.
Then he sat by the waterfall to collect his thoughts.
Then a nap, because his brain was tired.
Then a swim to wake himself up.
Then it was suppertime.
Then he watched the stars.
And then it was bedtime.
This went on until Mrs. Doll said:
"My dear, that isn't the way to write a book! Go into your study after breakfast and write. Dinah will bring your lunch on a tray, and you'd better not work later than five o'clock every day...."
So, Mr. Doll, not very eagerly, tried Mrs. Doll's way.

By the end of the week Mr. Doll did have a very pretty page, ornamented and attractive, and even though it was not a book, it was more than air.

To many writers, as it is to me, keeping notes is practically a compulsion. Notes refresh the memory with thoughts that may get too deeply stored in the innermost portion of the mind, and be lost. Most people, including writers, have ideas that slide, unasked for, into the forepart of the mind, lightly, noiselessly as a fleck of dust floats by in a sunbeam before our eyes. Sometimes the idea is not held, not nurtured, not invited to stay so that one may become acquainted with it; and it slides back into the dark from whence it had emerged.

Writers, artists, teachers, and all who are creative in their vision, must welcome the elusive thought, examine it, turn it around, consider whether it has value or not, and then, either reject it as useless, or round it out and use it. The same applies in fact to all readers. Indeed, it applies to all people who strive to live creatively, to "those of them," as Plato said, "I mean, who are quick-witted, and like bees on the wing, light on every flower and out of all they hear, gather influences as to the character and way of life which are best for them...."

To the writer, his memory and his impressions are insistent. He finds he must get them down on paper, enhance them in the light of his own imagination, use them as a springboard. This happens often years and years after the impression has been made.

Where, for instance, did those moths come from that flew out of the organ in the chapter of "The Organ Recital" in *The Middle Moffat?* They flew out of a bank vault from which a little old lady in front of me asked to have some jewelry removed. They fluffed all over the bank and all over us. They had had a nice breeding place in the green velvet linings of the little jewelry boxes. And I'm sure that once I saw one moth fly out of our little old pump organ, from the felt paddings somewhere. So that one moth and the bank moths combined for "The Organ Recital" chapter.

And how did the first chapter of *Rufus M.* get written, the chapter in which Rufus learns to write his name, an accomplishment which he achieved in the public library? One day, many years ago, when I was a children's librarian in the George Bruce Branch Library in New York, a very little girl who could not see over the desk arrived in the children's room. She wanted to take home a book. When she understood that to do this she must have a library card, and that to have a library card she must print her name, which, not being quite old enough for school yet, she did not know how to do, she was not deterred. She spoke little and she did not say that she could not write her name, which was, I remember, Barbara Cooney. She bravely jabbed great symbols on the application blank, which she made up for the occasion. Most little children see little difference between their kind of imitative jagged lines up and down and grownups' writing.

I told Barbara Cooney that her writing was nice, but that it did not spell her name. And I suggested that she go home and have her sister teach her how to print her name. She did not budge; she said nothing, but she was not going to go home. So I undertook to teach her to print her name. As I recall it — once a book has been written it is impossible for me to sever the imagined portions from the remembered portions of any incident — her whole day and mine were entirely devoted to her great achievement. For before closing time, she did have her card and her book and she knew how to print her name — B A R B A R A   C O O N E Y. Years later, in telling how Rufus learned to write the "offat" part of Moffat, Barbara Cooney came back, unasked for, into my mind, asking to be transfused into the chapter about Rufus' learning to write his name.

So, in writing, inventiveness and imagination become partners of remembered impressions, and all skip along together. "Now you, now me," they seem to say, none of them alone being sufficient for creating a book. In revising a book, which I do many times, sometimes a thought or an incident is taken out and put back into storage. If it is worth writing about, it will emerge again some other time while writing some other book and insist upon being included. With each writing of his book, the writer is like a singer striving, pushing, reaching higher for a still higher, and more eloquent, note. Now the intellectual concept, the conscious thinking about what has been emerging, outweighs the first outpouring. The writer must survey his work critically, coolly, and as though he were a stranger to it. He must be willing to prune, expertly and hardheartedly. At the end of each revision, a manuscript may look like a battered old hive, worked over, torn apart, pinned together, added to, deleted from, words changed and words changed back. Yet the book must retain its initial freshness and spontaneity.

It is only after the fourth revision that I feel I know my book. It takes a while to get used to the new book. The writer is a little shaken and uncertain for a time. Is the book, most of all, a good one? Was the best, most flavorsome honey put into it? How much a writer needs to be told now, "How beautiful!" when, finally, his book is off to the press; how lost he feels without it, having grown now to love it.

Sometimes the time is not ripe for the writing of a certain book. But, if certain ideas or a group of ideas and impressions keep bubbling to the front of the mind, then most likely the time is ripe to include them in a special book. In this light we may consider *Ginger Pye* and *Pinky Pye*. Initial drafts, notes for both of these books, were made about ten years before the actual books as we know them now were written.

Ginger was a dog we had when I was a child. After *The Moffats*, my first book, was finished, I wrote a story about this dog, Ginger. But my heart was not completely in it, for I was still preoccupied with Moffats. So I put these first sketches about Ginger away in my notes. There they stayed for ten years, while I wrote other books.

Then I began to think about Ginger again, for we had acquired a new and different dog, who reminded me of him. At first I thought I would put Ginger into a fourth book about the Moffats. But in the end I decided to place him merely in the same town and time.

So *Ginger Pye* is about our old dog, Ginger. Mr. Pye is based partly on my husband and partly on my childhood remembrance of a certain man, the father of a friend, who was an ornithologist, very well-known nationally but a modest, humble man whose importance the town did not suspect. Mr. Pye is also partly based on another ornithologist whom we met in the west in later years. And this man happened to be the owner of a pygmy owl.

Now this pygmy owl, out west, did not get into the book *Ginger Pye,* for it sometimes takes me years to realize that I have seen a good thing. And it was lucky he did not, for he belongs in *Pinky Pye,* where indeed he is. Have you ever seen how fierce a pygmy owl can look, and how beguiling? I remember how avariciously he ate up a bright green grasshopper his owners caught for him. This pygmy owl stored himself away in my mind, and the great intensity, owl intensity, that was his personality, engraved itself on my mind, too.

Mrs. Pye is based on many people, too: partly my mother, partly my sister, partly myself — that is the timid, overanxious, have-you-got-your-sweater part — and partly made up. Rachel and Jerry are two children based on all the children I've known. Uncle Bennie, who is an uncle from the moment he came into the world, is based on all little uncles — my brother, for instance, who was a little uncle, and a little boy who used to come into the Seward Park Library, whose name was Uncle Henry, and who was an uncle, though only six.

The search for Ginger is the theme of *Ginger Pye*. Our dog, Ginger, really was stolen on Thanksgiving Day when he was a few months old, still a very little puppy. And he did return, full grown, dragging a ragged long rope behind him and with terrible scars on his face, in the month of May. This book, being a search, permitted me to include in it many impressions that I had not yet been able to get into any other book, such as those of tramps and sunny fields, and walking along behind a cow switching its tail to get rid of flies, and the eerie sound of a certain whistle, a sort of wailing siren, that blew each evening at five o'clock, usually, it seemed to me, when I was in the sunny field. It always frightened me unbearably, and my sister told me it was the gypsies' whistle, summoning them home, at five o'clock. Usually when an impression finally finds a home in some book, one can forget about it.

The perpendicular swimmer in *Ginger Pye* is based on a boy I knew who seemed to me to prefer that mode of swimming to the horizontal. The unsavory character is based on all unsavory characters. Bit-nose Sam is based on a man who had his nose bitten off him by another man, a far-distant relative — the biter not the bitee — of my cousins. As children, we really had bought Ginger for one dollar. I don't remember how we earned *that* dollar, but the dollar that Rachel and Jerry earned is based on a fifty-cent piece that a friend and I earned dusting the pews of our church for her big brother Sam. Now this big brother Sam is the Sam Doody of both Pye books. The chapter "Dusting the Pews" was first written for a Moffat book, but I felt that it did not fit, put it aside, until years later, when it seemed right for Ginger's dollar.

Many of the characters of the Pye books, as well as the Moffat books, are based on my childhood memories, with much gathered in later years, and with embellishments of the imagination — memories of people who used to inhabit that town named, in my books, Cranbury. Mr. Tuttle, who looked like a tall man when he was sitting down but a short man when standing, is based on a man I used to study in church, whom we called the tall and short man.

The manner in which Mr. Pye first met Mrs. Pye, his future bride — that is, he knocked her down while running up a down escalator — is based on an incident related to me by my husband. One morning, years ago, my husband chanced, upon entering a deserted subway station, to witness his very dignified, rather severe boss, who wore a Vandyke beard, running up a down escalator to the top, thinking the station was empty and suitable for the fulfillment of an ancient wish. Wouldn't you know that my husband would come along at that moment and encounter his panting boss? And wasn't this fortunate for Mrs. Pye, because otherwise, years later, in my book, Mr. Pye might not have run up a down escalator that day, knocked down the future Mrs. Pye, who was on her way home, enthralled from having attended her very first opera, *Tannhauser* — which happens also to have been my very first opera, and married her? Mr. Pye might even have married somebody else, if my husband had not seen his boss run up the down escalator.

Well, ten years after the original notes about our cat, Pinky, had been made and set aside, notes which had nothing to do with the Pyes, for the Pyes had not yet been invented and put into a book, I thought to myself, "Now, since the Pyes are such a family for pets, why not give them Pinky? Pinky Pye." So I examined the early notes. I liked the string-bean game I found among them, and also the account of how Pinky had typed the word "woogie," thus becoming a typewriting cat. And so I was right on the trail, now, of *Pinky Pye*.

Where did that big fish come from that Mr. Bish caught bare-handed, when he was hot on the trail of finding little Owlie in the home of his brother ornithologist, Mr. Pye? Well, that fish really was a fish another dear friend of ours, not an ornithologist at all, had really caught bare-handed as it lay floundering at the edge of the ocean, much to the chagrin of the real fishermen, red-faced and broiling in the sun, who had not had a nibble all summer. So, that chapter I dedicate to the friend who caught the fish bare-handed, and other bits and parts of all my books I dedicate to this person and to that person from whom I have been given some compelling and individual impression.

And so, as you see, for all the muddling explanation one tries to give concerning the creating of a book, that creation still remains as mysterious and inexplicable as life itself. But we all enjoy pondering it. Here are my heartfelt thanks to all who have liked the honey I've gathered so far.

From *The Horn Book* for December, 1960

ROOTS

By Marjorie Medary

ONE morning on the Boston-to-Chicago express I asked the Pullman porter why the train was two hours behind schedule.

"Engine trouble last night," he said.

"Really! Do even the wonderful new Diesel engines break down?"

He smiled. "Yes, old steam engine had to pull us till we got to where the Diesel could be fixed. Diesel goes wrong pretty often."

"More often than old-fashioned engines?"

He nodded. "Too much machinery. Just too much."

I had been pondering the state of the world, as who does not these days, and the porter's last words fitted the pattern of my thought. What can be done to prevent our complicated modern world from breaking down with "just too much machinery"?

In Chicago I changed to a streamliner which flashed through the suburbs and then across the fertile flat fields of Illinois. The speeding train hummed with the radio's crooning ditties, rotund advertising phrases, and brisk announcements, and they blurred bewilderingly like the landscape whirling past the window. Is it all real, I thought, or only a fantastic dream — this chrome-streamed car, rocketing along the rails, soft-cushioned and comfortable, but buzzing with sounds from the whole noisy world?

Suddenly the view includes a winding river, then willows and the dark backwater of a slough. The wheels change their tune, the water spreads out on each side, and I know we are crossing the Mississippi. There are glimpses of low green islands, distant wooded bluffs, and a steamboat towing a line of barges.

Then the trees close in again and presently give way to the houses and streets of a small city. We draw up at a busy station, but soon we are off again. The streets melt into open country. I smile and relax.

At last I am at home. Softly rounded fields slope gently to wooded valleys. No flat monotony here, no granite-ribbed hills, but a land of pleasant undulations, suggesting its amazing fertility. Dark green of corn rolling away between golden stubble of oats and wheat and barley. Big red barns flanked by silos, and barnyards alive with pigs. Sleek cows chewing their cud in the shade at the edge of the pasture. Farmhouses set squarely at the corners of quarter sections, and roads running true to the compass for miles, north, south, east and west.

The radio blares on, but now I do not hear it, for my heart is at home — at home in both time and place. There is a past here that I know. This is the land which my parents and my grandparents helped to bring into its flowering. Here are my roots.

Doubtless hundreds of people daily repeat my experience in other regions, returning to the salty tang of New England harbors, the sandy pinelands of Georgia, the snow-crowned distances of Colorado, with the same tug at the heart. Their business addresses may be elsewhere, and they may have left hostages of the heart in remote places, but the sights and sounds, the tastes and smells of childhood have a lingering power. The human spirit is blessed with a deep nostalgia. The young setting forth on high adventure feel the need for a point of return — the need to be rooted somewhere; and the old returning after long absence are gladdened by a sense of well-being, sweeter because mellowed by the long subconscious craving for home.

What subtle blend of sensuous pleasure, inherited attitudes, instinct, and sentiment creates this nostalgia? If it were subject to scientific analysis or to statistical research, we might be amazed to find how potent is its influence in all the affairs of life. Certainly it has profound significance in the arts. It sings in the poetry of Whittier, Lanier, Sandburg, and glows from the canvases of Winslow Homer, Grant Wood, Millard Sheets. It is the source of cowboy ballads, Negro spirituals,

Navajo weaving, the designs on Pennsylvania Dutch furniture — all the folk arts and their products so eagerly collected today. In novels and short stories of the past it appeared as "local color." In modern parlance it inspires "regional writing," and publishers launch series of books — "Rivers of America," "American Cities," "Land of the Free." In the field of children's books there has been much regional writing, although only recently has it been so labeled.

What is the significance of the regional feeling in the streamlined world of today and in our plans for the One World of tomorrow? Should we not try to keep it, both in America and in other lands, to help, like the old steam engine, when the world tends to break down from too much machinery? How can we best strengthen those regional affections in which culture and civilization are rooted?

Most of the forces of modern life are directly opposed to the regional spirit. Radio, motion pictures, airplanes and all other forms of rapid transportation, the shifting of industries and hence populations — all these tend to obliterate differences of custom, speech, and dress. We listen to the same news commentators and wisecrackers. Girls from Maine to California have hysterics over the same movie hero, and boys from Florida to Oregon read the same comics. Women envy the same scarlet-tipped fingernails spread glamorously through the same magazines. Travelers complain that hotel menus from Boston to San Francisco are distinguished only by a dreadful monotony.

Will any regional feeling survive this standardization? There are straws in the wind that seem to point both ways. On the one hand, interest in state and local history and the preservation of landmarks has increased appreciably in the past thirty years. Centennial celebrations of several Western states have had nation-wide publicity. Commercial interests are quick to exploit such regional feeling. Travel bureaus and ad writers for sundry commodities dig up odd facts of local history or legend to enhance sales appeal.

On the other hand, there are evidences of an inverted kind of regional pride. Groups in some sections of the country are so intent on showing their progressive spirit that they bring pressure to bear against textbooks in which any story or picture shows their region as backward in economic development or other than "modern" in its home life, dress, and customs. Such regional pride would be laudable if it were not based on a distorted idea of what represents progress. For standardization is not necessarily a synonym of progress, as we are learning to our sorrow.

Fortunately, even in a completely mechanized world, certain regional differences are bound to persist because they are due to climate and topography. A child of the Louisiana bayous is likely to grow up with interests and tastes and aspirations different from those of a child in the Montana cattle country. All the regimenting influences of machines and big advertising and organized entertainment probably will not quite obliterate those sensuous impressions of childhood which are the basis of our feeling for home and potent in their shaping of the whole personality. Sooner or later almost everyone who has loved the surroundings of his youth agrees with Wordsworth that

>   These beauteous forms,
> Through a long absence, have not been to me
> As is a landscape to a blind man's eye:
> But oft, in lonely rooms, and 'mid the din
> Of towns and cities, I have owed to them
> In hours of weariness, sensations sweet,
> Felt in the blood, and felt along the heart;
> And passing even into my purer mind,
> With tranquil restoration.

The regional spirit owes much to heredity, to family and local tradition and history, and is usually strongest in those whose ancestors have been identified with the region for three or four generations. While all sorts of regional books help to stem the tide of standardization, historical books can perhaps exert the strongest influence. For although the customs, speech, and modes of thought which have distinguished a region are fading, they can still be caught by a sensitive writer and preserved as if in amber for all time.

Knowledge of the past is a lively stimulant to regional interest, whether native or acquired. Anyone who has moved to a strange section of the country can testify that as soon as he begins to delve beneath the surface of daily life into the tradition and history of the region, bonds of affection for his new home begin to grow. He is putting out roots. How desperately those roots are sometimes needed, only those know who have contact with persons recently uprooted from their European homes. Stories of our American past cannot, of course, mend their wrenched and shattered lives, but they can give a sense of stability and of the possibilities of growth in a new soil.

Roots are essential to growth in the world of mind and spirit as in the world of plants. The very word *culture* is based on that assumption. Every society that has produced fruit worthy of the human spirit has been deeply rooted. But roots are of the past, not of the present; and children and their elders need a vivid sense of that past.

American culture is inherently rich just because it has so many roots. It is not a sturdy oak like the English, nor an ancient ash like the Scandinavian, nor a flowering linden like the French. It is a forest of oak and ash, linden and maple, palm and pine, spread over half a continent. Each state, each community has different roots because Americans have come from the four corners of the earth. Florida, Connecticut, Texas, Minnesota, Utah — each differs from the others as greatly as Spain, England, Greece, and Finland differ. Each has a proud history for the enrichment of our national culture.

Happy the child who begins his acquaintance with the past by hearing a grandfather say, "Now, when I was your age..." But in modern life, alas, oral tradition plays little part. Even granted the grandfather close at hand and the inclination and eager ear, the child of today cannot hear tales of America's pioneer age, for the ranks of even the youngest pioneers have thinned to a meager line. In their places as grandparents are those who can barely remember what life was like before automobiles, movies, airplanes, and radio. In how many homes are they telling stories of those simpler days? Unless children hear such stories from their elders, their knowledge of the past depends on history textbooks, historical fiction, motion pictures, occasionally the theater, and always radio. Are these giving them true accounts of the past, interpreted with sincerity and imagination?

Once I heard a young woman say that to her the past was nothing but a lot of old furniture cluttering up the present. If there are many who share her feeling, it must stem from our modern preoccupation with things, especially mechanical things — gadgets. But if our civilization is represented only by these things — automobiles, washing machines, cigarette lighters — then our culture is incapable of growth, for things can be multiplied, but they do not grow.

We need not worry lest the past clutter up our children's lives. What we should fear is that our present is failing to add new growth to their past. It is said that the rootlets of a great elm spread through the soil in a circle as wide as its branches. Like the roots of a tree, the roots of a culture grow. Historical fiction at its best is part of this new growth. Every imaginative recreation of the past is not only a new flowering but a new root.

Mere trappings, however — hoopskirts, stagecoaches, pewter porringers, serapes, ten-gallon hats, sou'westers — do not give the truth of the past or of a region. Stories rich in such picturesque and antiquarian matter, but feeble in characterization and thin in plot, have brought discredit upon junior historical and regional fiction. Children are suspicious of this pink-pill literature designed by their elders to give them a dose of history. Unless in their books real persons are engaged in action and struggle that smacks of real life, they quickly turn away to the fantasies of Superman.

But given historical fiction worthy of the name, the normal boy or girl will identify with a hero in buckskin or a heroine in crinoline as readily as if they lived in the next block. More readily, perhaps. Children are closer to the past than their elders are because they are reliving, as all persons do to a certain degree, the progress of our race from its primitive beginnings to the present. The life of the past — primitive, barbaric, or in the handicraft stage — has a natural appeal for the young. And young folks have time and energy to absorb it, along with plenty of reading about the present and its problems, time to find their roots and to grow in wisdom, provided their elders give them guidance and example.

By all means, then, let us encourage more regional books depicting both the past and the present, books written by men and women rooted in the region, who feel its pulse in their blood, so that their stories throb with the rhythm of its life. And let us encourage in boys and girls a lively interest in their regional history and in the arts and crafts native to the region. So we shall give them the strength that comes from roots clinging deep in rich soil and hidden rock, the blossom and fruit that come from rooted strength. For let us remember that only the person who feels an abiding affection for some particular spot of earth is able to understand the varying manifestations of such affection in others. And it is from such understanding and sympathy that a peaceful world must grow.

From *The Horn Book* for May, 1951

"WHERE DID YOU GET *THAT* IDEA?"

By *Elisabeth Hamilton Friermood*

ACCORDING to my mother nothing was impossible if people had enough imagination plus the gumption to work for what they wanted. While her hands were busy washing clothes, ironing, scrubbing, or sweeping floors (in the days before washing machines, electric irons, and vacuum cleaners), she told stories — stories she had read, stories of her childhood, stories of our ancestors. And at our bedtime, she read aloud from library books. No one, my mother said, ever need be poor with a public library within walking distance. Walking distance in those days could be two miles or more with no complaint from the walker.

By the time I was thirteen, my brother Tom began a plea that was to shape my life: "Tell me a story, Sissy." In those days there was little material in the public library for the preschool child, and once the meager supply was exhausted, I began creating tales just for him. His acquisitive mind, always wanting to know more about everything, kept me on my inventive toes. It was fortunate that I had such a persistent audience prodding my imagination.

As a child I knew the exact day of the month the children's librarian put the latest issue of the *St. Nicholas* magazine on the rack in the children's room. The following Saturday morning I waited on the steps of our Carnegie library for the janitor to unlock the door so that I could slip by him quickly and get my hands on that incomparable periodical before anyone else did. I was lost in its pages until it was time to go home.

I read my way through the library shelves: the Dorothy Dainty books, the Peggy Owens, the Little Colonels, the Little

Peppers, Mrs. Jameson's books, Mark Twain's, those by Mrs. Burnett, and of course all the Alcotts. Charles Major's *Bears of Blue River* was a favorite; I loved just holding it in my hands. What fun to read it to my brother and make him excited about the bear hunts too. And how we both loved *The Peterkin Papers!* Often we pretended ridiculous situations of our own, Tom as Agamemnon and I as Elizabeth Eliza. Even today we sometimes decide to refer our weightier problems to the lady from Philadelphia. Almost every Christmas we read aloud Kate Douglas Wiggin's *Birds' Christmas Carol.* Now, seldom does a member of my family leave for a party or a trip that I do not call after them Mrs. Ruggles' admonition to her nine children as they left for Carol Bird's Christmas party, "Never forget that your mother was a McGrill!" Bless Mrs. Ruggles and her family pride!

Tom and I were especially fond of the stories Mother told about one period in her childhood when she lived in a two-room log house on the banks of the Wabash River. It was natural that these tales should form the background for my first book, *The Wabash Knows the Secret.*

Ah! That first book! The writing, the rewriting, the rejection slips it collected as it went from publisher to publisher. In ten years that manuscript traveled to seven publishers and was rewritten completely three times before Doubleday published it in 1951. I recall Margaret Lesser's asking me to rewrite it that last time. I was so discouraged I came home and put it in my desk, deciding that I could not do it, that writing was not for me.

Then fate stepped in!

I received a letter from Bertha Mahony Miller, then editor of THE HORN BOOK, saying she wanted to publish an article I had sent her, an article called "Practicing the Preaching," which told how I introduced books to my preschool daughter, Libby, using the methods which, as a children's librarian, I had recommended to other mothers.

This acceptance, after years of rejection slips, was like a whiff of oats to a tired horse. "If I can write well enough for THE HORN BOOK," I told myself, "there's a chance that I can write well enough for Doubleday." I took the worn manuscript from the bottom drawer and got to work. THE HORN BOOK had set me back on the writing path.

Not only was I blessed with an imaginative mother, but also with a down-to-earth, storytelling Hoosier grandmother. There in her country kitchen she would sit in her rocking chair beside the cookstove, and puffing on her corncob pipe, she would say to me, "Now I mind the time when the whole kit and caboodle of us went to Missouri in covered wagons!" And she was off, and I, a wide-eyed child on a stool beside her, drank in her tales of the olden times. Grandma's tales gave me rich material for *Hoosier Heritage,* and her own indomitable pioneer spirit was a character pattern worth putting on paper. Her father, my great-grandfather, was probably the meanest old devil of his time. In this book I portrayed his cussedness realistically in the character of Pa Edwards. This, I was told by a student attending a writing-for-children class, was unorthodox. Presenting a parent in a bad light was not good for young people, and furthermore, the scene in which the heroine delivered her sister's baby was too daring for a teen-age novel. Time has proved the student wrong. Any lasting quality the book may have lies in the reality Grandma's salty tales gave it.

In the early 1900s my husband's family homesteaded near Artesia, New Mexico. Again and again during my married life my mother-in-law told of incidents about "when we were on the homestead." Her stories seemed too good to waste, so I began writing *Candle in the Sun.* Thank goodness my mother-in-law seldom threw anything away. She gave me pictures of Artesia in 1907, including one of the homestead shack; a pamphlet describing homesteading possibilities in the area; and letters she had received during that period. I had never been to New Mexico and wondered if I could get the place into words. To ease myself into the scene, I started the book in a place I knew well, my home town, Marion, Indiana. Then, traveling west with Kate Baker and her beloved papa, I viewed the land as a stranger, which, of course, I was. The nicest thing ever written to me about that book was a letter from an old-timer who had lived in Artesia all his life. "Just when, Mrs. Friermood," he wrote, "did you live in Artesia?"

There was no need to do much research for *That Jones Girl.*

I looked back at myself, my home town, my high school, and my senior year, the year Harold Friermood began carrying my books and walking home with me after school. While attending Northwestern University I had the good fortune to meet a fine actress of the day. A mutual friend arranged that I should go to the Blackstone Theater in Chicago for an interview with Margaret Anglin, playing in Oscar Wilde's *A Woman of No Importance*. At the time I was sure that I was meant to be an actress and that all I needed was the opportunity to prove my talent. I will never forget the kindness and understanding of that great lady as she talked to me after the performance on the bare, bleak stage of the Blackstone. Her wisdom was convincing, and although she offered me a walk-on part, I decided, after many sleepless nights, that acting was not for me. One of the fascinating tales she told me of her desperate beginning struggles was how she obtained the role of Roxane in *Cyrano de Bergerac*. Years later, when I wrote *That Jones Girl*, I patterned Louise Leander (Aunt Lou) after Margaret Anglin and included the Cyrano episode. The book's popularity is due in large part to Aunt Lou's glamor and common sense, both of which I found in Margaret Anglin.

Also during my university days I visited Hull House and saw the results of Jane Addams' life of service. In *Head High, Ellen Brody* I tried to depict not only Hull House but also the Chicago of 1903. I chose that year so that I might include the scene of the Iroquois Theater fire that had fascinated me ever since I discovered that it had occurred on the day I was born. Recently a teen-age girl telephoned me to talk about one of my books. At the end of the conversation she asked candidly, "Just how old *are* you, Mrs. Friermood?" "Read *Head High, Ellen Brody* and find out," I replied, explaining about the theater fire. A Chicago girl wrote, "Until I read about Ellen Brody I had never heard of Jane Addams or Hull House." This was reward enough for the pains I had taken with the book.

Again and again, while reading about Chicago, I came upon references to the Chicago World's Fair of 1893. A book with a world's fair as the background would be interesting to do, I thought. Since I didn't want to do another story about Chicago just then, I settled upon the St. Louis World's Fair of 1904 as the scene for *Jo Allen's Predicament*. I love apple blossoms. The memory of an orchard in bloom near Grandma's home inspired me to invent Mrs. Snow and her extensive orchards so that I could revel in describing the trees in their delicate blossoming. The Fair, the Ferris wheel, the invention of the ice-cream cone, St. Louis, the apple trees, and Jo Allen's dilemma gave me a year of vicarious pleasure.

The manuscript delivered, I told myself, "I'll probably never write another book, I am so empty, not an idea left." Then, at breakfast on May 16, 1958, we were listening to the radio news. General Charles de Gaulle was being recalled to leadership in France. "Why do the French have such confidence in the General?" our daughter Libby asked. Always the children's librarian, believing that youth's questions should be answered at once, I hopped up and brought the "D" volume of the encyclopedia from the study and read aloud the article about De Gaulle. As I always do with a volume of the encyclopedia in hand, I flipped through the pages. So often exciting items jump out at you during this procedure. I was not disappointed. A familiar city skyline across the bottom of a page struck my eye. It was Dayton, Ohio, where I had spent many years as a children's librarian. Above the picture I read, "In 1913 a terrible flood disaster threatened to destroy Dayton. Today Dayton has one of the greatest flood protection projects in the world."

I slammed the book shut and announced to my startled family, "That's it! The subject for my next book — the Dayton flood and how they *got* that flood protection project!" *Promises in the Attic* was on its way; the flood waters of the Miami River soon ran through my living room in a muddy stream. What a good thing that the General's name began with "D"!

A copy of Bulfinch's *Mythology* beside my writing chair provided the seed from which grew *The Luck of Daphne Tolliver*. The character of Mama, choosing names for her large family from the gods and goddesses, began to evolve. Once my husband and I built an outdoor fireplace during our vacation. We visited many junk yards before we found just the right iron grating to complete our project. Junk yards, I discovered, were fascinating and filled with unbelievable treasures. I remembered this experience, and Daphne Tolliver became, as the New York *Times* said, "the first teen-age heroine in the junk business."

At the time a number of junior high-school girls often gathered around my writing chair to talk books. As the junk-dealing Tollivers got on paper the girls listened, then advised the road they thought the tale should take. Many of their ideas were included.

During our daughter Libby's first year at Wellesley College I received a letter from a friend containing a brochure from a Kentucky settlement school she had visited. It told of the death of one of the school's teachers, Ann Cobb, a Wellesley graduate, who had come to the Kentucky school in 1905 to teach for one year. Two nights after Ann Cobb's arrival, the school was totally destroyed by fire. The courageous words of the two founders, "We'll put it up again," so influenced the young Wellesley graduate that she spent the rest of her life as a teacher there. Here, I thought, was an idea worthy of a book. *Ballad of Calamity Creek* grew from that two-page pamphlet on Ann Cobb. The real Kentucky woven coverlet Luciana Roselli used as the background for the bookjacket and the real mountain-made dulcimer she placed in the foreground give me great pleasure.

During National Library Week in 1961 I was the guest of the public library in my home town, Marion, Indiana. As I was leaving after the week's festivities, two friends gave me a large envelope, containing, they said, material that might interest me. It proved to be a collection of stories clipped from various Indiana newspapers concerning a rascally family that had lived in my home county in pre-Civil War days. What a dishonest, cheating, ornery family they were! First coming to Grant County as an Indian trader, the father had charged the Indians a dollar for each needle. Worst of all, the diabolical oldest son had, by disgraceful means, married the most beautiful girl in the vicinity, a girl who, like Cinderella, was as good as she was beautiful. All this melodrama, according to best authorities, was not suitable for a teen-age novel. But I could not resist it; I enjoyed writing *The Wild Donahues* right through the fixed horse races, the counterfeiting, the escapes by Underground Railroad, and the scalping of the despicable Mike. These true happenings were more exciting than any I could invent.

Riding home on the train from New York after delivering the above manuscript to Doubleday, I murmured to myself, "Well, Elisabeth, what next?" I looked out the window, and at that precise moment, the train was passing Calvary Cemetery! "Hmmm. A cemetery! I wonder if there has ever been a teen-age novel with a cemetery for its background." With eyes closed, I leaned my head back and looked into the past at remembered periods, scenes, and people. Accelerated by memory, imagination's wheels began turning.

When I was in the fifth grade we moved, and I had to change schools; a tragedy then for a ten-year-old girl, an opportunity now for a writer. In the fifth grade at the new school I became acquainted with two girls who were friends, one white, one golden brown. These girls were in my classes through the years, graduating with my high-school class. Their friendship and the cemetery my train had just passed grew into *Whispering Willows*. Research for this book took me to the Midwest to visit many cemeteries and to spend time with two undertakers of my acquaintance. The older one told me of the little white hearse and white ponies used in his establishment years ago; he even had a picture of the equipage. It looked so pathetic I knew I must put it in the book.

Getting a story on paper is an exciting challenge. The period background must be accurate in all details. A friend of mine collects old *Ladies' Home Journals* as a hobby. Deciding upon a certain year for a tale, I call her, and usually the period I want can be found in this gold mine. The advertisements are as valuable as the articles and pictures. Would Tess Trumper wear button oxfords in 1910? Would Ginger O'Neal want a willow plume in 1913? Would the Tollivers use Fels Naptha soap in 1917? Would Ellen Brody buy Skinner's satin in 1903? No guesswork at all with the *Journals* for that year at hand.

Characters must speak up for themselves. If they do not, I discard them and invent others who do. Once, while I was writing *Candle in the Sun,* Libby asked, "What is Kate Baker going to do now?" I answered, "I don't know, she hasn't told me yet."

My heroines are real girls as I write; I see them move and hear them speak as one does in a motion picture. I then tell the story as I see and hear it projected on the screen of my imagination.

Knowing that the idea for the next book may pop up at any moment makes life interesting and exciting.

From *The Horn Book* for December, 1965

II
GOALS AND GUIDELINES FOR WRITERS AND ILLUSTRATORS

True literature, then, is a form of communication — be it oral, picture, alphabet or composite code systems — which weaves a mystical curtain enhancing the uniqueness of life, at the same time de-emphasizing the humdrumness of it. Literature breathing this living element is often referred to as "creative writing". And if it is to deserve this term, it must be sparked with originality, integrity, and plausibility. Without these three distinct, yet interrelated, elements there can be no "creative literature."

From "Who'll Kill the Mockingbirds?" by David C. Davis

A craft is a level of art which is worthy of anybody's respect. One cannot be a craftsman without a gift, however modest. There must be a brain, not only in the skull but a brain in the fingers. The craftsman rejoices in the things his hands make and his mind conceives. Illustration today is one of the last strongholds of the craftsman.

From "The Art of Illustration" by Henry C. Pitz

Articles

THE WRITER'S VIEW OF CHILDHOOD *by Philippa Pearce*
THE ACID TEST *by Marion Garthwaite*
WHO'LL KILL THE MOCKINGBIRDS? *by David C. Davis*
THE COMMON GROUND *by Ann Petry*
BENCH MARKS FOR ILLUSTRATORS OF CHILDREN'S BOOKS
by Warren Chappell
THE ART OF ILLUSTRATION *by Henry C. Pitz*
AN ILLUSTRATOR'S VIEWPOINT *by Barbara Cooney*
STORY AND PICTURE IN CHILDREN'S BOOKS
by Bettina Ehrlich

THE WRITER'S VIEW OF CHILDHOOD

By Philippa Pearce

WE STAND ACCUSED. Even though the accusation is not violent, not even explicit, still you will detect it in the amused glance and pitying smile. Some writers for adults, when they think of children's writers at all, despise us as the Peter Pans of literature. The charge is that the view of childhood in children's literature reflects not only a recognition of the limitations of immature readers but also the writer's own shameful limitations — his own immaturity, his own childishness.

Among writers for children examples are unkindly quoted of intelligence and literary sensitivity at work in some kind of over-close relationship to the experience of childhood: Lewis Carroll, James Barrie, Kenneth Grahame. Perhaps there are many more, and living, too, waiting to be exposed. After all, every adult must have a peculiar relationship (in the sense of an individual and private relationship) with his own childhood. No wonder if the relationship is sometimes peculiar in another sense. A man can never entirely free himself of the child he once was, and that ghost-figure haunts him during this curious action of writing books for children.

There seem to be two main motives (apart from a sensible regard for cash) in the writing of good books for children. One is to re-create the author's own childhood or childhood interests for self-entertainment. The other is to entertain a particular child or group of children. The child may be a real audience, as Lloyd Osbourne was for Robert Louis Stevenson when he wrote *Treasure Island*. Or he may be imaginary. You can identify an imaginary audience for Mary Norton's Borrowers stories in "Paul's Tale" in the anthology edited by James Reeves called *A Golden Land* (Hastings). There the child Paul is listening to his aunt's story of a dear little man in a foxglove cap who lives in a bluebell wood. But Paul, whose tastes are different, interrupts with his tale of a *real* little man, about six inches high, not very attractive really, with his skin thick and wrinkled like a twig's, his scuttling, rat-like gait, and his croaking voice. Paul caught him and kept him in an old cake tin with holes bored in the top and sent him — on the end of a long string — down rabbit holes to find out what was going on and report back. Paul is freely imaginative, practical, and (like so many children) callous without intention. Perhaps that makes him a character for adult reading rather than for children's; certainly "Paul's Tale" could usefully be prescribed for all adult writers of children's fantasy. But Paul's callousness is chiefly in reaction against his aunt's sentimentality. One feels that he has a heart responsive to the *right* appeal, that he is the reader for whom the Borrower books are written.

Yet, in these books, Mrs. Norton was also re-creating a fantasy of her own childhood, for this is how she describes herself then, a shortsighted little girl: "When others saw the far hills, the distant woods, the soaring pheasant, I, as a child, would turn sideways to the close bank, the tree-roots, and the tangled grasses. Moss, fern-stalks, sorrel stems, created the *mise en scène* for a jungle drama. . . . One invented the characters — small, fearful people picking their way through miniature undergrowth; one saw smooth places where they might sit and rest; branched stems which might invite them to climb; sandy holes in which they might creep for shelter."

So perhaps those two main motives are really one. Significantly, Stevenson wrote to a friend about the completed *Treasure Island:* "If this don't fetch the kids, why they have gone rotten *since my day."* The italics are mine. From those words it seems that Stevenson was really writing for children he knew even more intimately than he knew Lloyd Osbourne — for the children of his own childhood, for himself as he was then. Lloyd Osbourne became a convenient device by which he projected that child from the past into the present, to tell him the kind of story he knew for certain that that child would enjoy.

Notice that Stevenson was not re-creating even remotely the kind of thing that might have happened to him as a boy. He was, in fact, delicate and shielded from rough adventures. No, he was inventing just the kind of thing such a boy liked imagining: voyages, pirates, treasure, and all the rest. In children's books we should be prepared to find the fantasies as well as the realities of the author's childhood. Even what seems fairly realistic may have been heightened and distorted for a private purpose. An unusually honest writer for children said of one of her books: "The children themselves ... were quite simply the kind that at fourteen I would like to have been myself; extrovert, with clear-cut and developed values, plenty of courage, and good at games — I having been the kind of child who had and was none of these things."

Sometimes children's literature is written from the more obviously "real" experiences of childhood, as in Richard Jefferies's *Bevis* or Ernest Thompson Seton's *Two Little Savages*. For this recalling of childhood one needs to have a clear memory, a quickening sympathy for the child one was, and, above all, perhaps, a brisk disregard for the biased remarks of the adult one has become. Childhood is so easily romanticized: the further off in time, the brighter the gleam of that Golden Age; or, on the other hand, the formative years can be blamed and blackened as the origin of all adult unhappiness and failure. Both views of childhood are oversimplifications. They are a view from such a long, adult way away that the distance creates a kind of mirage.

Writing about and for children, one should have a view almost from the inside, to re-create — not what childhood looks like now — but what it felt like then. What did it feel like, for instance, to be little, physically little? What did it feel like to be a child among children? Mr. and Mrs. Opie's factual study of *The Lore and Language of Schoolchildren* has documented a children's culture in Britain of almost unsuspected richness and vigor — and also savagery. One should remember that as a corrective to what is represented in so many jolly children's stories.

Really, there is very much unpleasantness in childhood that we adults forget — and much that some simply dare not remember. For, let's face it, a good deal of childhood is strong stuff for adults and totally unsuitable for children. Psychologists since Freud have told us some home truths, and novelists have always been able to guess a great deal for themselves — Henry James, for instance, in *The Turn of the Screw*, L. P. Hartley in *The Go-Between*, William Golding in *Lord of the Flies*. The most intense experiences of childhood can be, in more than one sense, unspeakable, certainly far beyond anything that a child's vocabulary of words and ideas is capable of, either for understanding or expression. Henry James wrote: "Small children have many more perceptions than they have terms to translate them; their vision is at any moment much richer, their apprehension even constantly stronger, than their prompt, their at all producible vocabulary." So novelists are sometimes driven literally to take the words out of the mouths of their child-characters, in order to replace them with something less realistic but much more deeply expressive.

But writers for children clearly have to use a language understood by children, more or less. ("More or less" only because some meanings may enter a child's mind and wait there for a later time of full understanding.) The children's writer must acknowledge himself unashamedly as a writer for children, without, for example, sly whimsicalities meant for adults reading aloud rather than for children being read to. He must write of children's interests, which are wide enough, anyway, and in children's language of understanding, which is a good way ahead of children's language of expression and always ready to be advanced still further. At the same time, he must do much more and be much more.

Through the re-creations of childhood one should feel the quality of an adult mind. Mrs. Hodgson Burnett, for instance, is a writer of moral seriousness but also of sentimentality; she is the creator of Little Lord Fauntleroy. Through Mrs. Norton's fantasies one feels the comment of a mind no less serious but much tougher; she is the creator of Paul. So, in any good book for children, we should expect the two parts of an author's life to come together: his own childhood experiences or interests, re-created fictionally, and his own maturity, reflected in the significance he chooses to give them. Both parts must be present and within the limits of what young readers can intellectually grasp or intuitively feel. Everyone knows that children are bored with writers with no understanding of childhood; but, equally, children will eventually begin to see through a writer, however entertaining, who is childish in outlook. Children themselves are facing toward maturity and taking steps toward it: an adult who stands still, peering backwards into their faces, is very soon going to become an embarrassment, and useless — even an obstacle — to their advance.

Then, is it not a curious, perhaps dangerous, discrepancy that the very child-heroes with whom this ever-developing child-reader is supposed to identify himself never grow to full maturity? In a good children's book, however, the child-characters, although not actually growing up, always appear capable of it. The children's writer not only makes a satisfactory connection between his present maturity and his past childhood, he also does the same for his child-characters in reverse — makes the connection between their present childhood and their future maturity. That their maturity is never visibly achieved makes no difference; the promise of it is there. The reader cannot predict what the mature individual will be; one can seldom predict that, even in real life. But there will be the certainty that the child-character already means something now, and will mean something more later; he'll grow up after the end of the book. Such a character is a fit companion for the imagination of an actual child who is actually growing up.

From *The Horn Book* for February, 1962

THE ACID TEST

By Marion Garthwaite

THERE ARE lemon trees, fine bearers, too, that produce big, juicy lemons so mild they are almost sweet. But to my notion sweet lemons are anomalies, lacking that *raison d'être*, the sharp and acidulous tartness needed to point up the flavor of meat and fish and salad greens.

Children want their witches, their giants and ogres, sour, too. They want them ugly, wicked, and dispatched, as all evil should be. That's what they're there for — the witches, the dragons, the giants, the whole horde of "wizards and wuzzards." They are there to be vanquished by a boy with the courage to face them down, or by a girl with wits enough to fool them and escape across a bridge of a single hair.

Of late years authors have been watering down witches, gentling them until they are well-intentioned creatures who mean no harm. If a child is too high-strung to listen to exciting stories, he shouldn't hear about witches. He needs some comforting stories that keep his world serene and warm and secure. This is right for most preschoolers, for many children up to the third grade. After that, or even before, if the children are conditioned to it, the Baba Yaga can come sailing in, seated in her stone mortar, sweeping away the path behind her with her besom. For children used to this kind of story, witches should have teeth in them, preferably iron and champing.

This applies to pictures of witches, too. The earlier artists, like Arthur Rackham, knew how to limn fearful witches. Henry Pitz doesn't mince matters, either. His witches and ogres, and Tenggren's, too, mean business — dirty work at the crossroads — fearsomely wicked creatures.

When children have been read to at home, progressing by easy stages from Mother Goose through the old accumulative tales, and then three this and three that, and on to the tougher stories, they can face fierce antagonists with equanimity and relish.

There comes a time when children need to realize that the world is not always serene and warm and secure, that it sometimes takes courage and quick wits and a grim hanging on before witches and hobgoblins can be routed. Like the hobbit, children have two sides to them. There's the side that wants to stay close to warmth and security. But there's also the Tookish side that yearns for far places and adventure and derring-do.

We can't let them go off at a tender age on ventures of their own — too much traffic. But we can give them vicarious experiences to fire their imaginations or to condition them to meet the challenges of an age gearing itself for flight into Heaven-knows-what. It doesn't make sense to keep children wrapped in wool while they miss out on a toughening process, with no understanding of the courage it takes to face struggle or the cleverness it takes to outwit a cunning adversary.

Some of our teen-agers realize they have been softened up instead of steeled. The thinking ones don't thank us for having made things too easy. They are scared, scared they aren't really brave, scared they won't know enough in a world that is tightening its standards of knowledge and reasoning, scared that they might not be able to cope. Cope with what? They aren't even sure of that, and their own fears are much worse than any witch or ogre ever invented.

As a storyteller I am convinced that the children who cringe are enjoying the cringing. They feel safe enough on a lap, in front of a fire, or gathered about a storyteller where there is friendly interest and a warmth of tone that says all will be well in the end — just wait — you'll see.

When the wee red man demands the carving knife to cut off the king's head, a boy will groan, *"Oh! No!"*, and then be lost again in the hilarious story. Children find this tale, told by a storyteller like Josephine Gardner of San Francisco, funnier and funnier the gorier it gets.

The cerebral-palsied children at the El Portal School in Hillcrest, California, are good listeners. They started out with an attention span equal to the early nursery tales with which they were familiar. The day they first heard Howard Pyle's "Three Little Pigs and the Ogre" we talked about ogres ahead of time. What was an ogre? The guesses from the children were, "He's a kind of a wolf," or "I think he's a bad giant."

"Yes, he's a kind of a wolf. He's a kind of a giant. He's always bad. And he's nearly always *stupid!*"

That did it. They enjoy hearing about the stupid old ogre being so gaily outwitted by the three little pigs. Children often feel stupid themselves. They want to hear about big, overgrown creatures being stupid.

These handicapped children identified themselves with the smartest of the three little pigs. They learned to take all kinds of stories — a grim fight to the death between Robin Hood and the savage, horse-hided Sir Guy of Gisbourne; the clang of lance against helmet as Arthur, barely healed of his wounds, once more thunders against the Black Knight; the hungry old witch clutching at Stoutheart and the maiden, as the power of the stone that keeps them flying just out of reach grows less with the setting sun.

There's acid in that old witch from South America, gobbling up the hard-shelled turtles that weigh her down to her doom.

If our villains are halfhearted, if our bandits give back the gold, or our witches fly about doing good deeds, our children can always sit glued to television sets — any time they choose in most homes — watching good triumph over evil by the simple and stultifying process of shooting it out.

There was nothing tame about the old stories. Cuchulain got his name because he became a watchdog for the man whose warden hounds the boy had strangled with his bare hands. Beowulf tore the arm of the monster Grendel from its socket and followed the evil creature to his lair beneath the sea where he fought the dragon's mother to her gory end.

Who dragged whom how many times around the walls of what? What boy sent a slung stone from the brook deep into the forehead of a giant whose spear had a shaft like a weaver's beam and a head that weighed six hundred shekels of iron?

These are stout old stories, full of battle, full of mouth-filling words that picture life and death "running beautiful together" and being met with courage and faith.

I am sure that the vivid stories we heard, the ones my mother or my grandmother read to us, were an emotional release for my brother and me. We used the stories for all kinds of creative activities. We acted them out, made all the costumes, provided all the props, and performed them at the slightest encouragement. We re-created the stories geared to our own experience and created fresh drama to meet our own limitations. The more horrendous the villains the easier it was to act them out.

We liked witch stories, but not stories of gentle, friendly witches. No such sissy stuff for Malcolm and me. We wanted witches who ate people. We were pleased when somebody pushed a wicked witch into the oven or ran off with a willy-willy-wag and the old witch's bag of gold.

Children don't want everybody good. H. H. Munro made this point in his story-within-a-story called "The Story-Teller." The children in that poking-of-fun at all tame storytellers were enchanted when the wolf ate up the insufferably good little girl, all except her good conduct medals. Even *he* couldn't swallow those! The children decided it was the most beautiful story they had ever heard.

On the other hand most children want evil vanquished. But they want the wicked bad enough to deserve it. When the old witch orders Hansel to stick out his finger to see if he has been fattened up enough to roast, anybody can see with half an eye that she is cooking up trouble for herself. I have never found a child who minded the dreadful penalties dreamed up for the wicked in the old tales. Barrels full of nails, pits full of vipers — if the wicked ones have earned it, serves 'em right!

Once when I was telling "Snow White and the Seven Dwarfs" I decided to temper the ending. To a man, the children protested. "You forgot the part where she had to dance in the red-hot shoes until she dropped down dead." Justice had not been done.

Children know it's just a story, a lively tale that goes galloping along to a satisfying end. In so many of these old folk and fairy tales the children see themselves in the same situations, where the small and the put-upon, the weak and the simple can match wits with the biggest and the worst, the slyest and most crafty. They can win out, too, if they are brave enough and kind enough and keep their wits about them. In the folk tales kindness and good manners pay off again and again.

We need to tell or read the old tales of witches and ogres with tongue in cheek, twinkle in eye, laughter in heart. In the voice, too, if the children seem to be taking the story too seriously.

But on the whole, pallid witches that don't bewitch, or gentle dragons that fail to drag people off, may lull our children (and of course this has its place with the too young or the insecure), but they won't do much to stimulate them. They won't do much to entice our young people into a creativeness of their own.

If our children are going to sail off into space in capsules, they should be brought up on the old-time witches who made it on broomsticks. There's no telling what they'll meet at the end of the ride. A firsthand acquaintance with a few dragons or Baba Yagas, Difs or wicked witches might not come amiss.

Witches should be sour, like good lemons, and as tart and zestful.

The only good witch is a really bad one. That's the acid test.

From *The Horn Book* for August, 1963

WHO'LL KILL THE MOCKINGBIRDS?

By David C. Davis

Who killed Cock Robin?
    I, said the sparrow,
    With my bow and arrow,
    I killed Cock Robin.

All the birds in the air
    Fell to sighing and sobbing,
    When they heard the bell toll
    For poor Cock Robin!

But would they have cared?
    Had it not been robin,
    Kind, gentle Cock Robin,
        Would they have cared?

Had it been Mockingbird
    Who fell from the arrow
Sent by the sparrow,
    Who would have cared?

WOULD THERE have been a trial? Ask yourself how you would have felt — that is, assuming that you can enter the bird world of fantasy and think as one of its members. How would it have been to have such a fellow as a *Mimus polyglottos* (which is how he's classified by ornithologists in the human kingdom) in the midst of an otherwise busy, normal society? What kind of a neighbor would he make, with his ability to embarrass you with mockery, lead you on wild-goose chases by mimicking your friends, and in general make himself a nuisance? As a citizen he'd be a dismal failure, and who could blame a bird for turning his eyes in the other direction if a wayward arrow, loosed by Sparrow, or any other bird, should down the irritating Mockingbird? In such an instance, would you have demanded a trial? Perhaps not.

Why worry, why speculate about what might have happened in this bit of traditional verse? Hasn't this mid-twentieth century enough to be concerned about without bringing in a hypothetical murder among the birds?

However, some of those who are involved with literature for children might see a parallel — and not such a farfetched one as might be supposed — between the mockingbird and its human counterpart. Mockingbird writers, these human counterparts of the *Mimus polyglottos*. But who are they? What about the writers who had unusual success with a book or two — and seem to think the formula can be used for another set or two? Can't they be termed mockingbirds? *Mimus autoglottos*, perhaps? Then there are the writers who could well be classified as true *Mimus polyglottos;* they imitate the styles and plots of pace-setting books to the extent that they seldom discover whether they are capable of individual contributions. And, sadly enough, there are the writers who, either consciously or subconsciously, lend their names and reputations to false trends and fads, which often enough are excellent financial risks. Would it be too far wrong if they were called *Mimus falsettoglottos?*

If it is not too far from reason to concede that mockingbird writers exist, can we say that they are evil? Probably not necessarily so, if we take into account the principles that have guided individuals ever since the first man became critical of his neighbor's actions.

It would be foolish to say that writers are basically different from other humans. Granted they were born with a singularity which gives them their own ways of perceiving, assimilating, registering, and reproducing thoughts and experiences. But so were actors, musicians, politicians, and salesmen. If writers are born with a specific potentiality, they must demonstrate, as must others, that they are fulfilling that potentiality. It is a writer's successful communication of insights and experiences that can stimulate readers to make the most of their own qualities.

True literature, then, is a form of communication — be it oral, picture, alphabet, or composite code systems — which weaves a mystical curtain enhancing the uniqueness of life, at the same time de-emphasizing the humdrumness of it. Literature breathing this living element is often referred to as "creative writing." And if it is to deserve this term, it must be sparked with originality, integrity, and plausibility. Without these three distinct, yet interrelated, elements there can be no "creative literature."

Children's literature has its share of writers who feed the souls of the young. Carroll, Lear, Greenaway, Crane, Brooke, Potter, Farjeon, Dickens, Norton, Lawson, Holling, Krumgold, White, Sawyer — the list runs into the hundreds of authors who have kept in balance the elements of originality, integrity, and plausibility. There are, on the other hand, writers who have succumbed to the blare, the dazzle, and the Barnum-like inducements of an easier manner of writing.

The autoglottos mockingbird writer is not quite honest with himself. He skips lightly over the fact that in literature each creation must stand on its own merits. He sings the same refrain over and over, never noticing if subsequent versions lack something. And soon, regrettably, both author and story are drained of vitality.

Margaret Wise Brown wrote much that was appealing to young children. But the drearily repetitious strain in her simple here-and-now sentences destroys even the more pleasant effect of a Muffin or a lonely rabbit, duck, or dead bird. Penetrating examination of recent picture-story books for the very young will reveal that many reputable writers and artists show definite signs of being affected with the malady of self-imitation. Even Garth Williams, who imprinted Wilbur upon our minds, has taken on the habits of his own distinctive rabbits and has overpopulated the illustrated trade book field with soft, fuzzy-looking animals.

The signs pointing to mockingbird tendencies often go unnoticed and, even when they are detected, appear to be of little consequence — until it is too late. The tragedy of the change from a writer with originality to one without originality is that the author's much-needed talent lies fallow as he fails to stretch out to greater heights of accomplishment.

True, the autoglottos ape only themselves, while the polyglottos seldom look for individuality within themselves, preferring rather to follow a leader. Such writers absorb the story forms or plots already established. They are imitators in the strict sense, sometimes receiving encouragement from reviewers who haven't taken the time to discover where the stories or characters might have originated and from the purchasing public, which often buys books because they are reminders of something vaguely familiar. *A Bear Called Paddington* by Michael Bond is scarcely heir apparent to the kingdom of Pooh. Those sentimentally attached to bears will follow Paddington's disastrous triumphs; but, if he overstays his visit in America, even this reasonable facsimile will grow tiresome.

The most overrated piece of writing reeking of blatant imitation appeared recently in Norman Juster's *The Phantom Tollbooth*. Had the book been given reliable critical analysis, it would never have reached the pages of a national magazine for previewing. To the children who love *Alice's Adventures in Wonderland, The Wind in the Willows,* and *The Hobbit,* this was a hodgepodge of words, dull, unrewarding, and completely lacking in humor, satire, or subtlety. It must have been a slight touch of this polyglottos illness that tempted Tony Palazzo to illustrate *Edward Lear's Nonsense Book.*

These specific examples are multiplied when one considers the contagious aspects that result when writers follow theme and subject trends. The overabundance of horse stories, justified by some who cling to the myth that children at certain ages must have horse stories, is an outstanding example. Pioneer episodes to satisfy correlation techniques applied by unthinking instructors is another. Watered-down "adolescent novels" respond to the vacuum in which the mid-century teen-ager is supposed to exist. Federal funds for science materials have caused an eruption of mediocre material that has put much science teaching back in the nineteenth-century period of fiction-coated fact. Family stories, school stories, Peckish boys' deeds, girls' romances, the emergence of Africa, the social class scene in India, atypical children, and the dozens of other faddish interests have given multiple birth to needless printed pages. And the advocates of "children reading *just for fun and relaxation*" have damaged the time-honored concept of reading for satisfaction and growth. Who is to say that the child who skims through the undemanding pages of *The Three-Seated Space Ship* has been relaxed any more than the one who shares the travels of *Adam of the Road*?

A book cannot be of value in contributing to a personal or curricular need unless it is of excellent quality. The introduction of false or unimportant material to satisfy a curricular need is unsound; drugging a child with mockingbird reading material under the guise of teaching him, or pleasing him, or relaxing him is fiddle-faddle! Polyglottos writers deserve a more critical eye than has been turned on them. Admitting that little can be done to protect the rights of the original sources, still there must be an obligation on the part of those who have some power to exert in selection and buying to filter out only the best of the works of piggy-back writers.

Discouraging as it is to witness the superabundance of imitators, it is even more disappointing to recognize the species of writer which can only be described as falsettoglottos. In plain language, falsettoglottos are simple, old-fashioned "backsliders." When reputable authors, who normally keep in balance the elements of integrity, originality, and plausibility, and who have a long record of healthy books to their credit, slip, it is disheartening. And unfortunately, the matter doesn't always end with one slipshod story being published. More often, that one story becomes a Typhoid Mary and unwittingly spreads the killer germ.

The backsliding that Theodore Geisel experienced when he began his romance with restricted vocabulary illustrates an interesting point. Dr. Seuss is a great humorist, and those who know him as such can forgive him for his minor errors (if he keeps them minor); but it is up to him to determine whether future historians of children's literature will credit him with being a children's humorist or an easy-to-read opportunist.

A foremost poet, teacher, lecturer, and critic — in *I Met a Man, The Reason for the Pelican,* and *You Read to Me, I'll Read to You* — indicates that those who seek to inspire in one sense sometimes fail utterly in another. The limited vocabulary, impressionistic illustration, and lack of culling hamper the very interest in poetry that John Ciardi authored in *How Does a Poem Mean?* It is an admirable objective to engage beginning readers in the delights of poetry; but should not the topflight American poetry reviewer serve the same sauce to his own "peoms"* that he has served to others?

A perceptive writer like Mr. DeJong produces such memorable stories as *The Tower by the Sea, Along Came a Dog, The Wheel on the School,* and *The House of Sixty Fathers* — and a gear slips. *The Last Little Cat* and *The Singing Hill* appear on the scene and only an occasional flicker and a flash feebly ignite from the pages.

Other gifted writers have developed overextended plots and labored characters at the expense of distinction. Why should we be disturbed? Is it that we are not tolerant of the failures of these authors whom we so much admire? Or is it that we question not the fact that the stories were written but rather the fact that their authors allowed them to be published? Do they not realize their own exalted obligation to their readers?

Does the human genus of the mockingbird clan need to breed? Are formulae and imitations to be celebrated over the imaginativeness that exists in literature? Is our business machinery overshadowing the art and craft components of writing? Is it possible that children's literature is degenerating to repetitious drivel? Is it time to determine whose responsibility it is to avoid such a fate? Literature for children affects too many people too early in their impressionable years for adults to fail to give it serious consideration. For this reason these questions should not go unanswered.

If we are truly concerned, the initial step is to determine who is responsible for high standards. First are the writers themselves. Next are the publishers with their particular problems and insights. Third are the reviewers and professional consultants. Last are the purchasers — teachers, librarians, parents, or children. No one group can be held singly responsible, yet all must accept responsibility.

Writers must always be conscious of the elements of living literature. If they do not define distinguished material as that which reveals originality, integrity, and plausibility, then they must broadcast their own working definitions as do research

---

*peom — a group of words put together for the purpose of making a poem, but failing to reach the goal.

workers in other fields. Writers must be alert to trends, fads, and government subsidies that tempt. *They must not gamble with integrity.*

Publishers should balance business considerations with the art of selection and the understanding of quality craftsmanship. These three aspects of the publishing world require wisdom and courage. Publishers may rely too often on an expanding group of reviewing experts who lack the insight to judge. Selecting stories for publication is an art — not a one, two, three-step science. Because it is an art, more editors must not only transmit to writers why they select as they do but also take credit when they choose wisely. The batting averages of editors should be a credit to their profession and known to interested parties.

Reviewers help to establish the level of children's literature. Previews, book lists, and reviews that simply redigest the material on the book jacket do little to promote higher standards. Lessons that have been taught by master writers and critics Bertha Mahony Miller, Anne Carroll Moore, Padraic Colum, Howard Pease, Mary Gould Davis, Anne Thaxter Eaton, and C. S. Lewis need to be remembered by contemporary reviewers. Fresh approaches should be tested and the lockstep procedures broken if we are to improve many of the reviewing techniques now in practice. A book should first be judged for its apparent worth and then given a second review a few months or a year after publication. A true and therefore valuable review requires reflection, and reflection demands time. Literature cannot be reviewed in the same way that the American public chooses from the new models of automobiles.

Sharing responsibility also is the fourth group of individuals who influence the quality of literature for children — teachers and librarians. They are the contact points between the book and the reader. This segment of the reading world should be certain that it understands the nature of writing and literature before it pushes the contact button. Trifles such as reader's level, vocabulary difficulty, subject interests, correlation, enrichment, or extension of experience should not overshadow the task of determining which books are made available and what the reader *as an individual* needs, wants, or can benefit by experiencing. Such professional persons must train the young reader to accept the responsibility of selecting quality books, a goal which may best be reached by adults first establishing concepts of distinction in the child's mind.

Joining these professional groups to complete the ranks of the purchasers are the parents and other adults who roam through the bookstores. To these adults, of course, the booksellers themselves have a responsibility. No excuse for stocking shelves with inconsequential and unworthy books can be offered for any bookseller. Yet, only if responsibility has been accepted by writers, publishers, reviewers, and purchasers, can booksellers be held accountable for what they make available.

When people become aware that the price of a book cannot be the basis of selection and that both expensive and inexpensive publications may contain inconsequential material; when the value of a book is not thought of in dollars and cents, or color or print, but in its power to make the reader believe and become a part of a story or subject; when a child wants to own a book, reread it, and place it with his favorites on his own personal bookshelf — then will we know that we are, in part, accepting the responsibility that is placed upon adults.

Who'll kill the mockingbird tendencies? Will the breed cease to prosper if each group accepts its responsibilities? Will they diminish with inspired, informed writers, publishers, reviewers, and purchasers? Will the formula writers, the imitators, and the backsliders be brought to trial?

The people who care about children and books have the answers — and the obligation.

From *The Horn Book* for June, 1963

THE COMMON GROUND*

By Ann Petry

WHENEVER I think that I have defined what I believe or what I am doing, or saying, or thinking, I find myself laughing, because I invariably think of a story that Robert Graves tells in 5 *Pens in Hand*. He says that the story is a very old one, but I had never read it until I found it in his delightful book.

An old lady was taking a pet tortoise by train, in a basket, from London to Edinburgh, and wanted to know whether she ought to buy a dog-ticket for it, as one has to do in England if one takes a cat by train — because cats officially count as dogs. "No," said the ticket inspector, "no, mum! Cats is dogs, and rabbits is dogs, and dogs is dogs, and squirrels in cages is parrots; but this here turkle is a hinsect. We won't charge you nothing, mum!"

It seems to me that this world of ours, in which a turtle can be classified as an insect, contains other and more serious confusions and contradictions. All too often our world fits Herodotus' description of a Greek market as "a place set apart for people to go and cheat each other on oath." That aspect of the world is revealed in newspapers, on the radio, on television.

The world of children's books obviously offers another set of values, for it is a world diametrically opposed to the Greek market place — and it is something more.

The same Herodotus who described the market place was, according to Edith Hamilton, the first person to give Greece the idea that an expression in prose could have the worth of a line of poetry. The expression in prose of a poetic idea is the

*An edited version of a talk given by Mrs. Petry at the Central Children's Room of the New York Public Library on November 16, 1964.

something-more always to be found in the best books for children, books that seem to have been written by people who had a touch of honey on the lips. If you are willing to accept the Greek idea that a true poet's lips are touched with honey, then many of the people who write children's books are poets.

Here is a sample of prose-poetry from Howard Pyle's *Otto of the Silver Hand*. Otto is a little boy living in a monastery, and his best friend is Brother John.

> But most of all they loved to lie up in the airy wooden belfry; the great gaping bell hanging darkly above them, the mouldering cross-beams glimmering far up under the dim shadows of the roof, where dwelt a great brown owl that, unfrightened at their familiar presence, stared down at them with his round, solemn eyes. Below them stretched the white walls of the garden, beyond them the vineyard, and beyond that again the far shining river, that seemed to Otto's mind to lead into wonder-land. There the two would lie upon the belfry floor by the hour, talking together of the strangest things.

When Brother John speaks of a vision he had in the garden, he says, " 'I was walking there, and my wits were running around in the grass like a mouse. What heard I but a wonderful sound of singing, and it was like the hum of a great bee, only sweeter than honey.' "

The Courage of Sarah Noble by Alice Dalgliesh is filled with poetry and poetic ideas. It is in the very sound of the words *Keep up your courage, Sarah Noble. Keep up your courage.* In 1707 John Noble and his eight-year-old daughter, Sarah, were en route from Westfield, Massachusetts, to the wilderness of Connecticut to build a house in New Milford. During their journey

> ... they came to the cabin where the candle wood was lighted early.
> They knocked. The latch was lifted and a woman stood in the doorway looking at them.
> *She is not like my mother,* Sarah thought. *Her face is not like a mother's face.*

Another example: Joseph Krumgold's *... and now Miguel* is filled with poetry, and with poetic ideas. Miguel wants only to go with the men when they take the sheep up into the high mountains to graze for the summer; he knows that then he will be regarded as a man.

In our family there is always one thing, and that is the sheep. The summer passes and the winter comes and soon it is Easter and the time for spring; but all the time, no matter when, there is the sheep. In our house we may be very happy. Like the time my littlest sister, Faustina, was born. Or very sad. Like when Young Blas was hurt by the mowing machine. But these things they come and go. Everything comes and goes. Except one thing. The sheep.

For that is the work of our family, to raise sheep.

What effect do these splendid books have on children? Do they remember them?

Of course; not only do they remember them, but quite often they act out a scene, a story from a favorite book. In his journal Coleridge speaks of the role that books played in his early childhood. He says that his one desire always was to crumple himself up in a sunny corner and read, read, read. He often acted out what he had been reading.

To this day I am affected by Howard Pyle's *The Garden Behind the Moon*. I was born and grew up in a small town in Connecticut. It is located where the Connecticut River goes into Long Island Sound, so the town is almost surrounded by water. (I have always felt that I had a special understanding of Mrs. Susan Fosdick in *The Country of the Pointed Firs*. She felt very strongly about what she called landlocked folks. When she heard a story about a minister who suddenly stood up in a small sailboat and nearly capsized it, she said, "I do think they ought not to settle them landlocked folks in parishes where they're liable to be on the water.") Anyway, I was brought up close to the sea — to gulls and sand and salt water and pebbly beaches. I was familiar with the smell of the marshes at low tide. I knew the difference in the smell of the air when the tide was going out, and I knew how it freshened when the tide was coming in.

Perhaps *The Garden Behind the Moon* would not have had the same effect on landlocked folks. But whenever I see moonlight on the water, see that long path, glistening, shining — what Howard Pyle called the moonpath — I have been tempted to try to walk on it straight out to the moon.

I can remember kneeling down at a second-floor window in my aunt's house, my nose pressed against the window screen, aware of the damp smell from the sea — the tide was coming in and the air was cold and moist — smell of the sea and the marshes, smell of the metal in the screen.... I must have been about eight years old, and I yelled out of the window at one of our neighbors, a middle-aged, gray-haired woman, "Hans Kraut, your wits are out! Your wits are out!"

Hans Kraut was like Brother John in *Otto of the Silver Hand*; his wits ran around in the grass like a mouse, and the boys in the village used to run behind him, shouting, "Hans Kraut, your wits are out." I do not know how or in what way our middle-aged neighbor resembled Hans Kraut. I doubt that she did. I was simply acting out a scene from *The Garden Behind the Moon*.

You may well say to me, Fine, wonderful; but that was a long time ago. What about today? Right now. Does the same thing happen now?

Yes. It does.

Recently one of my neighbors was twelve years old, and I took him a birthday present. Though I rang the doorbell of his house, nobody came to the door. I could see Judy, his ten-year-old sister, at the back of their yard, where they have a small orchard. I walked down to the orchard, gave her her brother's present, and also gave her an unbirthday present for herself. Then I paused to admire a tree house that her father had built for her in an apple tree. He had painted it yellow.

I said, "What a wonderful tree house. It has a door and two windows."

She said, "That is not a tree house."

I said, "It isn't?"

"No," she answered. "It's a claim shanty and I am going to spend the first of those blizzards in it before I move into town."

I smiled and said, "Oh, yes, I see." I remembered Laura Ingalls Wilder's description of the claim shanty in *By the Shores of Silver Lake*, a little house almost lost in the grasses with its roof sloped all one way, as if it were only half a roof.

And now I live right next door to that claim shanty because a ten-year-old is playing the part of Laura in the Laura Ingalls Wilder books.

I have talked about other people's books and have quoted from them. What about my own?

Certainly I have tried to add the something-more for which I have expressed admiration. My only comment is to say sadly that a writer's reach always exceeds his grasp.

I don't know that I have ever questioned my own intentions, and the degree to which I have carried them out, quite as seriously as I did just a few weeks ago. I had been at the library in the small town where I live. As I was about to leave, a little girl came in to return a book of mine, a book I wrote about Harriet Tubman. She was carrying it hugged close to her chest. She laid it down on the table, and the librarian said to her, "You know, this is Mrs. Petry, the author of the book you are returning."

I must confess that I was dismayed, because though I have received letters from children and from adults who had read my books, and though I have had children tell me they enjoyed something I had written, I had never had a face-to-face encounter with a young reader who was actually holding one of my books. The child looked at me, and I looked at her — she didn't say anything and neither did I. I didn't know what to say. Neither did she. Finally she reached out and touched my arm, ever so gently, and then drew her hand back as though she were embarrassed. I copied her gesture, touching her gently on the arm, because I felt it would serve to indicate that I approved her gesture.

Then I left the library, but I left it thinking to myself: What have I said to this child in this book? What was I saying in the other books I have written for children and for young people? What am I really saying to them? Of course, I have been saying, Let's take a look at slavery. I said it in *Harriet Tubman* and again in *Tituba of Salem Village*.

But what else was I saying? Over and over again, I have said: These are people. Look at them, listen to them; watch Harriet Tubman in the nineteenth century, a heroic woman, a rescuer of other slaves. Look at Tituba in the seventeenth century, a slave involved in the witchcraft trials in Salem Village. Look at them and remember them. Remember for what a long, long time black people have been in this country, have been a part of America: a sturdy, indestructible, wonderful part of America, woven into its heart and into its soul.

What else was there in these books for the child who had touched my arm? Why did she touch my arm?

Perhaps, I thought, because there is something more in the books than the excitement that lies naturally, innately in the stories themselves. These women were slaves. I hoped that I had made them come alive, turned them into real people. I tried to make history speak across the centuries in the voices of people — young, old, good, evil, beautiful, ugly.

There is, however, something more than that. For there is a common ground on which all the people involved in the world of children's books — authors, illustrators, editors, publishers, librarians, teachers, critics, and reviewers — there is a common ground on which we meet, or perhaps I should say a belief that we share with that little girl in the library in Old Saybrook.

The shared belief? The common ground? What is it? It is the very antithesis of Herodotus' description of a Greek market as a place where men go to cheat each other on oath. This belief is, I think, summed up by Archibald MacLeish in that magnificent book, *The Dialogues of Archibald MacLeish and Mark Van Doren,* edited by Warren V. Bush:

> I know for myself if I were put through the orange squeezer and squeezed to the point where the pips began to squeak . . . [and he repeats this] I do think if I were squeezed down to the point where the pips began to emit high, shrill sounds, I would have to say, that what I surely do believe in is the unspeakable, infinite, immeasurable, spiritual capacity of that thing called a man; a capacity which expresses itself in so many ways, but expresses itself nowhere more perfectly than in the capacity for friendship, which is really a capacity for love.

From *The Horn Book* for April, 1965

BENCH MARKS FOR ILLUSTRATORS OF CHILDREN'S BOOKS

By Warren Chappell

ONE OF my weekly pleasures as a *Punch* subscriber is seeing each new masthead drawing by Ernest Shepard. Punch and his dog Toby respond to the artist's inventiveness and rich experience as readily as did Pooh, Tigger, and Eeyore, at an earlier time, and seasons and events are made to move around them. Shepard is a professional pen-draughtsman, and they are rare these days. It is easy to trace his line right back to Leech, recalling other *Punch* artists like Tenniel, Keene, and Caldecott. He has a kinship with our own Edwin Abbey, who lived in England for some years. I have been told that he is part Spanish, which could give him a sense of relationship with Vierge and Rico.

Ernest Shepard, Sir John Tenniel, and A. B. Frost have managed in the *Pooh* books, *Alice*, and *Uncle Remus* to put their names as indelibly on these works as did the authors. They are like actors who have created roles and forever devised their stage business to their successors. It is interesting to note that all of them worked as professionals, drawing against weekly deadlines for periodicals. There is no hint of naïveté in their approach and no sign of any advisory intervention by a child psychiatrist. We must all regret that Stevenson and Mark Twain were not blessed with such perfect pictorial collaborators. From some of his comments it is evident that Mark Twain's graphic sense was not highly developed but he did know enough to be dissatisfied with his illustrators, and when Dan Beard was about to do drawings for the *Connecticut Yankee*, he wrote that he hoped Beard would read the book.

If we are going to call the children's book illustration of Shepard, Tenniel, and Frost ideal, in its way (and time has done just that), then we can learn a simple lesson: There should be no such category as children's illustration, for none of these men changed hats to undertake their celebrated drawings. We might then go even further and question the whole concept of illustration as something special and apart, rather than as a natural medium like painting or print-making. There have been more great artists who have been illustrators than not. And it is well to keep in mind that some of the greatest illustrations were not even made for publication, notably Rembrandt's for The Bible and Daumier's for *Don Quixote*, yet they are *book* illustrations.

Artists like Van Gogh and Picasso can be admired for their creations, and can stimulate and attract imitators, but they are sports and cannot teach. The bench marks of an illustrator should be sought in the works of those universal spirits who found so many of their themes in literature and who had what Baudelaire called "a kind of fierce spirit of competition with the written word." This was to describe Delacroix whose work, the poet observed, "sometimes seems to me a kind of remembrance of the greatness and passion of the universal man." One could hardly hope to find a better statement of what should be an illustrator's goal.

It should be taken for granted that an illustrator of books must know his craft. He should have not only a knowledge of the means of printing but a deep tactile sense of its capacities. He must be able to project his expression past the plate and the press and onto the sheet, for it is the printed result that is the end in view. Craftsmanship of the highest order will not make a great artist. It is the exception when menial engravers ascend the heights of art, as did Blake and Hogarth. Great artists, however, have always managed to be masters of the necessary craftsmanship.

"A classic must be about something and by somebody," said Carl Van Doren, in a short speech addressed to the subject "How to Write a Classic." This aphorism might just as well apply to artists as to writers, and it would be obviously absurd to expect a large bucket of imagination from a small well of experience. So, an illustrator needs to know much more than the means of making drawings which will print. He should aspire to become a man of broad culture. Of necessity, his art must be his way of life, and his expression of life should be illuminated by his personal vision and his spirit.

In the days when artists learned through apprenticeship, a part of their training was to make copies from the large collection of drawings which were a part of the resources of every studio. Art was passed on, like an inheritance. But the beneficiary was in no way restricted; he made his own individual use of his legacy and in time passed it on, perhaps with some increase. For those illustrators who want to be a part of the continuity of exploration, to try to make their passage on the main stream of art even though it might have to be along the shallower banks, it is still important to look at what has been done and to try to master it through understanding. Otherwise they might be like the young student at the Berlin Academy who announced, in the early 'twenties, that he had found he could draw on stone, with grease, and print from it. "Wonderful," said his teacher, "you have invented lithography a hundred and twenty-five years too late."

It is worse than hazardous to try to assemble a portfolio of drawings and prints for study by a mythical group of apprentices in a Universal Studio. But there are some artists who seem to arrange themselves into a hierarchy of illustration and whose places there cannot be very hotly contested. Certainly their works contain essential bench marks for an illustrator. At the top I would put Rembrandt, "that sublime figure in the history of art." The lessons to be learned from Rembrandt are infinite, for his range of expression, as draughtsman, is so wide as to embrace almost the whole gamut of drawing. One looks in fascination at his simultaneous achieving of form and symbol, at his breathing, broken line that maintains the tension which is inherent in search. One can follow his inventiveness through a series of drawings on a single theme, as he moves around the subject like a painter moving around a model. Above all, there is a universal quality in his statements which lifts their themes above the level of incident. That is a prime objective for an illustrator, just as a portrait painter should want to achieve more than a likeness.

Below Rembrandt, put Daumier, Goya, Delacroix, and Callot, despite the fact that the last-named came before the first, in time, and had a great influence on him in both style and subject matter. For our purposes, especially, I would like to see Daumier lifted above the other three, for he was a professional illustrator and journalist and, like Rembrandt, he drew structurally and had the genius of fusing form and symbol. Again, I want to quote from Charles Baudelaire. "As an artist, Daumier is distinguished by his assurance. He draws like the great masters. His drawing is broad, facile, a constant improvisation, yet never divorced from reality. He has a marvelous, almost superhuman, memory which serves him in place of a model. All his figures are well poised, always convincing in their movement. His gift of observation is so sure that one finds in his work not a single head unsuited to the body that supports it."

It is the measure of Daumier's genius that, after a lifetime of illustration and journalistic drawing, he could turn to painting and do it with the same authority which had characterized his graphic work.

Goya is close to us in his draughtsmanship, and his violence is certainly not a stranger to our time. However, his chief messages to our mythical apprentices should lie in his boldly designed compositions and in his capacity to carry his passion past the plate and into a print.

Delacroix has been referred to earlier, in quotations from Baudelaire. He was one of the giants of the nineteenth century and was a passionate reader of Shakespeare, Dante, Byron, and Ariosto. He was constantly taking themes from literature and his series of lithographs for *Faust* won Goethe's praise as being more than a complement to the text. One can learn from Delacroix because Delacroix spent his life in learning.

Callot is one of the most obvious ancestors of illustration as we know it. In him one sees the beginnings of several lines of illustration, especially the decorative, and above all he presages its eventual setting apart as a minor, and craft-aspect, of art.

In the drawings, paintings, and prints of these five artists any illustrator can find the nearest to absolute standards he should hope for. After all, perfection can only be achieved by the uninformed! Our apprentices must be searching for a broader understanding of the nature of drawing, its symbols and conventions, in all their varieties. They should want to see pictorial narration at its greatest, with incident providing the particularized setting for universal experiences. The making of a picture and the achieving of form are an artist's lifetime problems and he would do well to try to understand the searching improvisations and the constant efforts toward greater realization which were made by the masters. Perhaps then he might keep himself as dissatisfied as they were.

Of course, there are many other portfolios in the Universal Studio to which our apprentices have access, and in them will be the works of those who have made particular contributions to illustration. Among them are the revelations of Blake, the social commentary of Hogarth and Gavarni, the caricatures of Rowlandson and Busch, the historical reconstructions of Menzel, the illustrations made for children by Caldecott, Tenniel, Frost, Lear, and Nicholson, and the exuberant drawings of Doré.

I wish to conclude with a quotation from Boardman Robinson, a great draughtsman and illustrator and my dear friend and teacher:

"The practice of illustration, as I see it, is in one respect quite different from easel or mural painting, for it necessarily refers to something outside itself. The subject matter, the literary content, assumes a new significance, and the illustration must reflect this. From my point of view, the illustrator should not enter upon his task with too fixed a preconception; he should not have in mind too pronounced a pattern. The illustration is not pre-composed, but it must be allowed to grow, so to speak, from the seed of the impulse. Upon reading a poem or a work of fiction or history, I *see* a picture, and I go to work, usually without sketches, and I try to bring the picture to life, to develop and make actual that subjective impression. This subjective impression is, by definition, my own, not the author's, although he provides the stimulus. My impression is not his, nor is it that of any other reader."

From *The Horn Book* for October, 1957.

THE ART OF ILLUSTRATION
By Henry C. Pitz

ILLUSTRATION can be and sometimes is a racket. It is also a trade, and, better still, it is very often a craft. At times it reaches the upper levels and becomes an art. I think the only level we need deprecate is that of the racketeer, which, happily, is not really present in the field of children's book illustration, although it lurks sometimes in advertising and magazine illustration. But in a sense, illustration is, as we have said, a trade — not a fact to be ashamed of. One has to know one's trade, and I would say that almost every good children's book illustrator does just that.

A craft is a level of art which is worthy of anybody's respect. One cannot be a craftsman without a gift, however modest. There must be a brain not only in the skull but a brain in the fingers. The craftsman rejoices in the things his hands make and his mind conceives. Illustration today is one of the last strongholds of the craftsman. Modern industrial life has wiped craftsmanship out in large areas, and we are the losers thereby.

The children's book illustrators, I think, are a special breed of human being. They are not always greatly gifted; but, as a whole, they are the most devoted and dedicated group I know. Most of them give all they can, which fact leads me to remark about two viewpoints we can take about children's book illustration.

Like all illustrators, I have at times cursed the whole mechanics of printing — publishing, art directors, and editors. We all have moments of exasperation when we feel hemmed in by trivialities, misconceptions, and handicaps of various kinds. We think that, if we were free of them, we could function much more eloquently. When I am in such a mood, I can find any number of faults with our children's books: the way they are reproduced, the way they are illustrated, the way they are written, and so on. But I am an ambivalent kind of person, and I find it quite easy to shift my ground, change my focus, and find another answer.

I have been particularly conscious of that answer in the last few years. Some little time ago a publisher asked me to write a book on children's illustration, and I thought I would be delighted to do so. It has turned out to be much more difficult than I expected, even though I have spent most of my life in this field. I am not unfamiliar with the illustrations of the past or present, but I still find my knowledge inadequate.

One of my weak spots has been the work of foreign illustrators. On a recent trip to Europe I had letters of introduction to many artists and publishers and spent much of my time in bookshops, trying to find out all I could about what is happening in the children's book world in the Scandinavian countries, in Germany, Switzerland, Austria, Italy, France, and England. My reaction to what I discovered was one of bitter disappointment. Any time that I am tempted to be harsh in my criticism of American book illustration for children, I have only to think of what I found on the other side of the Atlantic. Of course, there were some excellent things, but the over-all picture is not exciting in the least.

Perhaps there is a perfectly good reason for this lack of excitement abroad. When we look at American illustrations, I think one of the first reactions is to note their diversity. They speak in so many voices. One finds individual voices having their say. Nowhere in any of the European countries can one find anything comparable to that. Even when we say things badly, we usually say them with a certain amount of vigor and conviction. This is no wonder, of course, when we consider the artists who are making the pictures for these books and the people who preside over the manufacture of them. Last evening I wrote down a few names as they came to me, some of the American-born illustrators: du Bois, McCloskey, Politi, Ishmael, Ward, Provensen, Weisgard, Krush, Daugherty, Hader, Lenski, Gramatky, and Milhous. These are just names I picked at random, but they call up a wealth of racial and cultural background. Out of this diversity must come something multicolored and exciting.

Remember, too, that some of our finest illustrators, though

not born here, have become Americans by choice. Why did Rojankovsky, Kredel, Wiese, d'Aulaire, Balet, Duvoisin, and Tenggren come here? Not to chase dollars, I am quite sure. They came because there were opportunities here.

In my more expansive moods I feel like saying that we live in what is a golden age in children's book illustration, without being fully aware of it. I have the feeling that twenty-five or fifty years from now people will look back upon this age as a very brilliant one. Perhaps illustration will go on to greater heights, but posterity will not disparage us.

How does the work of the present hold up against that of the past? I have a pretty good collection of children's books of the past. A few summers ago I was in a little New England town which has a remarkable library. Although it is kept fairly well up-to-date, the bulk of it was assembled in the 1880's and '90's and contains a wonderful collection of children's books of that period. Certain histories speak of that era and of the early years of this century as a golden age of illustration. Assuredly, there were some very fine things among those books and magazines. In the bound copies of *St. Nicholas, Harper's Young People,* and in the adult magazines, too, there are some brilliant, wonderfully fine illustrations, as good as anything done today and sometimes better. But they are buried among a great deal of mediocre work. I think we need not hesitate one moment to measure our work with that of the past. We come off well by comparison. We are fortunately drawing on a great reserve of talent which gets weeded out drastically, because, as Fritz Eichenberg has said, "Illustration is a discipline," and discipline very rapidly discourages the weak of will, the weak of purpose, and even the weak of talent.

Another line of credit should be given, I think, to our editors. The editors of children's books are almost all women — sharp and bright and well informed, and quite daring. As a matter of fact, I sometimes think they are occasionally too daring. Sometimes they succumb to the temptation to be chic. I can think of some children's books that were lauded in the past. When they are five years old, they are like last year's hats — beginning to be repulsive. The weakness here comes from excess of virtue. These editors are looking for lively, expressive, eloquent work, and they are sometimes overeager.

One of the interesting things about my trip abroad was that very often, when an exceptionally good set of illustrations was shown me, I already knew the illustrator. In some cases I even knew the set, because the American rights had already been secured by one of our lively young editors, or because the illustrator's work had already been exploited here. When viewing any large group of American book illustrations, one is in a sense looking at the book illustrations of the world. Librarians can well be proud of the volumes which they have on their shelves.

Fritz Eichenberg has said that librarians are very kind. There is no doubt about it. But I wish at times that they were more blunt, even unkind. I wish they would stand up for their own opinions, whether or not they are right. Librarians have a tendency to be easily talked down and converted to the theories of persuasive speakers. I wish them to be more resistant, more critical of the books which pass through their hands. Intelligent evaluation is needed in every field of endeavor.

American children's book illustration has elements of greatness in it. It has been fortunate in the people who have been attracted to it. Its triumphs have been many, but now, as it becomes less personal and more and more big business, a new doubt and a new challenge loom ahead. Can its creative vitality remain healthy under giantism?

From *The Horn Book* for October, 1962

AN ILLUSTRATOR'S VIEWPOINT
By Barbara Cooney

ADORNMENT of the written or printed word, illustration as we call it, is an ancient practice, an art not to be dismissed lightly. I use the word "art" because I believe illustration is, or should be, an art. Too much distinction is made today between "fine art" and "applied art," between "fine art" and "commercial art." Somewhere between these terms hovers the word "illustration." Yet all these terms are of comparatively recent vintage in the history of art. In ancient Greece all art was covered by one word: *tekhne*. The classical artist used his skill where the need arose. The artist today whose pictures lie within book covers should work with as much care, skill, and understanding as the artist whose pictures hang on the wall in gold frames.

Fifteen centuries before Christ the text of the Egyptian papyrus rolls known as *The Book of the Dead* was illustrated with brilliantly painted pictures. Illustrated books were not uncommon in early Rome. In the Middle Ages throughout Europe monks laboriously and lovingly ornamented their vellum pages, and in Persia the manuscripts were a delight to the eye. Now, why did men take these pains to adorn their words? What was the function of this adornment? It was certainly something more than that of the alluring wrapping around a toffee candy; it was more than a "come-on" to entice people to read; it was more than just factual instruction. Books were adorned because they were treasures. They were the storehouses of wisdom, wit, beauty, and knowledge; and, as such, they were treated with reverence and made beautiful. The binding, the ornamentation, the illustration, the very letters themselves, all were made to be as beautiful as possible. Decoration, then, is the first function of illustration. A second function that it often performs is that of elucidating or interpreting the text. A distinction must be made between mere pictorial representation or instruction and interpretation.

Furthermore, while decoration does nothing more than decorate, elucidation must decorate as well as elucidate. These two principles apply as much to today's machine-produced books as they did to the Egyptian papyri and the manuscripts of the medieval world.

Certainly, the illustrated book is not a necessity. Neither is the opera. Neither is the ballet. But is it not satisfying to see with one's eyes, to feel with one's hands, a book that is illustrated and printed well? Man's senses overlap. An idea can be communicated by literature, by music, by drama, by art, and by combinations of these, one art enhancing the other. How well an illustrator transfers an author's idea to his own medium is the measure of his success as an illustrator. Dickens cannot have been too dismayed over Cruikshank's Fagin, nor Harris over Frost's Br'er Rabbit, nor Carroll over Tenniel's Alice. Also, as a symphony can be variously interpreted by different conductors so can a text be illustrated, and illustrated well, by different artists. *The Arabian Nights* and *Don Quixote* have had various successful interpretations. It is difficult to choose between the pictures Rackham and Shepard made for *The Wind in the Willows,* or between those made by Thomas Nason and Aldren Watson for *Walden.* As a composer can be dismayed over a bad interpretation or the poor execution of his music, so can an author be dismayed when his book is badly or thoughtlessly or incorrectly illustrated. But this does not discredit illustration as such. A book *jacket* may be likened to a candy wrapping, but not the illustration proper. The two principles, decoration and elucidation, remain as the true functions of illustration.

A book does not have to be illustrated in order to be beautiful, but it must be well-designed. That too is an art, an abstract art. I am sure the general reader has little conception of the work that good bookmaking entails. I am afraid many authors don't know much about it either. The majority of publishers, I think, are in the book business because they love books. They want to produce books that are a pleasure to read, to look at, and to hold. But bookmaking is, after all, a business nowadays. Unfortunately, the publisher must consider dollars and cents. Bindings can no longer be encrusted with pearls and rubies.

Authors cannot expect gold tooling. Nor can designers have unlimited margins. Fortunately, paper is less scarce than vellum used to be. We do not have to run our words together or abbreviate them to save space as the monks did in the Middle Ages. There is enough paper. But it costs money. So do ink and glue and cloth. But even with the limitations of the cost of production an author has the right to expect good bookmaking. He deserves to see his words printed in good type with good ink on good paper in a well-designed book, the text and design forming a harmonious whole. A book harmonious in all ways means that everyone concerned in its making — the editor, the designer, the production head, the illustrator (if there was one), the printer, and the binder — all have worked in accord; all have tried to interpret the meaning and the mood of the author's words and put them in tangible form. Knowing this, an author should choose, if he can, a publishing house that will give his words this sort of care.

Besides being aware of the complexity of producing a book, it might help an author whose words are likely to be illustrated to know a little about the problems of illustration itself. Assuming that the author has had his manuscript accepted by a good publisher, one immediate problem is the choice of an illustrator. He should be a competent artist and craftsman; he should be in sympathy with the text; and, of course, he should be available. The first duty of a good illustrator is to know his manuscript cold. No illustrator worth his salt makes factual mistakes, substitutes blond hair for brown or shirts for jackets. Another problem confronting an illustrator is the distribution of the pictures throughout the book. These must be more or less evenly placed, not bunched together in groups with great stretches of unillustrated pages in between. They should flow through the book in a rhythm that is interesting to the eye, neither anticipating the action nor coming too long after it. A half-page drawing here, a full-page one there, here a spot, there a spot, and so on. The illustrator tries to vary his pictures somewhat as a movie director tries to vary his shots, to avoid monotony. The difficulty is that points of pictorial interest are rarely spaced evenly in a manuscript. Think of the long stretches of conversation that can go on and on, page after page. Though they may be fun to read, they are likely to be unillustratable. Understandably, illustrators cannot help but have a different viewpoint from writers.

There is, there cannot help but be, much shoddy illustrating in this day of mass-produced books. But there is much good illustrating, too. If children want their books illustrated, as admittedly they do, and at the same time do not like the illustrations in the books they find in their library, I think then that the books in that library must be poorly illustrated. I do not know the condition of book-publishing in general across the Atlantic. I have seen fine children's books published in England, as well as in other European countries. Were these exceptions? Do these children have access to these books? Do they have access to books of ours such as, say, *Moby Dick* illustrated by Rockwell Kent; *Wuthering Heights*, *Jane Eyre*, and Poe's *Tales* illustrated by Fritz Eichenberg; *The Treasure Trove of the Sun* illustrated by Rojankowsky; or any of the *Little House* series illustrated by Garth Williams? If they have seen these books or books whose illustration is of similiar quality and do not like the illustrations, I might conclude that Ruskin was right when, telling an English audience that they, as a nation, did not truly care for art, he said, "I say you have despised art! ... You know nothing of your own faculties or circumstances. You fancy that, among your damp, flat, fat fields of clay, you can have as quick art-fancy as the Frenchman among his bronzed vines, or the Italian under his volcanic cliffs.... You care for pictures, absolutely, no more than you do for the bills pasted on your dead-walls. There is always room on the wall for the bills to be read — never for the pictures to be seen." This is a harsh judgment. There should be fine illustrators in a country that produced the deans of present-day illustration: Bewick, Cruikshank, Morris, and Burne-Jones, Millais, Tenniel, Caldecott, Crane, Greenaway, Potter, and others in the grand tradition. Perhaps they have turned from illustration because it has less prestige nowadays than "fine art" or panel painting. Or perhaps other forms of art are more lucrative? They must be hiding in the hedgerows somewhere.

From *The Horn Book* for February, 1961

STORY AND PICTURE IN CHILDREN'S BOOKS

By Bettina Ehrlich

WHEN we hear the words, "a children's book," we think of a book made up of text and pictures. We think of these two things as of a unity. And indeed the unity of the word with its pictorial illustration is essential for a book for young children.

In an illustrated book for adults or semi-adults the story must be clear and understandable even if the illustrations are taken out. In a children's book they may, at times, be inseparable. But even then the story will always be the primary substance of the book; the story is the tune, the illustration its accompaniment. The merit of the story lies in itself; the merit of the illustration lies only partly in itself and to a great extent in the manner in which it serves the story. Hence a good picture is not necessarily a good illustration.

In awareness of this predominant role of the story, parents, educators and publishers are more careful and discriminating in their choice of text than in their choice of pictures. No doubt, they realize also that the word can do more harm than the image. And there are probably many more people who have a competent judgment on the written word than there are people competent in their judgment of pictures.

All this, along with the restrictions sometimes imposed on color reproduction, leads to the result that there exist more well-written children's books than well-illustrated ones.

There are two points in writing for children which I should like to stress.

The first concerns the "difficult words." I believe that every book for a child should contain some words which are not familiar to him. There is, in some quarters, a certain fear of confronting him with expressions he does not, at first sight or hearing, understand. I do not agree with this view, because I have found that the word he does not understand, or does not *quite* understand, will be the word he loves best — especially if he is an imaginative child. And how can a child enrich his vocabulary if he does not find new words here and there in his books? The development of one's vocabulary and one's means of expression is important not only for the sake of a richer diction, but also in order to open a wider area of thought and to attain precision of thought. The adult may sometimes find it a bit of a nuisance to have to explain words to a child, but I consider this trouble very worthwhile. Many children will neither ask for an explanation nor even care to get it, because the vague, the not-quite-explicable, has a great charm for the young mind. The all-too-easy book is, in a way, as unsatisfying and perhaps more to be avoided than the too difficult one. Of course a book for children should not abound in complicated words to the point of affectation, but one here and there will act as gymnastics for the mind and that is all to the good.

Naturally we wish to see our children carefree and happy, and the aim of modern education is to eliminate from the child's mind all the terrors of learning which beset it in pre-Freudian times. This is, I think, one of the greatest achievements of our days, and the merits of all the endeavors made in that direction and of the results attained need not be elaborated. However, we must be careful not to go too far in letting this our desire for carefree and fear-free minds lead us into spiritual mollycoddling so that we make everything too easy and too simple for the child. Everybody agrees that a child must train his muscles in order to develop them. The same should apply to the mind, if we want to forestall spiritual laziness and atrophy.

This leads me to the second point about writing for children. The tendency to mental mollycoddling sometimes makes the adult resent any sad passage in a children's book or the description of any of life's calamities. I find not only that children can stand quite a bit of this, but also that they enjoy it!

It is the adult who, having met sorrow, fears it. Not the child. And it is the adult, not the child, who has this insatiable hunger for "amusing" children's books. The child has an innate longing to get acquainted with all spheres of life and we should not underestimate this longing nor sacrifice its fulfillment to our own understandable, but unreasonable, wish to see the child merry and laughing all the time. The gruesome, the eerie and "creepy" are, I believe, unsuitable mental food for children; but a few little tragedies will add to the tension needed in a story and should be quite welcome provided the child's belief in ultimate justice is not disappointed, and the tigers who beset Little Black Sambo finally melt in the sun, or the wolf who eats Red Ridinghood is shot and she feels no worse for her stay inside him.

I should like to illustrate the aforesaid by a personal experience I shall not easily forget. I had given a little seven-year-old girl named Cate my book, *Cocolo Comes to America,* and met her again two or three weeks later. She said, "D'you know what I like best in your book?" "What, Cate?" "I like it best," she said calmly, "when Cocolo is run over by a car." "Do you really?" I said, and probably I looked a little upset, for she added, "Yes, this and also when he gets married."

This left me thinking. Danger and love, the two eternal subjects of the Human Drama, impressed this little child more than any of the other incidents in my story, including funny ones.

I am, however, a firm believer in the happy ending for young children. The teen-ager, on the other hand, will not have to be pitied if found closing a book with a tear in his or her eye. To cry over a book is one of the delights of youth and a bookshelf for the young which contains nothing to bring forth tears is as incomplete as one with nothing to laugh about.

The question of illustrating children's books needs some careful investigation.

One day, shortly after my first children's book had been published, an artist friend of ours came to see us. Naturally I could not refrain from showing him my book. Looking at the pictures quickly but intensively, he said, "They're all right. Children will be able to read them well. Because, as you probably know, children *read* pictures — like this." And producing a babyish and friendly grunt he began to dab his forefinger on the various little details of one picture, as a person who reads might follow the printed lines with his finger, thus rendering a perfect imitation of a small child with a book.

What he had so exquisitely expressed I had, up to that time, only felt vaguely and instinctively.

I had, however, in previous years made a rather thorough study of children's paintings, had watched their creation and discussed them with the children. I had learned then that the child's painting is a *picture writing* and that it grows from entirely different roots and motives than do the paintings of adults.

The truly visual perception develops at a fairly late stage in the child and this is precisely the stage at which, very often to the disappointment of the parents, the child will gradually or suddenly stop painting. It is roughly the age of ten or a little later. Anyway it is the time when the child begins to see things as they really appear to the human eye and when he can read and write without difficulty.

The first factor, the birth of visual perception, discourages artistic reproduction in the average child as being too difficult. The second, the ability to write and read, makes painting as a means of expression superfluous and illustrations as explanatory additions to the word no longer essential. Therefore, the book in which the illustration has a predominant part will be considered "babyish" by the child of over ten and though he may enjoy it, his dignity will forbid this enjoyment to become too manifest.

The small child paints and draws to express his thoughts and wishes and not from the desire to reproduce the visible world around him. He usually paints objects which he loves or wishes to possess. (Mum and Dad and little self before the house; an airplane, a horse, etc.) He will also draw without flinching objects he has never seen, a thing the adult artist hardly dares to attempt, unless he takes refuge in the uncontrollable shapes of non-objective art.

The child combines in his paintings shapes he has seen and can remember and others which he freely invents (these, too, however, representing objects!) without being aware of any difference between the two and with inimitable ease and power of composition. Hence the great charm of children's paintings. To the child himself, however, this charm is non-existent and only very few children cherish their own paintings for more than a few days. If a child shows a tendency to preserve them, this, more than the quality of the paintings, might be taken as a sign of artistic disposition.

Furthermore, and this is important, the child cannot read, nor does he want to read other children's "picture writing," i.e., look at other children's pictures. For every child's picture writing is a secret writing, understandable only to its creator and in need of explanations for everybody else. It is a writing made up, to a greater or lesser extent, of *personal symbols*.

Now, when we remember that as soon as a child can read lettering he wants clear, impersonal lettering — letterpress and not handwriting — we immediately understand that he will demand clarity also from the illustrations he has to *read*. Above all, they must be composed of universally valid symbols and not of personal ones such as those he uses himself.

This leads us quite naturally to see which are the most important qualities in illustrations for the young child.

The story told in the picture must correspond completely with the story told by words. If it is said in the story that a house stood near a forest, the forest must show up in the picture of the house. If a person in the story is described as wearing a green hat, green the hat in the picture must be. If green is denied to the illustrator by limitation of color imposed by economy or any other consideration, the only way out is for the author to change the text or for the illustrator to abandon the illustration of this particular passage. Incongruities of text and picture are unforgivable to the child and considered to be as absurd as it would seem to an adult to read, "His green hat was red."

On the other hand, a child will not usually mind a black and white drawing which illustrates a passage where color is mentioned. Imagination will fill the gap. But it is far better to avoid mentioning colors too much in a book which will be illustrated in black and white.

The importance of bright colors for children's book illustration is, I think, generally much overrated by the adult who buys the book and consequently by all those in the bookselling trade who cater to the child via the adult.

It is true that smaller children have a tendency to grab brightly colored objects, especially red ones. This, however, is really a consequence of their undeveloped faculty of visual discernment. Only a few children can distinguish subtle shades of one color or remember subtle colors. The defined and outspoken is easy to distinguish and red is the color that "strikes" the eye most.

However, when it comes to illustrations in a book, the contents of the picture, its "readability," and a certain quality which I should like to call "intimacy" or "lovability" are more important. The picture should offer a lot to read; it should, above all, go into detail. A picture which offers few facts and which one has finished "reading" in a second is unsatisfying for the small child however great its artistic merits in design, composition and color may be.

It cannot be emphasized enough that the picture is not taken in as a whole any more than the type face of a page is taken in as a whole by the reading adult. The picture is *dissected* into its details, and the more meaning it conveys the better. I think this must be the explanation for the fact that children often adore pictures which, to the eye of the discriminating adult, show no beauty and no artistic achievement.

It is often most disheartening for an illustrator (if, as he should, he watches out for these things with detachment) to see what an ugly picture book a child may adore! Just as much and perhaps at times even more than one of artistic value. The child has probably found on these horrible pages, or perhaps only on one, or in one little corner, something lovable. Who can tell from what sources love may spring!

Should this discourage the artist from doing his very best? Or the publisher from encouraging the very best? Certainly not! I deeply believe that if a child is brought up on beautiful pictures (as on other beautiful things), he will benefit greatly in later life by developing a sense for beauty which will enrich his life enormously. He will develop this sense quite unconsciously, of course. I think we must introduce beauty into the child's life in a sort of surreptitious way to begin with. Just as a child absorbs vitamins with his orange juice without knowing it, so he should absorb beauty from many things, and among them from his picture books. What care the parents invest in a well-balanced diet for the child's body! But is not much thrust before the child's eye which cannot but corrupt a sense for beauty?

However, let us not forget that the orange juice, apart from its nutrition value, also has a very good taste! Thus the picture for the child, if its beauty is to be palatable, must take into consideration the facts outlined before: it should convey information, meaning, story, detail. In order to produce good as well as beautiful illustrations for children the artist must love children and understand their needs. He should also, to a certain extent, have a lively recollection of his own childhood, an ability to creep back into it and to recall what it felt like to be little. However, he should never try to paint like a child!

The imitation of children's art is a great danger in contemporary illustrations of the more sophisticated brand. Never can this method lead to a good result. The adult artist has neither the naïveté nor the imagination to produce the picture writing of the child, and to attempt it is as objectionable as it would be for an adult writer to express himself in baby language or to spell as a child does. No one would appreciate that. "Talking down" to children has fortunately been condemned. Yet "painting down" to them is not only endured but often encouraged. I think this is the gravest danger that confronts the modern children's book. The child, like every unspoilt human being, wants perfection and not regression into artificial babyishness.

One word, I think, should also be said about a certain type of balloon-headed children and pets which crop up all too frequently in children's books. The desire to create lovable and cuddly creatures, especially little animals, is, I suppose, responsible for this fashion. But a drawing, however free and personal, based on the profound study of nature will, I believe, convey the lovable and the moving much better. The wrinkles on a puppy's forehead, the enormous beak of a baby chicken, are features that make us love them but I cannot see that the fact that a creature is hydrocephalic makes it particularly adorable.

Yet proportion, in a much more dramatic sense, means a lot to children because they are continually confronted with the problem of size in their daily life, being themselves small compared with their surroundings, their parents, older children, etc. Therefore the counterplay of big and small is an important factor in illustrations as well as in the stories for children. Charlie Chaplin is, I believe, the greatest master in this field. He, like no other living artist I know of, has expressed to the point of perfection the philosophy, the ridicule, the pathos of "Big and Small" in its visual and its spiritual aspects.

Because size also plays a big role in the child's possessiveness and natural greed, the elaboration of fascinating proportions in children's book illustrations may be of greater value than the use of bright colors.

If I now try to sum up what I believe to be most important in writing and illustrating for children I would say it is: to give them, apart from the obviously needed facts and information, a wide and manifold idea of the world, beauty and emotional wealth.

From *The Horn Book* for October, 1952

III

RECREATING OTHER TIMES

Now there is no yardstick for measuring ordinary people. They must grow in fiction, as they grow in real life, from their environment, and when it is a question of bringing them out of the past, that environment must be built, stone by stone, from the ground upwards.

From "From the Ground Upwards"
by Cynthia Harnett

Articles

FROM THE GROUND UPWARDS *by Cynthia Harnett*

SHAKESPEARE OF LONDON *by Marchette Chute*

THE TREEGATE SERIES *by Leonard Wibberley*

"WATCH YOUR LANGUAGE — YOU'RE WRITING FOR YOUNG PEOPLE!" *by John and Patricia Beatty*

ROSEMARY SUTCLIFF, LANTERN BEARER
by Eileen H. Colwell

BIOGRAPHY: THE OTHER FACE OF THE COIN
by Rosemary Sprague

DIMENSIONS IN TIME, A CRITICAL VIEW OF HISTORICAL FICTION FOR CHILDREN *by Carolyn Horovitz*

FROM THE GROUND UPWARDS

By Cynthia Harnett

SOME TIME ago a friend said to me, "I wonder why there are so few historical novels about ordinary people. I'm tired of plots, and spies, and life in high circles. I'd like to read about ordinary men and women — people like you and me — how they lived, what their problems were and how they coped with them."

That was said more than ten years ago, and, although it may have been true of historical novels then, it is probably less than true now, since social history has become fashionable. But for me it was seed dropped on ground ready to receive it. I was already writing for children and had long cherished an ambition to write history for them. But I, too, was weary of the conventional historical thriller, about the boy who sailed with Drake or outwitted the wily agents of Napoleon. Now this would be different. It was an idea which meant getting down to the bare ground and scratching about until one found something alive, something that would grow.

I started by looking around me. "Ordinary people like you and me." One of my neighbors was an architect; there were architects in my own family; within a few miles of me stood houses, great houses and smaller ones, built by some architect or other one hundred, or two hundred, or three hundred years ago. Very well. I would deal with the family of an architect who was building a great house in, say, 1690, at a time when the old rambling medieval manor houses were falling into decay and being replaced by fine new mansions, spacious and stately and built of brick.

It was splendid fun. Two hundred and fifty years ago was recent enough to have left plenty of traces behind it. Even if the tall trees flanking the great houses today were not always the identical ones planted when the house was built, they could easily be saplings from the same stock. As I drove up and down from London to my home near Henley-on-Thames, I could spot house after house, and cottage after cottage, which must surely have been there two hundred and fifty years ago. Soon it became an enthralling game to watch for landmarks which the children of my architect might have seen on *their* journey from London. Gradually the picture built itself up. The story began to grow. It was written and sent off, and I looked around for the next.

So far everything had been comparatively easy. All the material was at hand. But now I wanted to go further back in history. Two ideas presented themselves. I would like to do a story about young apprentices in medieval London (I am a Londoner myself); or I would like to write about a wool merchant of the Cotswolds in the days when the wool trade was the life blood of England. I had treasured this subject ever since, as a child, I had made rubbings from the brasses on the tombs of Cotswold merchants, where they are shown lying placidly with their feet on a wool-pack, or on the back of a sheep. But either of these subjects would be a very different matter from writing of 1690. About five hundred years, not a mere two hundred and fifty, would separate me from my ordinary people.

Now there is no yardstick for measuring ordinary people. They must grow, in fiction, as they grow in real life, from their environment; and when it is a question of bringing them out of the past, that environment must be built, stone by stone, from the ground upwards. The adventures of a wool merchant must grow from the realities of the wool trade, and those of a London apprentice from the streets of London. It was at this point that I began to appreciate the value of maps. However great the changes in five hundred years, the hills and valleys are the same; the rivers run in the same courses, and the prevailing winds blow from the same quarter. Men build their dwellings with the same need for shelter, and make their roads to follow the contours of the same slopes. So I bought a large scale map and went down to the Cotswolds to work it out on the spot.

The first thing that struck me was how little had changed. When I began, with an empty map, to fill in all I could discover which had been there in the fifteenth century, the skeleton quickly emerged, and before long the bare bones were nicely covered. Since the little town of Burford, the center of the story, was already mapped and documented in great detail by an accomplished local historian, it became an easy matter to work out every movement of the characters and to go over every step of the ground myself.

But all this preoccupation over maps might have remained a backstage performance if my eyes had not suddenly been opened.

I was in a children's library with two boys, aged eleven and twelve, who were eagerly showing me books they had recently enjoyed. One of them produced a *Children's Guide to London*, lavishly illustrated.

"What did you like about it?" I inquired, thinking of my medieval apprentices.

"It's got maps," he said promptly; and the other chimed in, "Yes. Dad took us to London on Saturday. I'll show you which way we went."

Two heads pored over the pages, and a hot argument developed as two forefingers traced out contradictory routes. I was forgotten. But I didn't mind. I had learned my lesson. For the future I would include maps in my books.

The City of London, to which I turned for the apprentice story, is a historian's paradise. There was no difficulty about finding maps in this case. There are so many books on old London which include maps giving all the main streets and landmarks; and, though twice in three hundred years London has been almost razed to the ground — first in the Great Fire of 1666 and second in Hitler's blitz — its ground plan has changed little. But Burford had made me greedy. I wanted detail — detail of side streets and alleys and churches and taverns and great houses. So I made for myself, partly from printed historical maps and partly from a superimposed map of modern London, a chart of the principal medieval streets and set about filling in all the detail I could collect. The most valuable source was John Stow's *Survey of London* which was first printed in 1598, nearly seventy years before the destruction by the Great Fire. Stow had not only the precision of a geographer, but also the ferreting nose of an antiquary. As well as describing meticulously the highways and byways of his own day, he added much of their previous history and listed many of their past inhabitants — often with vivid anecdote to enliven things.

Making the map became almost an end in itself, and, if I were going to write the story at all, it was necessary to call a halt, for there was no limit to the search for detail. It will never be finished. It is too vast a subject. But the map answers its purpose, which is to bring the streets of old London to life, to the extent of knowing what a character will see when he rounds the next corner. It stands in the studio in which I write and draw as Stage Property Number One. With it are any ground plans I can collect of historic buildings which no longer exist, or have been rebuilt, such as the Palace of Westminster, London Bridge, or old St. Paul's — to name only those which I have already used. The search for these plans adds another spice to life, and often the shabbiest, most out-of-date guide book yields up a treasure, like the plan of the manor of Woodstock, which I found just as I was needing it for *Stars of Fortune*.

When Bendy, in *Caxton's Challenge*, moved from London to Westminster, he set a new problem, for Westminster is a couple of miles outside the walls of medieval London, and therefore, so far as I was concerned, unmapped. There were ground plans of the Abbey in plenty to help me, and also of the King's Palace. But I could find no map earlier than the seventeenth century to piece it together as a whole. It had grown up on a series of islands divided by brooks, but of that nothing is visible today. The islands have vanished, the brooks gone underground, the present Houses of Parliament replace the old Palace, Westminster Bridge is comparatively new, and an arterial road — Victoria Street — is cut at a tangent and alters the orientation almost beyond recognition. Even after making a map of it, there is great difficulty in picturing Westminster as it was in Caxton's day.

But with the City of London there is no such problem. The medieval lies close beneath the surface of the modern, and evidence survives in the most unlikely places. For instance, when I was looking for the site of the ancient Tower Royal, I glanced up at a radio shop and saw, just above it, the words, "Tower Royal," on a label, as the street name of a small alley.

I was fortunate enough to be writing *The Drawbridge Gate* before the war devastation had been cleared up. Stripped of its later buildings, the ground was like a map of John Stow's London. It was possible to identify almost every by-lane which he had chronicled. More than that, the scarred ground was broken open to reveal parts of the actual buildings burned down in 1666. Searching near the river to find the spot where, according to Stow, my merchant's house was located, I looked down into a bomb crater and saw the side of a wall of squared stones situated, just as Stow said, in the angle of two small streets. It took a moment to grasp that this was not just the *site*, but actually part of the very house itself, built in the reign of Edward III and still intact under the debris of five centuries.

It was on the same day that I sat down on a low wall facing the remains of the blitzed St. Michael Paternoster, Dick Whittington's church. It was a Sunday; the City was very quiet; and as I ate my sandwiches, a black cat moved quietly out of the ruins where Dick Whittington's house had once stood. It hopped up beside me and in the friendliest way shared my lunch. When I got up to go, the cat rubbed itself, purring, against my leg, and then went back whence it had come. I almost seemed to hear Bow Bells — then silent in their ruined tower — ring out the old jingle, "Turn again, Whittington, thrice mayor of London."

From *The Horn Book* for October, 1961.

SHAKESPEARE OF LONDON

By Marchette Chute

IT IS the business of a biographer to bring to life someone who lived in the past, and this is not always easy to do. If no personal documents have survived, no letters and no reminiscences, it is hard to reach back to the real human being who once lived and breathed, since it is out of small day-to-day matters that a clear sense of personality is built.

It is difficult, for instance, to write a biography of William Shakespeare. Unlike his friend Ben Jonson, Shakespeare did not have a fascinated interest in himself or a conviction that posterity would wish to know about him, and there is almost no record of him as a human being except a few dates, the admiring remarks of some of his friends and a very noncommittal will.

Still, a great many biographies of Shakespeare have been attempted and I thought I would like to try one too.

My only previous experience in writing biography had been a life of Geoffrey Chaucer, the first full-length biography that had ever been written on him. Very little information is available about that great medieval poet, but I found that if I lighted up the background of his life with sufficient clearness the figure of Chaucer himself could be silhouetted in front of it. An outline portrait is not so satisfactory as a three-dimensional one, but at least it is better than nothing. It seemed to me that it might be possible to use the same method with Shakespeare; at any rate, it would not hurt to try.

This method of writing biography involves a great deal of reading, since it requires a close and thorough knowledge of the period. There is no path backward into those earlier centuries except through books and documents, and the more the better.

Fortunately I had one great asset. I live in New York and so I have the use of the New York Public Library; and I already knew from my work on Chaucer what a wonderful library it is.

The New York Public Library, like the city itself, is an easy-going and democratic institution. No one needs credentials to use it. All you have to do is to ask for any book you want and it will be available within fifteen minutes. Yet for all this casual, kindly atmosphere it is one of the great research libraries of the world, with more than three million books waiting to be used. It does not specialize on the Elizabethan period, and yet when I finished my research I found that ninety-five per cent of all the titles I wanted had been available to me there and only a fraction had to be looked for in other libraries.

I especially loved the genealogy room in the library, where the parish records of the English towns are gathered together. In a place like that it is possible to rebuild Renaissance London, street by street and almost house by house. After I had finished writing *Shakespeare of London* I went to England for the first time, and when I visited London it was almost like coming home. The area which made up the old walled city that Shakespeare had known was as familiar to me as the city block I lived on in New York, and I found I could name every street before I came to it. I could never have written a biography of Shakespeare without the lavish, friendly, magnificent resources of the New York Public Library, and I am very grateful to it.

As far as the actual research went, I could see at once that there would be a difficulty in working with Shakespeare that I had not encountered with Chaucer. Chaucer has never roused any of the controversies that beset the name of Shakespeare, controversies so intense and so dogmatic that they are almost theological in tone. They began about a century after his death and have snowballed until they have reached gigantic proportions. Every aspect of his life has been argued over endlessly, some scholars taking one position and some another, and it is difficult to get a clear picture of the man himself when the area around him has been torn up so constantly.

I decided that for the time being I would not look up any of the catalog cards on Shakespeare or use any bibliographies, since I did not want to follow anyone else's pattern or use anyone else's point of view. It is only too easy to decide on a thesis and then start looking for the material that will support it, but it is a method that never results in a good biography. The material must all be collected first, and if the work has been done properly the thesis will eventually emerge.

I staked out in a general way the main areas of Elizabethan life in which Shakespeare had moved, and then I began to read. I read account books, law suits, parish records, government reports, diaries, ordinances, prison records and everything else I could get my hands on. I would arrive at the library two minutes before nine every morning (one never knows; the doors might have opened two minutes early some morning) and I galloped up the front stairs to the reading room on the third floor because I had a theory it took more time to use the back elevator. I was armed with half a dozen sharp pencils that were always blunt when I left, and I wrote my notes in a series of composition books, transcribing them as soon as I got home. The library does not loan out all the books in its research division, but that was just as well from my point of view; a single piece of information might lie dormant for a couple of years until I came across some other little fact that suddenly gave it meaning, and anything that is copied twice is much easier to remember. I am a quick reader and I managed to cover a good deal of ground. Sometimes I would spend a week on a book, and I think my record in the other direction was twenty-five books in one morning.

The purpose behind all this reading was to try to touch hands with the Elizabethan period. In Shakespeare's day there were no magazines or newspapers, and the letters were few and mostly formal. It is extremely difficult to catch the Elizabethans in their relaxed, unguarded moments, in the small things that make a period come alive. The day of the snapshot, as it were, had not yet dawned, and when the men of Shakespeare's day wrote anything down they sat as stiffly for their portraits as when they posed for some painter in their doublets and their hired jewels. They wished to be admired by posterity, which is a laudable objective but one that makes things difficult for a biographer. John Stow, for instance, wrote a huge volume about his beloved city of London, so that posterity would know all about its churches, its great men, its processions, its government and so on. Then he came to the Elizabethan theatre, which to us is the chief glory of the city and the age; and he dismissed the subject in one sentence because it was not sufficiently dignified to be worth his attention.

The only way to catch the Elizabethans off guard is to read everything that can be found about them, looking always for the reality behind the official language and the people behind the acts. It is not dull work, for people are never dull, and information can turn up in the most unexpected places. It was in a book on witches, for instance, that I found my most valuable information on the use of sleight-of-hand on the contemporary stage.

As I went on with my reading I could see that the episodes of Shakespeare's life took on a different color when they were set against the actual background of his own day. Some of the things he did which have been described as odd and unnatural became entirely normal. He hoarded grain in his barn at Stratford, for instance, because everyone else in Stratford was hoarding grain and the special economic conditions of 1598 made the action inevitable. On the other hand, Shakespeare did certain things that have been accepted as natural enough but were in fact unique. He was the only writer of the period who gave up a promising career in the book world, abandoned both his patron and his publisher, and spent the rest of his life writing nothing but plays for the theatre.

The more I went on with the research, the clearer it became that the key to Shakespeare's life was the theatre. In spite of the efforts of many of his biographers, who seemed to feel with John Stow that the theatre was not quite respectable, Shakespeare had demonstrably been an actor as well as a playwright throughout the whole of his adult professional career, and he could not be separated from his environment without grave damage to the truth. It was against a theatre background that the silhouette of Shakespeare would have to emerge if it was going to emerge at all.

By this time I had been working for about two years and had collected a great deal of material. But I still lacked what I wanted most — a picture of Shakespeare as a human being. I had a lot of facts but no way to arrange them, and I began to wonder if it would ever be possible to write the kind of book I had in mind. However, that is an unprofitable kind of wondering to indulge in, and so I started on a third year of work.

The major difficulty, of course, was that William Shakespeare had worked in a despised medium — the theatre — and it was therefore believed in his own day that he was a man of very little importance. It was not until many years after his death that his literary reputation began to rise, and by that time the world in which he had lived and worked had been destroyed. In 1642 the Puritans closed all the theatres in England, and when they were finally reopened it was in a tight, aristocratic atmosphere that would have been unrecognizable to the Elizabethans. The Elizabethans in their turn were unrecognizable to the men of the Restoration, who peered back across a chasm to what they felt were the barbaric old days and had no conception of the kind of world in which Shakespeare had really lived. Not knowing, they guessed, and their guesses were mostly wrong.

Nevertheless, these men of the Restoration were the first biographers of Shakespeare and they supplied most of the material on which all subsequent biographies have been based. The more I considered the matter, the more it seemed to me that this evidence was not really reliable, and I finally decided to discard any information about Shakespeare that was later than 1642. Whatever came before the closing of the theatres could be trusted; what came after could not.

This left me with very little information about Shakespeare as a man, but such as it was it was reliable. Moreover, the decision brought an unexpected dividend: all the contemporary material about Shakespeare moved in the same direction and formed a clear, consistent pattern, and I knew I would be able to write the book after all.

By this time I had read about ten thousand books and articles and could walk around in the period without stumbling. Just to make sure that I had missed nothing, I checked through the various bibliographies and the library catalog cards under "Shakespeare" but all the titles were already familiar to me.

As far as the actual writing goes, a book of this kind is not so much written as rewritten. It is one thing to have the pattern clear in your own mind and quite another to get it clear in the mind of your reader. One reason why I never sign a contract for a book until I have finished the last draft is that a contract implies a deadline. Anyone who tries to bring the past back to life is fighting a duel with time, and there is no point in getting involved in a lesser struggle with the same enemy and trying to finish the book by a given date. The manuscript may need to be rewritten only two or three times, or it may be that some parts of it will require a dozen drafts before they are satisfactory. There is no way of knowing and it is better not to make any plans.

The method I used in writing *Shakespeare of London* might be called picture writing. The story is not presented through explanations but through a series of images, leaving the reader to draw his own conclusions. It goes without saying that the details which make up each image must be carefully documented — that is, chosen from a reliable source — but it is equally important that they should be characteristic. The choice of the final, single detail will be much more effective if you have found a dozen similar examples in your research than if you have to choose from only two or three.

Too much detail will overload a book and make it difficult to read, and one of the problems in this kind of writing, where there is a large amount of material, is to keep the movement of the book under control. One way to do this is to focus on each image from some special angle. For instance, the general theatre material in *Shakespeare of London* is divided into three points of view. The first presents it from the point of view of the man who built the first theatre, which gave me an opportunity to describe theatre architecture and costs, civic opposition, the makeup of the audiences and so on. Then I described the problems of a young actor entering the theatre, with the emphasis on stage training, doubling, voice control and so on. Then, later on, I described the theatre from the production end — the problems of licensing, casting, costuming, advertising — and I did this by focusing on a sample production of *Romeo and Juliet*. Above all, I tried to keep to the contemporary point of view. When I took Shakespeare's company on tour I did not describe the various towns which the actors visited as they would look today or even as they looked to their own inhabitants then, but instead I described the various things that a London actor would have noticed about them.

Throughout the book I left Shakespeare free to enter whereever he would, and I tried not to push any of my own opinions about him on to the reader. I left him alone and hoped the reader would draw his own conclusions.

Nevertheless, I formed very definite impressions about Shakespeare as a human being. I was impressed by his gentleness, his selflessness, his dedication to the theatre and his conviction that the work he did was more important than the man who was doing it. I was equally impressed by the company that worked with him, the company that stayed in continuous existence for fifty years and that produced all his plays.

For several years I wanted to put something of this in a book for children, and finally I got a plot I liked and wrote *The Wonderful Winter*. It is the story of a lonely, loveless youngster who spent one winter in the affectionate, hard-working atmosphere of Shakespeare's company and describes what the experience did for him. It is also an attempt to bring middle-class London to life for a child. There have been perhaps enough books written for children about Elizabethan court life and conspiracies, full of Gadzooks and rapiers and glimpses of Good Queen Bess. I wanted to do a book about ordinary people who would be recognizable in any century, and especially I wanted to give children a picture of Shakespeare himself. I hope it is a truthful one. I have a strong conviction about the need for complete truthfulness in books for children.

I had a delightful time writing *The Wonderful Winter*. But I had an equally good time with *Shakespeare of London* and all the other books I have written. I start each one with a sense of excitement that lasts through all the years of research, through all the various drafts that have to be written, and even through the making of the index. Then, at that point, I suddenly lose interest. I have started to think about another book instead, and the whole process begins over again.

I am now working on my twelfth book, and I cannot imagine how I could ever have been interested in any subject except this one. In a few years it will be finished and I shall no longer be interested in it. But never mind; I can start at once on my thirteenth.

From *The Horn Book* for February, 1955

THE TREEGATE SERIES

By Leonard Wibberley

FIRST OF ALL I have always had a great interest in history — not the kind of litany of kings and presidents and knaves and heroes that is so frequently taught in schools — but the bright little incidents that gloriously illuminate a landscape which is too often mouldy with the bone dust of the dead. I am fascinated by such incidents as Simon de Montfort sending his barber to the top of a tree to call out to him the devices of the knights in the army approaching to engage him at Evesham so that he might know with whom he had to deal.

"Lilies argent on a field azure!" cried the barber, and de Montfort knew that the House of Mortimer marched against him. And so on.

In my youth I studied English history, and it was not until I came to the United States some eighteen years ago that I became first of all interested in and then captivated by American history.

Of all the wars of which I have any knowledge from history, it gradually became evident to me that none was as important for the Western World as the War of the American Revolution. Indeed I regard it as the most important struggle in the history of what we can call Western Man.

That is a big statement. But here are my reasons. There have been many many wars fought to overthrow tyranny. Such wars are not exclusively a feature of American history. There was, for instance, the English Civil War which resulted in the beheading of Charles I (an appalling action — to try and to behead a king for crimes against his people), and earlier there was the Peasants' Revolt in what we call Germany now and Wat the Tyler's Rebellion in England. But the Revolutionary War not only sought to overthrow tyranny, it also established certain inalienable rights for people, rights which if preserved would protect mankind from tyranny in all the centuries ahead.

What was fought on the North American continent then was a war for the rights of *all* men. The scope was wider than national. It embraced all mankind who loved freedom, and its effects are felt to this very day. Overshrill efforts have been made to deny that there was any connection between the French Revolution and the American Revolution. But the one stemmed from the other. Tom Paine was honored in Revolutionary France because he was part of Revolutionary America — because he adhered to principles of freedom enunciated clearly in America and passionately embraced by the French and later by the people of what were to become the Latin American Republics.

The point I want to make here is that the American Revolution demonstrated that man needs constant protection from his own government — his house must be inviolate, his right to speak his mind at election unbreached, his right to bear arms unchallenged. He was not to be made to testify against himself nor be put in double jeopardy of his life by the courts. The more one examines the effect of the Revolutionary War not merely on Americans but on all peoples, the more one is amazed by the enormity of that effect. The shot was indeed heard around the world and is still heard today.

Americans, alas, know little of this most astounding of all wars. There was Bunker Hill and there was Yorktown and there was a thing called Valley Forge. Men who can give you the exact placement of the regiments of Lee at Gettysburg have no idea which of the thirteen colonies sent troops to the siege of Boston. They haven't much idea of the men who fought in the war, and hardly think of them as people very much like themselves — troubled about what was the right thing to do, divided among themselves, some of them from families who had been in America for 150 years and some of them, like Tom Paine, recently off the boat from England. They were not the united band of heroes they have become in the schoolbooks. The New Englanders were a cantankerous bunch with "leveling" ideas that were utterly destructive of discipline and drove Washington to cold fury at times. The Pennsylvanians were frontiersmen who not long before Bunker Hill had marched on Philadelphia determined to shoot up the city. The people of the southern colonies were distrustful of those of the northern colonies and did not want to do much fighting outside their own area. Many of the men in the Continental Army had served in the British army and were at first loathe to fire on a redcoat. The health of King George III was drunk regularly in the Continental Army until the first of the German mercenaries arrived and the men realized that the King whom they thought of as a father was in fact a tyrant determined to have his way.

Colonies that were prepared to equip militia for their own defense were reluctant to send supplies and men to Washington to be employed outside their own limits. It was all very confusing — and very human. But at the bottom of it all, there was a basic dedication to the concept of a freedom that permitted a man to speak his mind even against his own government, his own congress, his own rulers.

The more I read about the Revolutionary War, the more these elements came clearly to me and the more I marveled at them and wanted to bring them to the attention of others. Out of this desire came the Treegate series of books in which I have attempted to trace the fortunes and feelings of a family of Americans of the Revolutionary War period.

I asked for and was given large scope in writing these books. I didn't want to write books in which one hero got in and out of a series of scrapes. I wanted to paint a large mural which would embrace as many of the figures of the Revolution as could be usefully depicted ... the dissolute Earl of Sandwich, pious Peace of God Manly, the fiery Maclaren of Spey nursing the old wound of the Battle of Culloden, Gabby the seaman with his love for a piece of fat pork, a mite rancid, Benjamin Franklin, Washington himself, aging Daniel Morgan with the scars of a whip across his back, Sam Adams organizing the Boston mobs, and many many others. Some of the figures are historic — some of them creatures of my imagination. These latter came to life as I wrote, standing as it were by my elbow and telling me of the weight of their muskets and how the birds sounded in the boding woods at Saratoga and how sharp was the January frost at Morristown.

This of course is the work of the novelist in the field of history — not to instruct but to enrich that which is already known; not to distort but to listen to the insistent whisper of forgotten voices penetrating the centuries.

There were, I am sure, people like Gabby and Master Gunner Simmons and Mr. Treaser in his Queen Anne coat, and Mr. Paddock — a self-appointed traveling university, and Peter Treegate and his stubborn, enduring father, John. History has no place for them. They belong in that other wing of history called the historical novel. They are the humble builders of the world, whose names are unknown, whose graves are lost, and whose lives made no stir beyond the circle of their friends.

They are you and I and everyman, and I have tried to give them back their voices, so that they can speak across the centuries of their time on earth.

From *The Horn Book* for April, 1962

"WATCH YOUR LANGUAGE— YOU'RE WRITING FOR YOUNG PEOPLE!"

By John and Patricia Beatty

BEFORE beginning a new novel some years ago, we took an informal poll of friends and colleagues at the University of California at Riverside on the extremely moot subject of the first-person book versus the third-person book. Everyone had a strong opinion, and every opinion conflicted with the next one we heard. The body of thought fell into two distinct categories: "Nothing written in the first person is worth reading" (for the most part a masculine viewpoint) and "I just love books written in the first person! They're so vital and revealing" (an opinion chiefly feminine).

Because we had decided that the chief character in the new book, *Campion Towers*, was to be female — having featured Richard Larkin in *At the Seven Stars* — we settled on a first-person presentation. So, the novel had our Massachusetts Bay Colony heroine, Penitence Hervey, telling the entire story "in her own write." The writing went along swimmingly as we avoided *thee* and *thou* and still managed to give a seventeenth-century flavor to the book. Penitence had many adventures in the dangerous England of the 1650s as she met the young fugitive king, Charles II, and rode toward battle with Oliver Cromwell's "Ironsides." We enjoyed taking Penitence, a wide-eyed colonial, through the countryside of Worcestershire, displaying our hard-earned knowledge of seventeenth-century England gently, we trusted, without bludgeoning the teen-age reader into a knowledge of 1651 which he would usually meet only in a graduate seminar. We felt that we had educated the reader in a pleasantly painless way and that we had stuffed in a great deal of easily digestible, accurate material about Cromwell, the ill-fated Earl of Derby, and Charles II. We even thought that if the readers of our novel were never exposed to another book dealing with mid-seventeenth-century England, we had given them a fairly good picture and had drawn a Cromwell and a Charles that would live for a long time in young memories. If we could lead anyone to a further interest in the English Civil War, all to the good — a wonderful dividend. If we could lead anyone to any further historical study, we would be as happy as clams.

So, novel finished and accepted for publication, we sat back, fat and happy, waiting for the book to come forth. After due process, the publisher returned the priced-out manuscript with the words "Fine book — but cut it!" Those last two ominous words had been heard before, of course, and by now evoked only a minimum of bad language. We sat down to blue-pencil out at least fifty pages of Penitence's glorious prose.

At about this time the HORN BOOK printed an article of ours, one in which we congratulated ourselves on the passion for accuracy we demonstrated in *At the Seven Stars*. We felt quite smug about our carefulness and were certain that the new book was every bit as accurate and detailed as *At the Seven Stars*, with its third-person treatment, had ever been.

We were about to send the truncated manuscript back to Macmillan and wait for the galleys to show up at Christmas, or Easter, or mid-June of a sabbatical year, or some other predictably dreadful time. But just as the customary supermarket paper bag was being cut up to wrap the manuscript for mailing, a terrible thought assailed us. A first-person novel presented a problem which we had completely overlooked. The book was not simply a novel — it was also a journal!

We had been careful to keep the conversations on an accurate seventeenth-century level, but we had neglected the narrative, which in a first-person book *also* had to be couched in the speech of 1651. Thunderstruck by the discovery of our oversight, we wondered what we were to do. And we made the wracking decision to check and rewrite, because it was the only one we could make. (Another decision came far more easily: never to do a first-person historical novel again.)

Once more we hauled out our two-volume *Shorter Oxford English Dictionary on Historical Principles* and, to boot, borrowed a concordance to the King James version of the Bible. Now all we needed was a good light, a stern sense of discipline, and infinite patience. All disputable non-seventeenth-century words were penciled lightly in the left margin of the manuscript and were erased if found suitable to 1651. If a word was not suitable, a substitute had to be found and written in. The concordance was checked first. If we were lucky, we found the word there. Mostly, however, we were not lucky. The next step was delving into the dictionary, hunting in the fine print for meanings and historical dates. All too often a twenty-minute search would be made for one word.

The new enterprise turned into a two-man, three-hour-a-day project that took six long weeks. Social life ground to a standstill while the pages of the great dictionary became dog-eared. The results of our work were a completely verified manuscript, a greatly enlarged knowledge of seventeenth-century vocabularies, this article, and a new pair of reading glasses for the distaff side of the writing Beattys.

Macmillan was patient about our wanting to keep the manuscript for "a little extra work" to get it more in line with a true flavor of the period. We did not tell our editor that we were checking more than ten thousand words about which we were unsure. Memory being the chancy thing it is, we looked up the same word over and over until we reached the point of list-making knowledge, which greatly speeded up the wearisome chore.

Naturally, we had to set up some criteria for the project. If a word was similarly utilized by us and by Shakespeare, we left it in. If it appeared in the Bible with the same meaning, we retained it. And if a word appeared in the *Oxford English Dictionary* as late as 1665, we included it, assuming that it was current in the language for some time before seeing print. The search became harrowing in the extreme when we sought to use a word in a verb form and found that it was known only as a noun — a common occurrence. We then had to delete and find a suitable substitute. All too often substituting did not come easily, and it was back to "Well, how did Cromwell say it to Ireton?" and thence to our volumes of Cromwell's letters, the original models for Penitence's conversations. Most of the time we could not find that Cromwell had ever said the word we needed.

We had delved into the everyday language of eighteenth-century upper-class England for *At the Seven Stars* and had thoroughly enjoyed it. We had found the speech rich and fascinating, and we thought that the period between Shakespeare and Dr. Johnson would not be so very different. We were wrong. And Cromwell's vocabulary should have warned us. The simplicity of his speech is overwhelming, sounding actually more modern than that of Samuel Johnson. (We avoided Milton as much too grandiose for a teen-age novel.) We found that in the narrative we were using words eminently suitable to the eighteenth century and that from Cromwell's day to Johnson's the everyday English language had grown considerably. The word *mob* had been confidently used. We soon caught this particular clinker, but saw people turn pale when they learned that we had dared use *mob* in a 1651 context. "What were you thinking of?" asked a scholar-mentor-friend visiting from Reed College. We told him we hadn't been thinking at all when we included that famous example of coined speech from the Glorious Revolution of 1688.

After we finished erasing and cleaning up the new book, to satisfy our own curiosity we checked a little set piece used to confound and stun a certain graduate seminar in eighteenth-century English history. The words would have made sympathetic sense to those two famous philanderers, Benjamin Franklin and George Washington. For HORN BOOK readers who might also be interested, it goes as follows: "So I took that living doll to a hop and a square got her away from me. He did a real cool job!" But Cromwell, chances are, would have found this as easily comprehensible as Urdu or Southern California surfing jargon.

Important to the action in *Campion Towers* is the Battle of Worcester, and one of our worst problems was having to use military language. We found that the usual terms employed so easily and so often by military historians today are almost entirely of eighteenth-century extraction. We needed to talk about patrols, passwords, caissons, and guns — all integral parts of the story. But there were no *patrols* in Penitence Hervey's England; there were *scouting parties*. There were no *passwords;* there were *watchwords*. A sentry was not *posted;* he seemed to have just been there! There were no *caissons,* but our *cannon* somehow got to Worcester and Red Hill. (The military situation was difficult enough, what with the soldierly words all wrong; our luck totally deserted us when we learned to our sorrow that the Battle of Worcester was the least known and most confused of all the many Civil War battles.)

Other forbidden words followed thick and fast, some of them remarkably surprising, to us at least, when we learned that they either did not exist in 1651 or had entered the language only in another form or with a variant meaning. Intrigued, we continued adding to our list of outlawed words.

Aisle and *amazing* were not acceptable for the period, nor were *bewildering* or *chunk, clump, carefree,* or *complex.* Penitence's little sisters might play with *poppets* but not with *dolls. Dismissal, eager, extra,* and *eerie* had not quite entered our language in the 1650s, or not in the sense in which we were hoping to use them. No one was ever *embarrassed* in that period. *Fireplace* was not yet in use, but *hearthfire* was. That circumlocution was a fortunate find for us.

Stairs in 1651 gave us almost as much trouble as military terms. Stairs did not have *flights* or *landings*. We are still in some doubt about how our heroine gets up and down the many steps in Campion Towers, the fictional "stately home." Candles did not *gutter* or *flicker* in 1651. They just went out, it seems. No one ever had *gooseflesh* in that unusually verbally self-contained age. No one ever *gossiped,* although the noun form was in common current usage — as was the ducking stool. There were no *riding habits* and, believe it or not, in the heyday of the Puritan hegemony, there was no one who was *hellbent*. We had not known that *jillflirt,* our fine term used in *At the Seven Stars,* was an eighteenth-century manifestation. We were forced to reverse English here and use the acceptable word *flirtgill*. People in the seventeenth century were not *ignored*, and they did not *lurch*. Nor did they *move over*, *minimize*, or go in for the collecting of *mementoes*.

Horses and equine behavior and trappings drove us wild. Seventeenth-century horses neither *nickered* nor *whinnied*; but they did *bite* and *neigh*. They never wore *hackamores*, a pure nineteenth-century Americanism. They could not be tied to *hitching posts*. The red horses at Campion Towers are either extremely well-trained, or they roam loose.

Our characters could not *ogle* one another, not even Charles II. We felt that the twenty-one-year-old king should have been permitted at least to *ogle* our pretty heroine, since in a young people's novel we could not be entirely truthful by showing him as much at home in the hayloft as at the Hague. Poor Charles was kept on a tight rein and permitted only a couple of swift kisses.

In 1651 no one gave *parties* or went in for *balls* or *routs*. Things did not go *plop*. (We became convinced that Cromwell's England was, in general, a mighty silent one, innocent of onomatopoeia except for the loud sounds of battle.) *Proper*, that wonderful standby of the nineteenth century, was unknown. Even in extremes of emotion, voices never *quavered*. For all the dangers — civil wars and the Great Plague — of the 1600s, the period was not *risky*.

A character could have an *ailment*, which might be *arthritis* but would never be *rheumatism*. People who wore rags and tags were not *shabby*, nor were somber, sober merchants *sedate*. No one in that day ever *sprinted* or *sauntered*. As a matter of fact, we aren't quite sure how they did get about. The *Oxford English Dictionary* betrayed us all too often by giving equivalents of a later date than the words we had chosen in the first place.

No one in the days of Royalist/Cavalier — Parliamentarian /Roundhead ever *schemed*. Predictably in such stern times no one was ever *thrilled*. And no one was ever *tense, terse,* or spoke in a *toneless* voice. No one ever drank a *toast*; gentlemen drank copiously and constantly in Cromwell's time, but they drank *healths*.

Under the regime of the Stuart kings people may have had

their ears cropped for various small offenses, such as publishing derogatory pamphlets; but they were never treated *unfairly, unidentifiably,* or *unfalteringly,* even though many of them could be best described as unfaltering. (Thank heaven, *grim* was left to us.)

We also encountered problems of an entirely opposite kind, and it became necessary to delete some perfectly acceptable words of 1651 because they smacked of Hollywoodese or were too twentieth-century sounding. *Darling* was one such word. *Fascinating* also had to be used with great care, for it meant the hypnotic stare of the serpent rather than sexual allure. Our heroine stares *fascinated* into a *hearthfire* looking for salamanders in a fine old seventeenth-century tradition. She certainly does not look *fascinated* into the eyes of her kinsman, husband-to-be Sir Julian Killingtree. (Penitence, poor trammeled maiden, and the erstwhile highwayman, full-time Royalist cannot even meet by *moonglow* and render up their *heartfelt* love. The language restrictions played hob with our love scenes.)

Other possible words of that day we either discarded or retained despite the fear of accusations of overmodernity. We could have used *glorious, sprightly, lively, whimsical,* and *witty*. Penitence could even have been a *charmer*, though she wouldn't have been *charming*.

We made our way by one shift or another through most of the language problems. But one in particular confounded us and almost brought the book to a complete impasse. Toward the end of the frantic rechecking of the novel we encountered the four-letter word *knob*. Here our bad luck with the little things of historical fiction struck again. At first glance, what is to be said about knobs? People had them, didn't they? We hadn't given a single thought to knobs, but an integral, un-changeable part of the book dealt with the often-found secret passage, or *priest hole,* of the English country house. The entrance to our particular passage is activated in the paneled wall of one room by a *Spanish knob,* a specific knob which alone features the device of a *fleur-de-lis* among hundreds of *Tudor roses*. There were Tudor roses as motifs all over Cromwell's England, and the *fleur-de-lis* was well known indeed.

As a sort of lazy afterthought, we checked out the word *knob*. Consternation! There weren't any knobs at all.

Door knobs are newfangled things. Three hundred years ago people got in and out of rooms and houses by latches and strings, for the most part. And knobs certainly were not part of the English paneling of that period. *Rosette*, as a substitute word, did not exist either; nor did anything that we could conceive of in the paucity of our panic-stricken imaginations. A few worried days passed, and then *button* mercifully popped up. And although the twentieth-century young reader may have visions of elevators and may wonder at Penitence's pushing of a *button* in the wall of that strange chamber at the end of the passageway (not *corridor* or *hall*), he will have absorbed a bit of exotic knowledge with far less anguish than we did.

It would be pretentious and silly to claim that many of the words eliminated, and even those cited here, were not actually current in the 1600s. Surely some appeared somewhere within letters of the period, letters that the *Oxford English Dictionary* has not yet caught up with. *Fleet* (in the naval sense) is a good example. But to press this qualification to its conclusion seemed a Herculean chore, so we settled on the obvious solution: If a word was not seventeenth century according to The Dictionary, it was rejected.

All of our efforts, chances are, will never be recognized. We can only hope that one day someone who "knows," perhaps some lint-picking pedant, will be agreeably surprised by the trouble taken with a children's book — and a novel at that. We will not hold our breath until this happy event occurs (an expression Cromwell would have understood quite well). Yet out of all the work watching our language for young people we have gained a new and deeper respect for the ever-changing, "never-changing" English language.

From *The Horn Book* for February, 1965

ROSEMARY SUTCLIFF—
LANTERN BEARER

By Eileen H. Colwell

IN SUSSEX, one of the most beautiful counties in southern England, lie the Downs, those green, undulating hills crossed by tracks centuries old. Here, in a small village not far from the sea, lives Rosemary Sutcliff, the writer of historical stories for children. Her early life was spent in north Devon, the background of her first book, but it is the Downs which are home to her, perhaps because they have seen so much of the history which is such a great part of her life. As she sits writing, her eyes can rest on green English lawns and trees, and in the centre of her bungalow is a tiny courtyard, full of bright flowers, which only lacks a household god to seem Roman!

Talking with Rosemary Sutcliff one realises again the qualities one has come to expect in her books — a keen intelligence, a lively interest in the many facets of life, an eye for beauty, a sense of humour, courage, and a shrewd perception of character. Writing does not come easily to her for she has the artist's desire for perfection. Each book costs her months of research — but that she loves and finds fascinating — and many more months of writing and rewriting the four drafts she usually feels she must make. Each descriptive phrase is as evocative as she can make it, every detail of her historical background is carefully verified.

Although she has written adult books, Miss Sutcliff prefers to write for children because of their responsiveness. She credits them with intelligence and the power of appreciation, and refuses to oversimplify her material and vocabulary. Her own interest in history was aroused by the historical stories her mother read to her at an early age, when ill health compelled her to spend many hours in bed. It may be that this rather shut-in childhood led her to look outwards into the wide landscape of history, and later to write historical stories herself. She realises the responsibility of the writer of this kind of story, for the attitude of children towards history and historical events may be formed forever by what they read in childhood. More than a meticulous accuracy of fact is needed if the reader is to receive a true and balanced picture of the chosen period. Few children have strong feeling for history or any conception of its continuity, for to most of them it is a difficult subject, full of names and dates, strange backgrounds and inexplicable customs. Fortunate are the young people whose introduction to history is through the medium of stories by such a writer as Rosemary Sutcliff.

Miss Sutcliff's first book for children, *The Queen Elizabeth Story*, was written in 1950, and since then she has had ten others published. These include two more set in the Tudor period, one in the Bronze Age, one in Norman times, one in the Civil Wars, and four in Roman Britain, the period which has captured her imagination most.

To read these books in the order in which they were written is an illuminating experience. From a writer of pleasant stories with an historical flavour for younger children, Rosemary Sutcliff has developed into a mature artist whose books can be read with interest by adults as well as children. Undoubtedly she has a genius for the re-creation of an historical period. She has learned to restrain her early overenthusiasm, which at times was dangerously near to sentimentality, and to tone down the lushness of her descriptive passages. There is much fine writing in her books, but it is disciplined now in the service of her story. Her style has become vigorous, direct, and mature.

For children, one of Miss Sutcliff's chief recommendations is her ability as a storyteller. Win a child's interest in a story and it matters little that its events took place a thousand years ago. Her choice of period is felicitous, for she seems to have a flair for forgotten or little-known facets of history in which her imagination can have full play and she plunges into a story so that interest is captured from the first sentence. *The Shield Ring* begins, for example:

> The thing happened with the appalling swiftness of a hawk swooping out of a quiet sky, on a day in late spring, when Frytha was not quite five.

At once we are in the midst of the tragedy of a child's loss of parents and home. Endings are equally satisfactory, for we are left to imagine what might have "happened next." Marcus in *The Eagle of the Ninth* thinks how:

> A new life, a new beginning, had warmed out of the grey ash for himself and Esca, and Cottia; perhaps for other people too; even for an unknown downland valley that one day would be a farm.

Of the hours of careful research that must precede these apparently effortless stories we can have little conception. So well does Rosemary Sutcliff absorb her material that she can imagine nothing, it seems, that is out of keeping with her period. Every aspect of those far-off times has been realised in her imagination, with the result that we are in the hero's environment itself, seeing, feeling and hearing as he does. Just as when we learn a language we are taught to think in it, so Miss Sutcliff thinks in terms of her chosen period. It is not surprising, therefore, that her similes are so apt: "It was a day like a trumpet blast," "The village seethed like a pan of warming yeast," "Frost as keen and deadly as the blade of a dagger." There is no period jargon, no archaic or obscure expression, to slow down the story and puzzle the child. This skillful and apparently simple re-creation of a time outside our experience is one of her greatest gifts.

It is perhaps in her reconstruction of religious rites and ceremonies that Rosemary Sutcliff shows her imaginative understanding of her characters and her period most strikingly, for she never dismisses what seem to be savage customs as barbarous and without significance. As a result we are given fascinating pictures of an unfamiliar way of life and find them strangely impressive. In *Eagle of the Ninth* Marcus sees the Feast of the New Spears and, Roman as he is, is moved to kneel in awe. He realises that "the mysterious unforgettable figure of nightmare beauty" is indeed a godlike figure to these people.

In *Warrior Scarlet*, a new king is chosen in the Bronze Age and, as he stands by his father's funeral pyre, half seen in the mist over the Downs, the people swear the solemn and moving oath of loyalty of these ancient folk:

If we break faith with you, may the green earth gape and swallow us. May the grey sea burst loose and overwhelm us; may the sky of stars fall and crush us out of life forever.

In the same book, when Drem came at last to his initiation into manhood, he gazed into the compelling eyes of Midir the priest and saw there a face that was not Midir's. He was aware of a "shining and unbearable glory, a power that seemed to beat about him in fiery waves; and he knew in a moment of terror and ecstasy that he was looking into the face of the Sun Lord himself...." This power of imaginative insight into the hearts and minds of ancient peoples adds depth to Miss Sutcliff's books and lifts them above the rut of competent historical stories.

What a memorable gallery of characters she has created, from Perdita Pettle, aged eight, the gentle little heroine of *The Queen Elizabeth Story*, to Beric, embittered outcast. Perhaps her male characters are more strongly drawn, but we cannot dismiss the study of Tamsyn, the lonely little girl who "didn't belong" in *The Armourer's House*, or Blai, the despised slave in *Warrior Scarlet*, with her pitiful belief that her father will come to rescue her. Rosemary Sutcliff's understanding of children, particularly those with some handicap, is sincere and intuitive, all the more perhaps because she knew pain and illness as a child herself. We remember Frytha in her desolate bewilderment, when she knew only that "the world had fallen to pieces and that it was very cold among the ruins."* Of how many refugee children during the centuries could this have been said! Drem's experience, when he realised that his trailing useless arm would shut him out from many things that other boys could do, must be that of countless children. With each of Rosemary Sutcliff's books her ability to draw her characters "in the round" has strengthened, until in her latest book, *The Lantern Bearers*, she has given us Aquila who, a man "lost in a great bitterness," comes through a spiritual experience to a "quiet place."

Many of Rosemary Sutcliff's readers are boys, a tribute to the vitality of her writing. Perhaps it is partly because she has described fights and battles so vividly, much as she dislikes

**The Shield Ring.*

them personally! She is not afraid to introduce pain and cruelty into her stories when the period requires it in the interest of historical truth. In *Outcast* the harrowing descriptions of Beric's life as a galley slave shock and move us. Yet, although her stories are set in bloodthirsty times, she has avoided the excessive violence and savagery considered necessary by some historical writers. Many characters in her books die a violent death, as they must, but because she does not dwell on the manner of their death, the young reader is not haunted by it. All children know that there must be death and pain and sorrow, but the sensitive and skillful artist can deal with these things in a way that helps boys and girls to accept them.

In all these books the underlying values are the right ones, an essential quality in books for children. Reading *The Shield Ring*, we realise that no price is too great to pay for freedom and that the bravest man is he who knows he is afraid and yet faces danger. In *Simon* we are shown the futility of war, which divides friend from friend and destroys so much that is good in life. Family life is portrayed as the natural thing and friendship is often Miss Sutcliff's theme. Loyalty, courage, tolerance of other men's opinions and rights, man's basic need to recognise some greater power than himself — all these are part of her stories.

Rosemary Sutcliff's feeling for "place" is strong and, as we read, we feel the misty rain of the Lake District, taste the salty tang of the wind over the marshes and see the wide expanse of the Downs. She can convey the atmosphere of a place or moment most vividly and impressively. To stand with Aquila in the fort when the last Roman soldiers have left Britain, is to be conscious of utter desolation. Running with Drem in the darkness, we feel and share the elemental "Fear that walked the forest, the Terror of the Soul"; battling through the great storm with Beric we are wildly exhilarated as the "great swinging seas fling in blow after blow." How evocative are her descriptive phrases! Hers is the heightened perception of the artist, for she was trained as one and, indeed, achieved some eminence as a painter of miniatures before she began to write seriously. Her trained observation has been invaluable to her and a pleasure to her readers. She sees smoke rising in curls and eddies "like fern-fronds made of jewel-blue air." Dawn comes in "the smell of the little knife-edged wind that shivered and sang through the hairy grasses." A dog has "wallflower brown eyes," and, as a wild swan takes flight, its shadow flies beneath it "like a dark echo along the ground." Note, too, the poet as well as the artist in the songs and verses scattered through her books, most of them her own.

All of us, even children, have had "shining days" in our lives. There are many such preserved in the pages of Rosemary Sutcliff's books. Drem's ecstasy when he holds his puppy, Whitethroat, in his arms and knows that he has earned it fairly and forever; Aquila with his sister Flavia and their blind father, looking over the Downs, for what was to be the last time, as the twilight comes "lapping up the valley like a quiet tide." Surely Justinius and Flavius in *The Silver Branch* must have remembered all their lives the night they dined with their Emperor: "Outside, the beat of the wind and the far-down boom of the sea, and within, the scent of the burning logs, the steady radiance of the lamps." The magic feeling of Christmas is in *The Armourer's House* for us all as Piers, looking out over snow-bright London on Christmas Eve, whispers: "Lights, and stars, and snow, and people in their houses, all holding their breath and waiting." Children reading will remember their own shining hours with a sharpened perception of joy and beauty.

Rosemary Sutcliff is recognised as one of the two outstanding authors of historical stories for children in England today, and through the medium of her inspired storytelling children can glimpse the pattern of history and man's perpetual struggle to fulfill his true purpose in life. Authors who can bring history to life for young people with such distinction could well claim, in Miss Sutcliff's own words: "We are the Lantern Bearers. . . . [It is] for us to carry what light we can forward into the darkness and the wind."

From *The Horn Book* for June, 1960

BIOGRAPHY: THE OTHER FACE OF THE COIN

By Rosemary Sprague

THE HISTORICAL NOVELIST, in this era of pragmatic indoctrination, is frequently under attack. In the first camp of opponents are those who criticize him for "withdrawing from present reality because of a subconscious reluctance to face it, and seeking through his books to live in the past." This criticism, of course, has as its origin the endlessly repeated cliché that, after all, this *is* the twentieth century, and by all that is holy and existential, we should *live* in the twentieth century, unconcerned with the past. The point of view, however, is not entirely valid. And in an age when psychiatry is plumbing the human psyche to the depths, endeavoring to discover in past traumata the reasons for present actions, it would seem only good sense that a historical novelist should explore into the past of a nation or a world and, by that same process, try to bring to light the reasons for the swift changes in our present world. The real historical novelist is indeed quite properly aware that there is no new thing under the sun, that today's present reality was yesterday's future reality, and that the reality we are reaping now is the harvest of seeds sown many yesterdays ago.

Such an *apologia pro novella historica* has a sobering effect upon those readers whose sense of history is not completely blunted, either by the current cult of present-mindedness or by their own continued stubborn adherence to the proposition that nothing really happened in their world prior to, say, 1932. But such readers are only a small percentage of the reading public. The majority of the opponents form the battalions which make up attack number two: "The historical novel is a fake, the product of the author's imagination. Perhaps the events depicted could have happened, but they just as easily might not have. How do you really know what went on in Britain in 1060 B.C. or in France in 1600 or in Spain in 1812? You, Charlie, were not there!"

What these battalions fail to take into consideration is that there are two kinds of historical novels. One, we might call the real kind; the other is that hybrid variety which sprang into existence during World War II and is still very much with us. The latter is outwardly characterized by the jacket featuring a portrait of the heroine in perilous décolleté and inwardly, whenever inspiration flags, by the opening of another bedroom door for two or three chapters, until something else occurs to the author. The hybrid fully deserves the criticism leveled against it. The genre bears not the slightest resemblance to the work of a Kenneth Roberts or an Edith Simon or a Thomas Costain in his better moments. That the real historical novel is so constantly lumped in the popular mind with this illegitimate "sport" is both exasperating and regrettable.

What the real historical novel does, or tries to do, is to open the door to another world. Not only does it fulfill the first requirement of fiction, that of telling a good story, it also reveals the past, as accurately as painstaking research can reveal it. In order to write my novels, I have battled French officialdom to the top echelons for permission to view a section of the Louvre closed to visitors in order to verify the location of a staircase; I have been admitted to the Galérie d'Orée in what was once the Hôtel de Toulouse and is now the Banque de France, and have nearly been arrested atop Bratoren Hill in Trondheim, Norway, because I was taking pictures, unaware up to that moment that the newly placed flag at the top of the hill marked the royal citadel. I have had to learn how to make a clock and build a ship, and have been permitted to copy Handel manuscripts in the British Museum — after they had been located. (They had been there since 1789, but had never been catalogued. I knew they were there and fortunately the curator knew where they were, so we did not actually *need* a catalogue!) I have had to become thoroughly conversant with the politics, economics, religious opinion, and intellectual *ambiance* of the entire world during those periods of which I have written. Often books and manuscripts written in the different languages of the various countries of that period had to be consulted. Important also were such little items as cooking, plumbing, gardening, clothes, roads, vehicles, and the necessity of acquiring that indefinable quality, unique to each period, known as *ton*, which set me to learning Old Norse for the Viking books and Renaissance Italian for *Heir of Kiloran*. (Norman French, German, and Latin I already knew.)

In other words, the historical novelist must, if he is to have any integrity at all and no matter how much he knows about modern art, languages, and civics, so immerse himself in the period he is writing about that he can quite literally feel that he is there, living in it — not merely viewing life as a panorama outside his window, but living it wholly, completely involved. If he does not or cannot do this, neither will his readers. He can even, if he goes deeply enough, acquire the attitudes and reactions of the people of whom he writes, though they may be completely antithetical to his own, as Kenneth Roberts does so marvelously in presenting the loyalist view of the American Revolution in *Oliver Wiswell*. Usually the historical novelist discovers that human reactions have not changed so much over the centuries as to make empathy entirely impossible. When he looks at the twentieth century, he sees that Spartacus the Gladiator, arousing the Roman mob to violence, is still with us. And so is the mob. Political opportunists are still cast in Julius Caesar's mold, and the voice of sanity still speaks powerfully through our few literate twentieth-century Ciceroes. Once this perspective is gained, the historical novelist can answer the accusation, "You were not there," with an unequivocal "I am here; and because I am here, I can also be there." A paradox, but a paradox of historical continuity which is reality itself.

But when the historical novelist turns to biography, the big guns are wheeled into position. "Isn't it marvelous," one is asked by the nicest people, "to be working with facts for a change, and not to have to imagine everything?"

Several answers to that question always occur to me, none of them precisely polite. The question conjures up a rather ironic cartoon, published several years ago in a magazine, in which a psychological research foundation, having found the couch inadequate and possessing neither spiritual nor emotional imagination, was conducting with electronic aid a study in depth of every facet of its chosen victim's life. The poor soul was covered from head to foot with various electronic devices attached by wires to a lowering computer; in one hand he carried a tape recorder and in the other a camera, while three TV cameras were trained on him. A brain-wave machine, set firmly on his head to track his thought patterns, was the crowning touch. W. H. Auden's comment on "The Unknown Citizen"

Was he free? Was he happy? The question is absurd!
Had there been anything wrong, we certainly should have heard

springs irresistibly to mind.

Nevertheless, it is this kind of clinical approach alone, rendering exact, scientifically verified information, that a biographer would have to have if he is to fulfill the requirement of "working with facts." And not only would this be an impossibility, but the facts themselves, so derived, would be far from self-evident. While a machine can indicate a quickening heartbeat, this information, which is vital to the heart specialist, is useless in and of itself to a biographer. Heartbeats quicken for many reasons — from love, anger, fear. The biographer, like the novelist, must know what specific emotion is involved. How can he find out? Lucky the biographer whose subject has been considerate enough to write a letter or to note in his diary on the precise day that the machine was computing the record, "I was so angry, my heart beat in my throat," or "She was so beautiful, my heart raced up and down like an elevator!" But suppose there is no letter? no diary? The biographer is left high and dry with the fact that the heart beat so many beats to the minute that day. If that is what he wants, that is what he will have, and much good may it do him! Who would care? Not even the computer operator.

Or, take that thought-wave machine. It is a device most admirably suited for clinical diagnosis of certain disorders of the brain. But, even so, medical experts are fully aware of its limitations. It can trace shifts in thought patterns, but we are rational beings, and *we think in words*. The machine has not yet been invented that can report the words inside the human brain which at any given moment project a thought. And until the machine knows those words, it cannot know what the individual is thinking or detect those subtle emotional overtones that differentiate mild exasperation from violent rage. And since thought alone gives rise to the kind of action which entitles an individual to have his biography written, the biographer must somehow, some way — call it mysticism if you will — get inside his subject's mind. In this process, which demands humanity, thought, imagination, compassion, intuition, faith, hope, charity, prayer, and frequently fasting, the exact fact that is the basis for the biographer's work often comes clearly to light.

I hope it does not seem presumptuous to say that the true historical novelist, who has great respect for and interest in biography, comes to biography with an important advantage over biographers who have never worked in fiction. What is the task of the historical novelist? To re-create a world. And the biographer? Precisely the same task. His subject, after all, exists or existed at a particular time, within a particular set of circumstances. This is not the occasion to debate the relative importance of heredity or environment, but simply to emphasize the fact (since facts are being stressed) that no man exists or has ever existed apart from his environment. He may either accept or reject it, but his very rejection indicates that he has acknowledged its existence; obviously he is influenced by his environment, whether he realizes it or not. The biographer, like the historical novelist, must, therefore, eagerly devote a tremendous amount of time and study to the re-creation of his subject's world. As Goethe remarks in *Dichtung und Wahrheit,*

> ... this seems to be the chief task of biography: to present the man within the relationships of his age, to show to what extent the currents of the whole oppose him, to what extent they favor him: how he forms out of this conflict a view of the world and of men, and how, if he is an artist, poet, writer, he reflects it back again.

Careful, intensive study of his era not only illuminates the particular subject of the biography, but is of great help in making the seemingly incredible credible to the reader. The historical novelist has this problem, too, but he has the protective wall of fiction and the reader's "willing suspension of disbelief." Also, he can occasionally omit a facet of a given period which the twentieth-century reader would find too difficult to accept. The biographer, however, is at the mercy of history. He is only permitted to deduct and surmise, provided that he plainly labels deductions and surmises; he *may not* alter or omit. And the first thing he learns (having already accepted the dogma that truth is stranger than fiction) is that those readers who have shouted most loudly for facts are the first to disbelieve or, worse, to ridicule any facts that are foreign to their long-accepted idea of reality. For example, my students are always astounded to learn that Tennyson and his wife were engaged for thirteen years before they were married, and are inclined to be rather derisive. Nevertheless, the long engagement was a fact. The students must be informed that in Victorian England a good father would be considered derelict in his duty if he permitted his daughter to marry before the man was able to support her properly; that such was the commonly held view of the time. (Strangely enough, when they recover from their skepticism, students not only accept the fact, but are even occasionally heard to murmur that it is too bad that that particular view of the world was ever altered.)

As Goethe implies, re-creation of the subject's world is especially important when he is a literary man fulfilling the demand of literature, that of mirroring his own time. Just as much of Shakespeare makes whole sense only when read against the background of the Elizabethan view of the kingship and the anointed sovereign, so Swift's appalling view of mankind in Book IV of *Gulliver's Travels* is more understandable when we keep in mind that he, an Irishman, is inveighing against British officialdom. And much of Browning's so-called "obscurity" vanishes, when it is put into the context of the poet's own intellectual frame of reference. "Caliban Upon Setebos" is admittedly a difficult poem, but seen in the light of a satiric thrust at the Darwinians, a subject widely discussed at the dinner parties of Browning's day, it becomes easier to understand. The brilliant casuistry of Bishop Blougram in "Bishop Blougram's Apology" becomes more fascinating, more important, when we discover that he is, in fact, a sharply etched portrait of Cardinal Wiseman, who at that very moment was doing his utmost to re-establish the Roman Catholic hierarchy in England, another subject hotly debated in drawing rooms and clubs. The school of criticism that maintains that only the words on the printed page are important and has sneered at the biographical approach to literature forgets that a mind thought the words before a hand wrote them and that the mind was influenced by the society from which it emerged.

In this re-creation of a world, then, biography shows its kinship to historical fiction; but an even closer relationship between them entitles biography to be called the other face of the same coin. Every biographer must, of course, cultivate the novelist's ear and eye: the eye that sees rather than merely looks; the ear that listens and does not just hear. The novelist uses these faculties to create his plot and characters. The biographer needs them to make his subject come alive. Sooner or later, there comes the moment in a biography — and they are more numerous than the average reader thinks — when no sources whatever will provide even a glimmer of the absolute fact which is so insistently demanded. A poem like Browning's "Childe Roland to the Dark Tower Came" has been interpreted a dozen different ways. The poet never gave his own interpretation, and the poem is crucial to an understanding of him. What does the biographer do? Two courses are open. He may, as has been done in many cases, plunge into Freud or Jung and wallow in those murky waters. But this is dangerous, because Browning is not available *in propria persona* to place upon a couch. The second course is to take the way of the historical novelist and say in effect, "Given this individual and this particular set of circumstances *which can be documented* and given this poem as an outcome of both, this was probably the way his mind was running at the moment. This could have been the creative process he followed." To the fact-demanders, particularly those governed by the psychological approach of the present age, such educated reasoning may seem most reprehensible. I submit, however, that it is much fairer to advance such a solution based on known and well-considered facts than to say categorically that Browning was in love with his mother or unhappy in his marriage, based on a *post hoc* Freudian analysis. Besides, psychiatric conjectures are inappropriate and inapplicable as well in the case of Browning. The real challenge for his biographer is to make his genuine integrity and goodness attractive to an age which tends to look on both with cynicism and derision.

Thus when the historical novelist turned biographer is asked which form he prefers, with the inference that he should prefer the latter as more accurate and factual, he must answer that both forms make the same demands of the writer, and both are written for the same purpose: to illuminate the past in which the present is anchored and on which our future depends. And also, because of the essential selectivity of the writer's art, the focus of both historical novel and biography is, or should be, upon one quality and one only — human greatness.

With this statement, we have come full circle to our opening consideration: the need today for readers to be conscious of the past and especially the need for them to become as aware of past greatness as they are now aware of past errors and defeats. All readers need this awareness; the younger to learn, the older to be reminded of that which is good. We have been put through a veritable orgy of castigation, all culminating in that woeful admission that past ages have not done right by the youth of today, as though they were somehow unique in the chaos they face. Young people need to be informed, quite ruthlessly if need be, that if they are to leave even as good a world to their descendants as our ancestors have left to them and to us, they must not only learn from past errors, but learn to emulate past greatness; and they must be *shown* past greatness. They must, in kindness, firmly be made to understand that theirs is not the only generation that has had problems to solve; that there have been wars and rumors of wars throughout history; and to quote David Dietz, "You can be just as dead from a tomahawk as from an atomic bomb." Or as Longfellow expressed it in his moving poem "The Children's Crusade," when the little band of children wept that they could go no further,

> But their dauntless leader said,
> "Faint not, though your bleeding feet
> O'er these slippery paths of sleet
>   Move but painfully and slowly.
> Other feet than yours have bled,
> Other tears than yours been shed.
> Courage! Lose not heart nor hope!
> On the mountain's southern slope
>   Lies Jerusalem, the Holy!"

Our children and our young people need to learn — need to be told — that standards and values which have proved their worth in the past are likely indeed to be useful now, in their own very present existential situation. They need to learn, too, that the end has never justified the means; that there is no royal road to honorable success; that there is no substitute for integrity; and that mankind has been saved only by those willing to commit themselves to the task of salvation and not by those who "play it cool." In a word, they need examples. To quote C. Day Lewis, as he expressed it in a lecture which he gave recently at my alma mater, "Men must always have something to look up to.... Each of us has a touch of the fine spirit, and this can be made finer only by looking up to the finest spirits of all."

It is these "finest spirits of all," plus the conviction that the greatness of the past can speak to the present, that should be the ultimate concern of both the real biographer and the real historical novelist. Their task is to present, in C. Day Lewis' words, "The heroic view of life, man at his loftiest and most intensely living moments." There have always been and will doubtless always be those who, for various reasons, point out the lesser and easier view. But the *heroic* view should be the concern of all those who work with young people and books, in the library, in the classroom, or with pen in hand. And not only our concern but our passion! Only as we ourselves possess the heroic view can we hand it on, and only as we hand it on can we ensure that this gallant company, which from the beginning of time has maintained and advanced civilization, will continue to endure.

From *The Horn Book* for June, 1966

DIMENSIONS IN TIME

A Critical View of Historical Fiction for Children

By Carolyn Horovitz

ANY STORY in the field of fiction deals with time, place, and people in a dimension slightly altered from the present in which the writer lives. Since such altering of life is inherent in fiction, it is not particularly illuminating to say that the historical novel differs from other forms of the novel in its characteristic use of time and place unless some consideration is given first to the meaning of time and place in the novel and how these are, or should be, different in the historical novel. Nor is it enough to say that we have a special type of novel, called historical fiction, because historical fiction covers works of varying types, ranging from the highly scholarly to the wildly adventurous.

In viewing the field of historical fiction critically, the concept of time must be faced as a central issue. Why *time?* Why has the author delved into another period, and what relationship has the story with that period? Does the story grow out of the time, or is it a case of a plot artificially imposed upon another period for the sake of color?

Hilaire Belloc in "The Character of an Historical Novel"[*] says that the prime test of success in historical fiction is not only in how well the past is made to live but how well its "inconceivable oddities" are made conceivable, its "incomprehensibles" illuminated so that the reader perceives the past as if it were the present. Such a fusion of scholarship and imagination means that time, as an element, slips from the self-conscious "historical" to a simple matter of living reality. With certain authors, scholarship may be subordinated to imagination. Yet the result may be one of essential truth. In her essay on historical novels, Esther Forbes makes this point, saying that for

[*] *One Thing and Another* by Hilaire Belloc. London: Hollis & Carter, 1955.

writers like Hawthorne, Tolstoy, and Emily Brontë removal of the story to a past time gives a necessary freedom to use a universal, time-transcending theme. Such use of time in the hands of lesser writers can be one of shoddy flamboyancy, a toying with the reader's gullibility.

In judging the distortion of another period, the question must be asked, why *time?* Is the story germane to the time, does it deepen the reader's feeling for the time? Is the story one that transcends time, or is it a debasement of fiction in the name of history?

Place in the historical novel, as in contemporary fiction, gives the reader a sense of reality. Eudora Welty, in a monograph, *Place in Fiction*, says:

> The moment the place in which the novel happens is accepted as true, through it will begin to glow, in a kind of recognizable glory, the feeling and thought that inhabited the novel in the author's head and animated the whole of his work.

At the same time that Miss Welty emphasizes the importance of place, she also stresses the necessity for the writer "to disentangle the significant — in character, incident, setting, mood, everything, from the random and meaningless and irrelevant...." She not only stresses place as giving vitality and depth to created people but also warns against the danger of overwhelming and warping the novel's structure with an overemphasis on place. Such disproportion she calls "showy and vulgar." Again, the matter of proportion goes back to the central purpose of the author. Place in the historical novel has the same importance that it does in contemporary work: it is needed to make the characters live.

Characters and plot — how are they made to seem real, to develop in an "inevitable" way? Or is this ever achieved? Certainly a story that does not carry the reader along is going to be dull, and one that does not evoke believable people is going to be lifeless. In a work of historical fiction it is too easy to put contemporary characters into another background. Such an error is a defect in depth of historical portrayal and may occur in varying degrees in works otherwise excellent. A great piece of historical fiction, written with absolute unity and depth of time, place, characters, and plot, is a unique achievement. According to Hilaire Belloc:

> ... a good historical novel — that rarest of rare things — is the best educational instrument imaginable. To know the past, or even a section of the past, is to add a dimension to experience. It does more to the mind even than does travel, and for the run of men who cannot evoke the life of the past through reading its chronicles, or even from any wide acquaintance with its material remains, fiction will give what is needed.*

It should be no surprise, if *Johnny Tremain*, by Esther Forbes, finds its way into the upper "rare" stratosphere of literary excellence. Lauded ever since it first appeared, it continues to be read and regarded as a fine historical novel. It is a book much praised, but it has not, as far as I know, been critically examined. It would be sheer foolishness to pretend that I will now bring to bear a perfected analytical device on this novel. The questions are really simple and seem perfectly obvious. Why did she use time, this particular time for this particular story? Miss Forbes tells in an article† about how she came to write this book, how it grew in her mind as she was working on another book of the same period. But that is not really the answer to a question which must find its answer in the book itself.

Basically, the story is one of character development, of a boy's struggle with his feelings of inferiority and worth, his attempts to find a place for himself, his problems about establishing relationships with people. It is almost as if he were a symbol of his time: a boy with promise and great natural ability but shackled by a sense of shame and inferiority. Aside from these symbolic values, this boy has the character and attitude of his own time, when men and boys were expected to make their own way. He is forthright, direct, and not unduly alarmed by the necessity of spending a night in the open or missing a meal. Only when he has missed quite a few

---

*Belloc, *op. cit.*

†The Newbery Medal Acceptance, *The Horn Book Magazine*, July-August, 1944.

meals and his hardships are those before which a man would quail does Johnny show signs of suffering. He is not described as showing these traits and qualities of the times; he actively displays them. Although he is a boy of all ages in his teasing and carefully guarded tender feelings, he is a boy of *his* time. In our day and age, such a boy would be sent to juvenile hall.

But in those days, Johnny was needed and soon came to be valued for his courage, just as he came to find values for which to fight and by which to live. In a time of growing, the boy grew in answer to needs greater than his own. The answer to the question, "why *time*?", is apparent in this novel. This boy is of the time, bred, illuminated, and developed. Although presented in far greater precision than a symbol, he does have symbolic value.

Place comes alive sensuously with the first sentence, the first paragraph:

> On rocky islands gulls woke. Time to be about their business. Silently they floated in on the town, but when their icy eyes sighted the first dead fish, first bits of garbage about the ships and wharves, they began to scream and quarrel.

Miss Forbes brings Boston awake at the same time that the reader plunges into a sense of place — smelling, breathing, hearing, seeing. The novel has base in this way, from start to finish; never is skillful use of place merely a garnish or a layer in a sandwich. Speech and clothes and manner of behavior are all of a piece, but not an undifferentiated piece. Life can be as different in the homes of the Silsbees or the Lytes or the Laphams as it can be in Bel-Air or Aliso Village.

This book does not merely deal with another time and place; it is impregnated with these elements. And the hero, in working out his destiny, is under the same inevitable compulsion that people in the past have always appeared to feel. There was no other way. Yet, during the telling, as during the actual happening, nothing seemed certain, nothing seemed inevitable. To Johnny the events of the day were felt, not as historic events, but as tragedies for his friends:

> Johnny put his hands to his face. It was wet and his hands were shaking. He thought of that blue smock his mother

had made him, now torn by bullets. Pumpkin had wanted so little out of life. A farm. Cows. True, Rab had got the musket he craved, but Pumpkin wasn't going to get his farm. Nothing more than a few feet by a few feet at the foot of Boston Common.

There is a sense of the meaning of life, of creed and ethics, of human behavior. Even the meanness of merchant Lyte was finally understood in some measure by Johnny. And Paul Revere's heroism was accepted casually with believability, credibility, coming through the illumination of small detail. One instance is the description of Revere's ride to Portsmouth, before his famous ride. The weather was bad that night:

> From the lowering December sky handfuls of snowflakes were falling, but as soon as they came to earth they turned to ice. It was a bleak, bad, dangerous day for the long ride north.

Revere's wife was in bed, recovering from having borne another child. She rapped on a windowpane at Johnny to come and get a note her husband had almost forgotten, a note about his sick grandmother with which to allay the suspicions of the British soldiers.

In this way, Esther Forbes brings about what Hilaire Belloc calls "the resurrection of the past" by the use of sudden illumination, proportion, and imagination:

> ... upon the discovery of the essential movements and the essential moments in the action; and upon imagination, the power of seeing the thing as it was; landscape, the weather, the gestures and the faces of the men; yes, and their thoughts within.*

Wonderful as Miss Forbes' work is, it is not a work which can be neatly pigeonholed as "suitable for children." It is "suitable" for anyone who wishes to read a good story of this period. The excitement of the times is used to its fullest extent in building plot interest; the boy's involvement in the Revolution is so intrinsic a part of the plot that reading about Johnny Tremain becomes reading about the American Revolution. If any book

---
* Belloc, *op. cit.*

can be called a prototype of all that historical fiction should be, this book merits that appellation.

Rosemary Sutcliff's *The Eagle of the Ninth* combines the presentation of the historic era of the Roman occupation of Britain with an acute sense of place. A feeling of belonging to a certain landscape becomes a vital part of the plot structure. She portrays remarkably the conflict between the Celtic tribal customs and the Roman way of imposing its own civilization wherever it went. The two elements are finally welded into an inseparable unity by one force of nature — the country itself. Strength of place, a certain foreshadowing of the future, lies in her description of Valentia, a deserted Roman province:

> But now the wild had flowed in again; grass covered the cobbles of the streets, timber roofs had fallen in, and the red sandstone walls stood gaunt and empty to the sky. The wells were choked with the debris of thirty autumns, and an eldertree had taken root in one corner of the roofless shrine where once had stood the cohort's standard and the altars of its gods, and had thrust a jagged gap in the wall to make room for itself.

Place works its will, not only on the buildings of the Romans but on the characters of the Romans as well. The hero of the story, Marcus, is at the end of the novel free to go where he wishes, back to the loved land of his childhood. But he elects to stay; Britain has become his home. This conclusion is no mere noble decision but the inevitable result of the strong sense of place inherent in this novel from the beginning. By the time the novel is finished, the reader even feels homesick, homesick not only for a certain essence of country and climate but for another time.

While the action in the plot is dignified and utterly credible, it moves to a climactic chase which crests onward to the conclusion. There is never any question about the appropriateness of this time and place as background; the characters are drawn out of the past; they behave in a way consistent with their times and still are utterly comprehensible. Much about the past is illuminated by this novel, particularly the relationship between Celt and Roman, the dynamics of two civilizations clashing. Used in a masterly, symbolic way to emphasize the underlying theme is the incident of the wolf cub and his allegiance, as a free animal, to his master. The author points out, through the wolf cub and also the Celtic freedman, that loyalty, allegiance, and friendship have value only when freely rendered. This idea is presented not as a moral but as dramatic development within the plot. If the plot is to have meaning it must be in the deepening of our understanding of man's relationship to man. That this presentation of the past does so with sharpness and acuity is not only a tribute to the writer's scholarship, her careful proportioning of a good story with believable characters, but is also a measure of her philosophical depth. She brings a degree of greatness to the feeling of love that a man from another place, a man of a conquering people, can have for a country not his birthplace, a people not his own.

Another book of the same time and locale, *The White Isle* by Caroline Dale Snedeker, suffers by comparison. Although a fine book, it does not have the same close-textured background. In *The White Isle* the story is told from the point of view of a young girl, a Roman patrician whose sense of injustice has been developed through an experience early in the story in which she has to face the prospect of an unwelcome marriage. She manages to escape the marriage, fortuitously, and then goes with her family to Britain. In this story, the characters change from the worship of Roman gods to belief in Christianity, a change neither credible nor incredible. I happened to find this conclusion less moving than the one in Miss Sutcliff's work, although a change in religion is one involving the innermost feelings. In this book the characters seem to lose some of their period authenticity as they approach the conclusion and this change of conviction. This is not a comment on the way they speak; the inner core of motivation and feeling seems to have snapped out of the past altogether; verbal explanations accomplish more than they should.

Mrs. Snedeker's work is valuable in that the characters do live; through them Roman family life is real, and the restrictions, ethics, and code of an upper-class Roman family are evident. Although the characters of the brother and sister, presented at the beginning of the novel, are well drawn, the dimension of their portrayal never deepens sufficiently to make the girl's final conversion to Christianity much more than an accompaniment to her romance. The story is well told, the action moves continually forward, and the time and characters are well related. A gentle quality pervades the entire book, and the writer's complete sincerity gives value and weight to her picture of life in Britain before the Saxons came, bringing, as she says, "sudden night."

Howard Pyle's *Men of Iron* is vigorously and directly told. He brings a strong note of authenticity to his time and place setting the plot squarely in the reign of Henry IV, using the king as a pivotal factor in his plot. Though the plot is one of vindication, it is clear that Pyle wished to show the training of a youth in medieval times. Thirty years after reading the novel I still had a vivid recollection of the trials of young Myles Falworth as he trained to become a knight. Rereading it these many years later, I was as engrossed as I remember myself to have been on the first reading. Such an old favorite is always in danger of being a disappointment on rereading. And when it proves to be more than worth its mettle, it is almost impossible to look at it with anything but the fondest approbation.

Pyle uses the intrusive author to tell whatever he thinks is necessary, yet — far from detracting from the story — he seems only to add to the flavor and character of the novel. He begins firmly, anchoring his story to historical happenings in his introduction, building on such a solid background of time and place that his further intrusions into the story are justifiable buttressings of fact:

> A quaint old book treating of knighthood and chivalry gives a full and detailed account of all the circumstances of the ceremony of a creation of a Knight of the Bath. It tells us that the candidate was first placed...

And on he goes for several pages of exposition which is not only palatable but necessary to understand what Myles must undergo to become such a Knight.

Simply and effectively, this book gives a keen sense of medieval life, the kinds of men it produced, and the challenges they had to meet. It unrolls an exciting story, one integrated in all events with the time and place. But this novel achieves still more; it gives the pith and marrow, the essence of an age. Long after the plot is forgotten, long after the information concerning what constitutes a Knight of the Bath has receded into the background, the feeling Pyle has created for this period will glow, unextinguished.

Mara, Daughter of the Nile, by Eloise Jarvis McGraw is a story that begins sensationally and builds expertly to an exciting conclusion. The background, Egypt in the time of Hatshepsut, is convenient to the story and presented deftly, obliquely. Time and place are definitely secondary to the story; a complicated one of spy and counterspy amid palace intrigues to place the young Thutmose on the throne. While this story moves swiftly, with skillful and ingenious plotting, it could be fitted to another locale. The heroine, being a rebellious slave, is free from the strictures of her time and background to a large extent and toward the end of the book becomes recognizable as a western romantic heroine instead of the slave girl in Egypt that she is supposed to be — and that at the beginning of the novel she was. She does change because of the events in her life, but she becomes more superficial as she becomes more noble. The difficulty of completely imagining the emotional life of another time is apparent in this story. Overcoming this difficulty by relying on a fast-moving plot is the solution used here. Although this is not one of those rare, great pieces of historical fiction, the writing does give a sense of life and place, of the relationship of ruler and people, slave and slaveholder, Syrian and Babylonian. Eloise McGraw does bring forth the past in flashes, and the novel is satisfying in that it whets the appetite for additional lore of ancient Egypt.

Before discussing Lucile Morrison's *The Lost Queen of Egypt* it is helpful to think of Emerson's comment in his essay on "History":

> Time dissipates to shining ether the solid angularity of facts. No anchor, no cable, no fences avail to keep a fact a fact. Babylon, Troy, Tyre, Palestine and even early Rome are passing already into fiction.... Who cares what the fact was when we have thus made a constellation of it to hang in heaven an immortal sign? London and Paris and New York must go the same way. "What is History," said Napoleon, "but a fable agreed upon?"

It is remarkable that Lucile Morrison's "constellation" of Egypt in the latter part of the Eighteenth Dynasty (1580-1350 B.C.) has so little of the "angular fact" to go on yet has the ring of authenticity of the history book. It is remarkable, not because the author disregards history but because the fiber which must be woven by the novelist to fit the facts together into a whole can be supplied only by the imagination. Yet Lucile Morrison has painted a picture of broad scope with deft, delightful touches of detail. The characterization of Ankhsenamon gives her depth and reality as a human in any time, but she is of her place and time to the core and consistently so throughout the book. The intelligence of the girl, combined with her sense of play and gradual development of the awareness of her imprisoning responsibilities as queen, gives warmth and depth to a novel which portrays the political and religious struggles for power of a time long blurred of its facts. By making her story and portrayal engrossing, Lucile Morrison has given the fact a more dignified position than if she had tried to weight her story beyond the need of the narrative. In her bibliography she lists books for those who would like to know more about the Eighteenth Dynasty Egypt. She is quite right in thinking that her book, ample feast that it is, has but developed an appetite for more knowledge. It has given the reader a gift of the imagination with which to read these books of "fact."

An historic novel can be presented in a familiar, almost miniature scope and still have the impact of a larger work. Such a story is *The Willow Whistle* by Cornelia Meigs. Written for younger children, who perhaps do not think about history as being different from any other story, this book gives a true and vivid insight into the ways of the Indians. The author makes no attempt to be comprehensive or tutorial in the sense that Howard Pyle was; the story is presented with deceptive simplicity. Yet there is good, carefully constructed plot, with distinct and real characters. Within the rather small framework of two children's adventures and friendship with a Sioux Indian, Cornelia Meigs presents a pattern of Indian life, beliefs, and differences between tribes. This story has emotional depth and a careful awareness of how much must be left unrevealed. To the end, a certain mystery remains, a definite gulf between two civilizations which cannot be bridged even by friendship, symbolized by the poignantly humorous episode of the Indians riding off with the Blue-Backed Speller, thinking that they have taken the white man's medicine.

Adam of the Road, by Elizabeth Janet Gray, presents a character as a device to show us England in the year 1294. And he does that beautifully. Using Adam to relate the reader to the background and times of medieval England, Elizabeth Janet Gray takes us on a tour of the countryside, showing us the people and typical occurrences of the time. The structure is rather rambling, and reminiscent of Chaucer's *Canterbury Tales*. The kind of life people had, the general culture, customs, and hardships are all revealed. But the book does not have the sharp, pungent quality of Chaucer's wit and tongue-in-cheek portrayal of character. The writer's skill is needed to keep this story from sagging. Only by sheer quality of writing and beautiful use of time and place does Elizabeth Janet Gray keep the reader's interest at a high level. A further disadvantage is the rather tepid quality of the boy, Adam. His inner struggles are not presented as a central part of the plot. There is no necessity for his having been what he was or having done anything that he did. At the opposite extreme of *Mara, Daughter of the Nile*, this plot shows such a careful restraint from adventure for adventure's sake that it seems ultrarefined.

It seems significant to me that on the John Newbery Medal, awarded this book, are the words "most distinguished." Peculiarly ambiguous, "most distinguished" can mean almost anything, but I sometimes suspect that it means something that adults can be proud of as having done for children. And certainly this is a book full of obvious merit: well written, carefully researched, carefully devised to avoid dullness. But I charge that there has been no headlong involvement with emotion in this book; rather, it is as carefully protective in its way as some of the older "moral" tales.

Paul Hazard has said that he likes books for children which "awaken in them not maudlin sentimentality, but sensibility; that enable them to share in great human emotions; that give them respect for universal life...." As to books of knowledge, he says, "I like them when they do not deceive themselves about the quality of knowledge, and do not claim that knowledge can take the place of everything else. I like them especially when they distill from all the different kinds of knowledge the most difficult and the most necessary — that of the human heart."

Although I have no quarrel with the awarding of the Newbery Medal to *Adam of the Road* — it cannot put the seal of perfection on any book — I would say that this book, admirable as it may be, lacks the chief ingredient which both *Johnny Tremain* and *Men of Iron* have so signally, and that is emotional vigor, the distillation of which Paul Hazard speaks.

Almost a morality tale, *The Trumpeter of Krakow* is a story fraught with suspense, but a story which could exist only in relation to its particular time and place of Poland in the fifteenth century. People are sketched in rather black-and-white tones, but the reader's involvement is emotional and immediate. Essentially a story of faith and loyalty, it is a reverberation from the story of the earlier trumpeter of Krakow. Eric Kelly has managed to resurrect not only a past time, a past place, but the essence of the period. In the way that his feeling for the past infuses every speech, every action, the past becomes real. This is a superb story and a superb history, neither one separable from the other. The writer has an architect's eye, an artist's sense of texture and color; and the mood he senses and creates brings to the novel an aura of lived experience. Not a feeling that now everything about Poland has been made clear, it is rather a knowing that mystery was in itself part of the time — a vague presentiment of fear and wonder. It is precisely this achievement which is unique about this novel, an achievement which no stack of history or geography books could give — truly a gift of an "incomprehensible."

To excite the imagination of a reader, to move that reader into consciousness of another time, to bring the perspective, immediacy, and continuity of all time into an emotional awareness is to give more than history; it is to give the meaning of history. Perhaps no single book of historical fiction, no single book of history, can achieve this. As Hilaire Belloc once said, and as I have often been aware, all the books one reads coalesce.

They are one big book. So with works of historical fiction: they can merge and blend and weave together.

No attempt has been made to select books representative of various periods in any way. The selection has been somewhat accidental, with the emphasis on quality. For these books have all measured up in an appreciable degree to standards of excellence: they are stories told in time because of need, the writer's need to tell of that time, and therefore reflect the delight and scholarship of the writer, as well as his understanding and emotional depth. If there is any danger in the guardianship of adults over the publication of books for children it is the danger pointed out by Paul Hazard, the danger of being overprotective, overcontrolling. Children, he says, protect themselves from such forces by simply not reading. That is the final criticism of a work meant for children: is it read? And the counter-question is: from what do they have to choose?

It is too little for a children's librarian merely to know the subject of a book, the general reputation of its author; the librarian must know if a book will delight or if it will need some special introduction; or if its failure to find response in readers is due to some inherent weakness. Works of historical fiction are valuable allies to developing reading interests. After reading one that is exciting for its plot and has set the reader firmly in the period, other works on the same period, factual or otherwise, partake of the same magic. A book which might be welcome after such an initiation might prove tedious if tackled first. A careful, critical appraisal of each book is not only a help in purchasing but is an indispensable service to the readers of such books. It is just as important to know the negative side as the positive. Perhaps the critical approach to children's literature has suffered from an approach of approbation, of a "seal of approval" attitude attached to works for children. Actually, children's literature is as varied and complex in its requirements for perfection as any other field. Nor is the subject matter limited to goodness and light and everlasting optimism. Evil and death and despair are in the children's room as well as the adult section. Johnny Tremain has his share; the story of Ankhsenamon is one of doom; Rosemary Sutcliff shows us the destruction of one way of life for another. That the final note is not one of suicidal despair is hardly a sharp differentiation from the adult section. At the end of his book, *The Uses of the Past*, Herbert J. Muller states what is pertinent for mankind, child and adult:

> Yet the tragic sense is the profoundest sense of our common humanity, and may therefore be a positive inspiration. If all the great societies have died, none is really dead. Their peoples have vanished, as all men must, but first they enriched the great tradition of high, enduring values. Like Burckhardt we might be heartened as well as sobered by the thought that we shall vanish into the same darkness, and live on in the same tradition. We might be freed from the vanity of grandiose hopes, as of petty concerns. We might learn that "ripeness is all," and that it is enough.

From *The Horn Book* for June, 1962

IV

THE MATTER OF POETRY

If Poetry is omitted from the lives of very young children or if it is allowed to play only a minor part in their experience, there is a serious danger that powerful, though undeveloped, feelings will remain only partially satisfied, and ideas, though not fully formed, will be confined to too narrow a range. This is a bold statement to make, and it is important to make it at the present time, when so many other agencies are at work in the world — whether willfully or not — to undermine the foundations of wholesome childhood, to seduce it from its normal pattern of growth, or to keep it ignorant of its cultural heritage.

From "Poetry for the Youngest" by Leonard Clark

Articles

A NEW GARLAND FOR A GREAT BOOK
  by Louise Seaman Bechtel
POETRY FOR THE YOUNGEST *by Leonard Clark*
POETRY FOR CHILDREN *by Harry Behn*
SPEAKING TO THE IMAGINATION *by Samuel French Morse*
"NOT THE ROSE ..." *by Myra Cohn Livingston*
WHERE ARE WE GOING WITH POETRY FOR CHILDREN?
  by Patrick J. Groff
FLIGHT PLAN FOR THE WINGED FOAL *by Dorothy E. Ames*

A NEW GARLAND FOR A GREAT BOOK*

By Louise Seaman Bechtel

"OH DEAR, my heart was ready to burst!" when I received the new edition of COME HITHER. Newly designed and decorated in beautiful taste by Warren Chappell; completely reset in "highly legible Janson"; gay with a garlanded jacket and a glowing, blue-green binding — it will delight its thousands of old friends and make many more new ones. The 771 new pages have xxi new pages of indexes. Salaams and gratitude to Mr. Knopf!

COME HITHER is unique among anthologies because the poet-editor approached his task in a specially creative spirit. He ranged more widely than any anthologist of poetry I know, over "rhymes and poems" from anonymous ancient songs, games, and ballads to modern poems of Great Britain and America, avoiding the most obvious, discovering little-known treasures, arranging all with inspired skill. Upon publication in 1923, it was recognized as a remarkable book, probably a great book.

In 1928, tantalized by interesting mail and by his own new ideas about some of the five hundred poems, Mr. de la Mare added still more to the pages of notes he called "About and Roundabout," more "notes" and more poems, even some "great" poems, bringing this fascinating section to 300 pages. His work stopped with the second edition of 1928, but you would not wish it brought "up to date," for the fact is you could not bear any more poems. The choices are perfect as they are, and in perfect balance. For quick evidence of this, read the section called "War."

*Come Hither by Walter de la Mare. Knopf, 1957. The first sentence of this review is quoted from page 177.

The exquisite fantasy of the introduction takes you back to the poet's childhood, to the way his own discriminating love of poetry began. With him, you find "the Key of the Kingdom," as he copies poems from Mr. Nahum's Volume One. At the dramatic ending, the boy suddenly is fearful, both of "Thrae" (spell it backwards) and of the real world he now must face. But he takes courage and joy from all he has read and copied, and then we know how "real" this fantasy is meant to be. This is made doubly clear as he talks of Mr. Nahum's very first poem, "Now the day is over," and on the last pages of the book, when the poet returns to the magical house and garden and gives us for the nth time a definition of poetry. (The key for Nahum is Human.)

The titles of the divisions of the poems are themselves a challenge to the imagination. They prove this a book not chiefly for children, though it is for all under twelve who find themselves ready for it. It is for "youth" and adults. It must be offered in both sections of libraries and bookshops, and shared in homes by young and old. In libraries, it must have its own small table, with a bouquet of flowers or herbs or evergreens beside it, and its special lamp and chair. Perhaps a sign can point to that corner, with a piper or dancer copied from Mr. Chappell and the words "To Thrae — Come Hither."

Introduction, poems, notes — read them apart, re-read them together. In those famous notes are surprises indeed, glowing bits of the thoughts and the wide reading of one who loved birds, animals, flowers, music; one who collected epitaphs, samplers, old children's books, madrigals; one who was learned about bells, gardens, fishing, cooking. You feel that all the while he knew all these things with his outer senses as well as in the pages of old books. There are poets' letters and diaries; there are acutely wise little essays on Chaucer, Shakespeare, Blake, and others. You are taught casually "how" to read poetry, both to yourself and aloud. You are lured to look up great books you had forgotten and to search for others you do not know. You learn more and more about WORDS.

Now and again you meet your guide in person: he comforts his small son by candle-light; he reads Alice Meynell by glow-worm-light; he walks far to look down on Widdicombe

Church; he visits Ludlow Castle where the Masque of Comus first was given; at Windsor he sees "the most beautiful set of armor in the world," made for the young Prince, Hally. Some of his curiosities may appeal to you more than others, as he spreads his rich fare. More important, you realize that this gentle, learned person knew well, above all, the human heart, the hearts of men of long ago and of today.

After certain verses in the notes, de la Mare says: "The men who wrote these words truly and solemnly meant them. They are not mere pretty flowers of the fancy, but the tough piercing roots of the tree of life that grew within their minds." As you live with this book, turning to it often in joy or sorrow, those roots will pierce your mind too.

From *The Horn Book* for December, 1957

POETRY FOR THE YOUNGEST

By Leonard Clark

> To learn to love books and reading is one of the very best things that can happen to anybody. So, too, with pictures and music. Poetry in particular wears well. The longer you care for it in itself the better it gets.
>
> <div style="text-align:right">— Walter de la Mare
Introduction to
<i>Tom Tiddler's Ground</i> (Knopf)</div>

IF POETRY is omitted from the lives of very young children or if it is allowed to play only a minor part in their experience, there is a serious danger that powerful, though undeveloped, feelings will remain only partially satisfied, and ideas, though not fully formed, will be confined to too narrow a range. This is a bold statement to make, and it is important to make it at the present time, when so many other agencies are at work in the world — whether willfully or not — to undermine the foundations of wholesome childhood, to seduce it from its normal pattern of growth, and to keep it ignorant of its cultural heritage. In his poem, "Ezekiel," Laurence Binyon called some of these agencies "the clutter and offal of man's invention."

Observation has shown that all young children possess an unspoiled "inner ear" for sounds and words and an untarnished "innocent eye" by means of which they behold the world and the people and things in it, as for the first time. Thomas Traherne knew this, and Blake, Wordsworth, and Walter de la Mare after him, to name but four poets of acute perception. In his poem, "Salutation," Traherne wrote,

> I that so long
> Was *Nothing* from Eternity,
> Did little think such Joys as Ear and Tongue
>   To celebrate or see:
> Such sounds to hear, such Hands to feel, such Feet,
> Such Eyes and Objects, on the Ground to meet.

This inner ear and innocent eye are, perhaps, the greatest gifts bestowed on childhood; but, because they are not easily recognizable or immediately capable of statistical measurement, they are often ignored, and, at worst, not realized to exist at all. In consequence, many grownups do little to train them to become sensitive and responsive instruments. Unless these gifts, these manifestations of the human heart and mind, are used and developed to the full, no true awareness of poetry is possible. For the inner ear and innocent eye are the means by which imagination is nurtured, memory crystallized, and emotions refined. When children enjoy poetry with understanding (it is equally true of adults), their imaginative and intellectual horizons are widened, the texture of their thinking is deepened, and their powers of language vastly augmented.

But if poetry is to take an honored place in the lives of very young children, it should be experienced regularly by them so that a tradition of familiarity with it as an art in its own right is established from the beginning. Therefore, a great deal of poetry should be read to very young children by grownups who are familiar with the ways of both children and poetry, who are in complete sympathy with what poetry has to offer, and who have, as it were, some of its ichor flowing in their veins. Sincerity — as in all other relationships between adults and children — is vital.

Few fields of poetic experience are closed to the youngest children. But in choosing what to read to them it can be laid down as a principle that poems with exciting meters and rhythms, sharply cut visual images, and the use of words in a fresh and novel manner (as if they had been new-minted at that hour) are the most suitable and the most likely to appeal to innocent eyes and inner ears, which are so quick to see and hear. And a second principle is to choose poems which tell simple stories, introduce stirring scenes of action and vivid dramatic situations, and describe in straightforward, powerful terms the more common natural phenomena. Such poems should always be of first-rate quality, of the stuff of genuine literature, with each poem normally concentrating on a single major theme. And in all this, it is wise to remember that it matters much more for the children if the greater emphasis is laid on the way the words in the poems *sound* rather than on what the words *say*.

Children should not be presented with verse which has been written down to their supposed level. A former poet laureate of England, Robert Bridges, had something to say about this in the preface to his anthology, *The Chilswell Book of English Poetry*:

> While in all other Arts it is agreed that a student should be trained only on the best models, wherein technique and aesthetic are both exemplary, there has been with respect to Poetry a pestilent notion that the young should be gradually led up to excellence through lower degrees of it; so that teachers have invited their pupils to learn and admire what they expected them to outgrow: and this was carried so far that writers, who else made no poetic pretense, have good-naturedly composed poems for the young, and in a technique often as inept as their sentiment.

For too long the youngest have been allowed to wander aimlessly in the candy-floss kingdom of Tinery-Tottery. They need stronger meat. The poems chosen for *them* should always have something to say which is worth saying. This does not mean, of course, that the architecture of a poem does not matter, but it should generally be enough for those who read to the youngest children to illumine the poems by a few, well-chosen remarks, sufficient to place them in their setting. But poetry should always be allowed to speak in its own voice. It follows, therefore, that the reading of poems to children is of prime importance. First readings, like first impressions, matter a great deal. Grownups should always read the poems themselves before reading them to the children, so that they get to know and understand them, to feel their divinity, and accept their conventions. When reading, simplicity and sincerity matter almost more than anything else. There is never any need to put on a special "poetry voice."

And so the love and the heritage will be passed on.

From *The Horn Book* for December, 1962

POETRY FOR CHILDREN

By Harry Behn

POETRY is a personal experience. So are children. And so, to me, is the various, wonderful, sometimes terrible world we are building for them to inherit.

I hope our children will be able to grow up whole and as they mature still find life full of meaning. I believe that poetry in childhood is essential to maturity. That is my theme.

The poems I shall mention are my own. In telling how I happened to write this one or that, or any at all, I hope to distil a few thoughts about the value of poetry.

Not long ago I learned something from a class of gifted children who came to visit me at my home in Connecticut. Seven girls, five boys, and their almost invisible teacher sat on the floor in a bright, airy Japanese room with a slow spring wind whispering in the pines and riffling the lake below.

I told my guests I was planning to write about poetry for children and asked them to help me. I asked them to tell me what poetry should be.

One of the boys said at once, "Anything that recites nicely without people."

I was surprised and asked, "Don't you like people?"

"Sure I do," he said. "But people are stories. A poem is something else. Something way out. Way out in the woods. Like Robert Frost waiting in a snowstorm with promises to keep."

I had no argument with him there. "And what do *you* think?" I asked the others. "And you and you?"

Here are some of the answers: A poem should be about animals, what you feel, springtime, something funny, anything you see and hear, anything you can imagine. Anything. Even a story!

Everyone giggled and looked at the boy who liked Frost. "Everybody's different," he said tolerantly, "but anybody who doesn't like Frost is stupid."

This time everybody laughed.

Then a small girl's voice chirped, "I think a poem should simply make music with words, that's all. The shorter the better. One of mine is only, *Clink, clank, clunk.* It's about a carpenter pounding nails in a new house."

A fat little girl stood up and said slowly, "Poems should be about monsters from Planet X because I have just written one about Planet X." She unfolded her poem and declared solemnly, "I usually write about my little brother who really is a monster, but he has measles, so I had to fall back on Planet X." She read her poem. It was very funny, full of bounce and alliteration suggesting serious-minded machinery.

Next, a foreign-looking boy stood up suddenly and read intensely, defiantly, a poem called "The Mountain."

> Did you think
> About the mountain?
> Did you think?
> Did you see it today
> or some other day
> in another way?

This gave me pause.

That evening, after the gifted children had gone, I did a good deal of thinking about *my* mountain, poetry for children. I had to go all the way back to infancy to remember the poetical taste of paint on a toy clown I was fond of, and then to my first day in kindergarten.

As you know, Indians are sometimes given totems that compel them to make songs whether they want to or not. Although I wasn't aware of it, I already had a totem. Indian totems are usually lizards or owls or some such creature. Mine wasn't even an animal, but a sort of invisible Episcopalian angel with conventional golden wings. He was very dignified but always amused by something, especially me. It was *his* idea to make a poet of me. This is how it happened.

On my first day in kindergarten, there he was, hovering about, fussing over me, nudging me on as I skipped around the mulberry bush, playing little tunes on his harp as London Bridge came falling down.

When suddenly I decided to walk out and go home, he slipped me a taste from a jar of library paste. It was delicious, and so I decided to eat stickily a little more, for which crime I was exiled to the cloak room.

This sunny, chalk-dusty room was also a storage room with a wide window and a window seat, and shelves stacked high with colored paper and boxes of colored chalk and cubes, pyramids and tetrahedrons of wood all brightly colored, and a few books.

Inside this delightful prison (which had a good echo) I howled until my teacher tripped in trembling and tried to quiet me. Hoping to read me into at least a snuffle, she reached for a book. That book might well have been *Sanford and Merton,* which my sister had already read to me and which I detested. Happily it wasn't. My angel (I am sure of it) handed down to my teacher a copy of Blake's *Songs of Innocence* conveniently open to a poem that said directly to me:

Piper, sit thee down and write.

And so, half a century later, I did.

In those days it was clear to me why Blake spelled tiger the way he did. Not that I thought about it in thoughts. But somehow I knew that a tiger in a jungle is one of nature's most beautiful and dangerous creations, but in a zoo is hardly a tiger at all, not a complete tiger. But Blake's Tyger burning bright in a dark forest is forever magically all the most glorious tigers that ever were.

That is how I learned the most important thing of all about poetry: Any thing or any experience, to become a poem, must be presented with a careful incompleteness of information.

I soon discovered that there are many ways of looking at everything. As there are many ways of looking at a tiger, there are many ways of looking at things we really know nothing about, such as time. To some, time is a cage in which one paces unhappily back and forth in hope of release. To others, to happy children, each moment *is* a release, into eternity, a voyage of refreshment with an instant return to an enriched present, as if Now is also perhaps Forever.

> Now evening is no longer really day.
> Some stars are out, but dusk is still not night.
> Now lightning-bugs are evenly as bright
> As stars, and with a dust-warm smell of hay
> Mingles the cool of grass mowed yesterday.
> Far in the windless wood a whippoorwill
> Proves over and over summer is with us still;
> But look again about you where the gray
> Has deepened into dark with many a star!
> And listen, as silence deepens, until you hear
> Katydids, who know what seasons are,
> Peacefully winding up the ticking year;
> Then you will know that Now is Forever, between
> Music and silence, the invisible and the seen.

Long ago I learned that art and play make *all* experience an adventure, old myths in the blood, this life as it is, or a daydream.

> In some far other time than here
> Are forests full of dappled deer
>
> Where wandering minstrel winds awake
> Shadows across a misty lake,
>
> Shadowy ripples rippling away
> To dreams of a still more distant day
>
> Where gardens greener than my own
> Grow round a mossy tower of stone,
>
> Where prancing steeds and knights of old
> Wear coats of armor bright with gold,
>
> And children dream, as still they do,
> Remembering what they never knew.

To range freely in paradox and across the contrary is a limbering exercise in a world we must admit will not conform to any static pattern. It is good to know that life is not reducible to a machine.

Too often we say of an opinion, take it and be wise like me, leave it and be a fool. Children know otherwise. They are at ease with the wholeness of the mind, incompletely furnished with fact as it is but alive throughout its full range. They may not know a hawk from a handsaw or a fact from a fancy,

he told me everything he believed. Perhaps the
[fir]st thing he told me was this:

> To plant a seed and see it grow
> Is something every child should do,
>
> And when it blossoms, how it grew
> Is something every child should know,
>
> And when its seeds are ripe to sow,
> A child may see the old made new.
>
> To grow and gently grow and grow
> Is something people should do too.

[led] me to wonder about time and the changes it [brings] as we grow up. Sometimes I think the only [difference be]tween children and us riper specimens of the [fami]ly that our growing has slowed down. It seems [that with al]l our knowledge, we might figure out some way [to be ha]ppier the more mature we get. But we aren't. [Wha]t has happened to the pliancy, and the persistence [w]e once nurtured in ourselves. Where is the self [as sep]arate and particular as it was everything? *River*

> Here am I where you see me
> Strong and brown.
> Still, I am far away
> Where yesterday I was.
>
> Here am I, shouting,
> Tossing my feathers.
> Still, I am far away
> Where I have not yet gone.
>
> I am a drop of dew
> Dripping to earth from a leaf.
> I am a sea.
>
> Here am I
> Where I was
> Where someday I will be.

[Now] then, here and there, I detect a sober effort to [find li]fe's wider meanings. Then the old-fashioned [pi]ety that used to scare us seems ridiculous. Today

but they are not to be sold out of either or into acceptance of either as all there is. What they look at they see. What they imagine, they also see, as the imagined, and each enriches the other.

They are used to looking at and into simultaneously, with the fully absorbed mind directed toward hopeful prophecy, and at the same time into the past of myth, from which we all have come, where they read an archeology deep with understanding.

In my childhood what seemed poetical to me was, almost always, lonely. Close as a sea-polished pebble or an autumn-colored leaf, far away as the song of a phoebe or wind in the eaves on a snowy night, all the most beautiful things were tinged with loneliness.

"Ah, Sunflower, weary of time, Who countest the steps of the Sun," said Blake. "O wind that bloweth all day long," said Stevenson. Why should those two poems move me so, even today? One starts with "Ah," the chorus of the other with "O". Both have archaic verbs, "countest" and "bloweth." Perhaps this strangeness creates a magical remoteness like loneliness.

Also, as Daisetz Suzuki said, the complete and perfect poem is simply "Ah!" or "O!" Pure wonder reverberating beyond the utmost brevity.

To a child, a flower is a complete poem, needing no metaphor, or even words. Few words are needed when an experience is fresh as a sunrise. What could be simpler than this haiku by Shiki!

> What a wonderful
> day! No one in the village
> doing anything.

Words are magical; those that burst up into images are miracles. From the dancing chants of Mother Goose to the whole-minded directness of haiku, the spectrum of early poetry is wide.

The gifted children assured me the subject of a poem may be anything. I think this is true — anything veiled in a shimmering distance to give it mystery, lifted as music lifts, or a kite on a wind, a kite being anything that absorbs interest.

How bright on the blue
Is a kite when it's new!

With a dive and a dip
It snaps its tail

Then soars like a ship
With only a sail

As over tides
Of wind it rides,

Climbs to the crest
Of a gust and pulls,

Then seems to rest
As wind falls.

When string goes slack
You wind it back

And run until
A new breeze blows

And its wings fill
And up it goes!

How bright on the blue
Is a kite when it's new!

But a raggeder thing
You never will see

When it flaps on a string
In the top of a tree.

A kite, like hope, lifts. But hope sometimes, as the wind dies, fails. In harsh times it is good to have a sense of humor, to be able to see in tattered hope something forlorn and slightly ridiculous.

Grownups may deflate a childhood experience in a different way; they may consider it just a fact, of interest only to curiosity. Three tadpoles in a mason jar is a fact. Tadpoles changing into froglets is a miracle. Watching a miracle is a different study from cutting up a frog to see how pulling his tendons makes his dead legs kick. Curiosity may lead to reading all about frogs, but knowing everything about frogs is not the same thing as having one for a pet, or hearing hundreds we face a clear and present danger with less panic. Beyond the effort to stir up news, I sense a braver attempt to see life as a process we still might shape toward a saner future for our children.

I am again aware of what I knew long ago when I lived and breathed poetry, aware of mystery and distance and a beautiful melancholy, aware that life is wonderful if elusive. But then, everything is elusive unless held lightly, with love, like one of my most enduring treasures, an evening many years ago in New Mexico.

> Hills grow small and flat and far
> Till four pale shades of blue they are.
> The yellow sky holds up one star
> Upon it like a silver burr.
>
> So still the twilight is that near
> And far the only sound I hear
> Is silence humming in my ear —
> No beetle's drum or cricket's churr,
>
> No twittering voice high in the air,
> Because no dancing bat is there —
> Only a stillness everywhere,
> Stillness without the slightest stir.
>
> In dusk that's neither dusk nor day
> The four far blue hills fade away,
> The yellow sky turns green, then gray
> As mothy stars upon it whirr.
>
> Don't breathe a sound and you may hear
> A twittering music far and near
> Of bats that dance and flip and fly
> Nipping stars out of the sky.

Poetry is reality, now and forever. Children taught me this, and so it's so.

From *The Horn Book* for April, 1966
Revised February, 1968

SPEAKING TO THE IMAGINATION

By Samuel French Morse

POETRY FOR CHILDREN really means poetry that children like, with all the latitude and variety of form and substance so easygoing a definition suggests. It means anything from nursery rhymes and tongue twisters to epics, from limericks to odes, from ancient riddles to the experiments of William Carlos Williams and Kenneth Patchen. Such lack of prejudice about what poetry can or ought to be, at least from the children's point of view, is unlikely to last long, not only because they soon learn the difference between real poetry and the unofficial poetry they may like best, but also because poetry becomes identified with what is "good" for them: in other words, what is inspirational, or edifying, "beautiful" or ennobling. Even more damaging to their pleasure is the taming of their imagination, justified as a kind of discipline, but more often the result of their elders' mistaking the ability to recognize trochaic dimeter or assonance for the substance of a poem. Unless they are tone-deaf or otherwise incapacitated, most children have a lively sense of rhythm and sound effects, and it is probably not important for them to start learning rhetorical terms until they have been allowed, in the words of C. S. Lewis, to "receive" what they read, without worrying about the ways they may "use" it. And although the pleasures of poetry involve the "pleasures of ulteriority" — "saying one thing in terms of another" (that is, in metaphor) or "saying one thing and meaning another" — it is not important to get at "the other thing" before the one thing has been seen and heard. A hawk cannot be a metaphor or a symbol for courage until it has first been seen as a hawk. If it is convincingly the thing itself first, it may (depending on the occasion) become something more.

For poetry is a way of seeing as well as of hearing, and its meaning is obviously both seeing and hearing. It would seem to follow, then, that the ways of seeing and hearing that children recognize and give their assent to most directly mean the most to them. Poems which capture their way of seeing and hearing are for them good poems, whether written by Chaucer or E. E. Cummings, Shakespeare or Richard Wilbur. But in one respect the modern poets have an immediate advantage over the poets of the past: the raw material with which they work — the particular sights, sounds, and idiom from which they build their poems — are likely to be readily familiar to children today. If the observation is accurate and the rhythms are strong, there will be no objection even to a lack of rhyme: one good example is "The Base Stealer," by Robert Francis:

> Poised between going on and back, pulled
> Both ways taut like a tightrope-walker,
> Fingertips pointing the opposites,
> Now bouncing tiptoe like a dropped ball
> Or a kid skipping rope, come on, come on,
> Running a scattering of steps sidewise,
> How he teeters, skitters, tingles, teases,
> Taunts them, hovers like an ecstatic bird,
> He's only flirting, crowd him, crowd him,
> Delicate, delicate, delicate, delicate — now!

Given a poet who has refused to let fashion or prejudice stifle his own capacity for wonder or surprise, who is willing to let go, and who respects his own way of seeing and hearing while exercising to the full his self-conscious craft — given such a poet, it seems likely that he will be admired and understood by children. He will not make the mistake of condescension or pretense that ends by being self-deception. If he is good enough, he may be another Edward Lear or Hilaire Belloc or Walter de la Mare. Since comparisons are largely odious, however, and since few poets, ancient or modern, have had the special gift of consistently writing well for children of all ages, the modern poet may have to be content with a more modest or incidental success with the young. Among contemporaries, David McCord and James Reeves are the most accomplished poets who have chosen children as their special audience. Their craftsmanship is never less than solid, and at its best is extraordinarily subtle; their prosody, indeed, offers some models of skill that more serious poets might heed. As for "grown-up" poets, as W. H. Auden calls them, one thinks of notable but occasional pieces by Cummings, Yeats, Williams, Edward Thomas, Marianne Moore, Wallace Stevens, Robert Frost, Mark Van Doren, Robert Graves, Abbie Huston Evans, and others: durable, delightful, and sure-fire.

Then there are poems by grown-up poets deliberately written for children. Sometimes the result is a poem not quite in the poet's own style or an unconvincing, uncomfortably mannered expression of an adult's notion of what pleases or ought to please a child. So long as the grownup sticks to what he *knows* about children — for example, the funny, exasperating, unbridgeable gap between his world and theirs — he is almost sure of success: children are as quick as the Duchess to recognize what they do to annoy, and they enjoy being appreciated for their subversive powers as well as for their more acceptable and charming qualities. In his best children's poems, John Ciardi has capitalized on just this difference between adults and the young, achieving in them a verisimilitude that his more conventionally fantastic inventions seldom possess, although his command of rhythm and rhyme is always engaging. Secure in his knowledge that children like what is familiar almost as well as they like novelty, and can take enormous amounts of the same thing, Ciardi has perhaps mined the same vein too often. He has, however, captured contemporary manners and relationships between generations and, without setting his sights on immortality, has provided timely entertainments. The variety one misses in his books can be found in anthologies, and notably in *Beastly Boys and Ghastly Girls,* edited by William Cole. The anthologist has an advantage over the poet with essentially one theme: he can choose the sure winners. His disadvantage, it hardly need be added, is that the winners are likely to turn up again and again; but once the young reader is prepared to explore on his own (though he may have decided by then that he really does want a lot of the same thing), the poet may be better off than the anthologist, particularly if he has real skill in playing his tunes or even his one tune in a variety of ways. It is virtuosity as much as integrity that gives the work of McCord and Reeves true distinction.

Timeliness and contemporaneity overlap, not only with respect to substance, but also with respect to literary fashions. The genuine success of Ciardi, William Jay Smith, Eve Merriam, and Stephen Vincent and Rosemary Benét, as well as the example of T. S. Eliot, whose *Practical Cats* furnished a not-altogether happy precedent for his imitators, and the increasing popularity of volumes for younger readers, selected from the work of such modern masters as Robert Frost, Carl Sandburg, Robert Graves, and Theodore Roethke, have tempted other grown-up poets to try their hand at verse for children. The results, predictably enough, have been various; for the luster attaching to the name of a writer gifted in dealing with experience from the point of view of an adult may not shine through his words when he attempts to write for children. Coyness, archness, unintentional condescension, mere prettiness — all these are risks that even the most gifted writer runs. All are evidence of a failure to gauge accurately the audience for which the work was intended. For, tolerant as children are of all sorts of extravagance and high jinks, they dislike being hoodwinked even more than they object to being edified.

Current fashion has dictated that verse for children should be amusing rather than serious, perhaps in reaction to a fashion that began with the success of Hilda Conkling's *Poems by a Little Girl* and *Shoes of the Wind,* those brief, sometimes dazzling images that were the marvels of another generation. Most of the poems inspired by those two books now seem more dated than even such dubious favorites as "The Inchcape Rock" and "Casabianca," which at least tell stories and have spirited, swinging rhythms. Although imagist poems frequently delight the sophisticated eye and ear with their delicate colors and fastidious music, they lack the intensity and boldness needed to give them staying power. Part of the pleasure of poetry, as noted earlier, derives from its capacity to suggest more than it states; but unless the reader can really connect with the poem, his response will be minimal. Much nature poetry for children suffers from a kind of overselection, for in the poet's attempt to avoid the cliché or the merely obvious, he may miss the essentials that will give his work real character.

To be accurate is not always to be original; and to be obvious is not always to be unoriginal. Humbert Wolfe, in *Kensington Gardens*, frequently managed the balance among poetic virtues with great skill, and nowhere better than in "The Grey Squirrel,"* which also has the extra dimension that gives it character for the adult:

> Like a small grey
> coffee-pot,
> sits the squirrel.
> He is not
>
> all he should be,
> kills by dozens
> trees, and eats
> his red-brown cousins.
>
> The keeper on the
> other hand
> , who shot him, is
> a Christian, and
>
> loves his enemies,
> which shows
> the squirrel was not
> one of those.

And even without benefit of rhyme, William Carlos Williams achieved the freshness, suggestiveness, and completeness that identify his work as the real thing, although such a poem as "Flowers by the Sea" is probably more effective read aloud than to oneself, at least to begin with:

> When over the flowery, sharp pasture's
> edge, unseen, the salt ocean
>
> lifts its form — chicory and daisies
> tied, released, seem hardly flowers alone
>
> but color and the movement — or the shape
> perhaps — of restlessness, whereas
>
> the sea is circled and sways
> peacefully upon its plantlike stem

Prejudice, preconception, fashion, condescension, pretentiousness: these are the enemies of the poet who would write for children as much as of the poet who writes for any other

---

*From *Kensington Gardens* by Humbert Wolfe (Ernest Benn Limited; o.p.)

audience. In the long run, it may be no more than the acknowledgment by the poet that children are as much a part of the world and of his audience as the grownup or the critic, which will help him to write well. Children seldom have to be wooed. But they must be respected for themselves, as human beings, and as more capable and often more honest than those who "know better" in judging what speaks to their imagination.

From *The Horn Book* for June, 1965

"NOT THE ROSE..."

By Myra Cohn Livingston

SHARING poetry with children, whether in the library, in the classroom, or at home, is a joy immeasurable for many. It is, in essence, what Robert Frost spoke of as the "delight to wisdom" implicit in the poem itself. But today, how many librarians and teachers must create a case for poetry, must explain the need for it in the child's world: perhaps to parents who have long since found poetry so much unnecessary baggage in their workaday and social worlds; perhaps to the child who has had no taste of it at home and is even a stranger to Mother Goose; perhaps to adult friends who dismiss the love of poetry as an idiosyncrasy.

It is difficult to define why poetry is important to the individual. Poetry is, after all, a personal thing; its meaning to each human being is private. It invades the innermost thoughts; it clings to and bolsters the inner life. It is not a something to be rationalized or explained; it is not an abstract principle; it is not part of an All-About book which arms with facts; it is not a piece of logic with which to startle others or to alter the course of scientific knowledge. It is not something to be classified. It cannot be proved.

Yet, could the very lack of dependence on fact be the dimension that makes poetry so important? Might one suggest to skeptical friends, to the parents caught in their business and social worlds, that the very lack of utility, gain, profit makes poetry more meaningful? Might one even suggest that, instead of buying pills to quiet, to exhilarate, to induce sleep, they spend money for poems? For poetry will provide the stillness, the jubilance men and women find so necessary in their lives.

At the symposium on Excellence in Children's Literature, led by Mae Durham at the University of California last summer, the poet Harry Behn spoke. Reminiscing about his own life with poetry, its meaning to him, he cited his early love for

William Blake. Perhaps, he mused, the very beginnings of long-remembered poems, whether "Oh rose" or "Ah, sunflower," explain more than he realized as a child. Is it not the "ahs" and "ohs" of poetry that satisfy man, quiet him, elate him?

This observation was intensified for me when an eighth grader in our Creative Writing class at the Dallas Public Library wrote:

> Oh and ah! for days of old,
> For times of queens and maidens fair,
> For knights that were both brave and bold,
> And dragons roaring in their lairs.
>
> Ah and oh! for olden times,
> When often finest silk was worn,
> When monks in abbeys rang the chimes,
> And peasants raised the wheat and corn.
>
> Yes, in days of long ago;
> In days of knights and maidens fair,
> In days of silk and chimes; ah, lo,
> I would that I be there.

Though not the best of poems, nor the best this girl has written, here is the child speaking. She is speaking of a desire, a dream, of "ah" and "oh" in the same fashion as Harry Behn does.

Such is the beauty of poetry: how it speaks to man, why it is so necessary to him; the everlasting longing for he knows not what, the very stillness, the absolute "now of it," as Mr. Behn would say. It is not the past, not the future, not the gain or the profit, but the essential religious-like awe; the satisfaction the individual feels in discovery, the nearest he can come, not to fact or abstract knowledge — there is another place for that in his life — but to achieving intuitive knowledge. This is a renewing knowledge, one affirming joy in the universe. It is self-affirmation, the discovery that he is at one with his world. Rather than grapple with utilitarianism or with the mode of society as it exists, man places himself in the midst of great beauty and harmony.

In short, man affirms poetry. He knows and clings to it for the increasing dimension and awareness it gives to his life. When I tell my Creative Writing students that I demand two things of their writing, I realize how much I am asking. I tell them: When you write a poem, either tell me something I have never heard before or tell me in a new way something I have heard before.

A new way! I am asking them for fresh imagery. I am asking them to develop their own sensitivities, to use their own imaginations. I am even asking them to discover something they may not have known they possessed. For without imagination, man is dead. And the world of imagination is as real as the world of Chavez Ravine, Cape Kennedy, or the bones and eating habits of the Tyrannosaurus rex.

Granted, then, that there is a place for poetry in the individual's life, that he is richer for it: what sort of poetry shall be shared with children? If, in Eleanor Farjeon's words, poetry is "not the rose but the scent of the rose," how can the right scent be detected?

There are two schools of thought on the sort of poetry children should read. One decries poetry written especially for children. The other upholds it. And something can be said for either side. If, however, one school had its way, we should have to reject Stevenson, Rossetti, and the others, writing from the child's point of view, who followed — Milne, Farjeon, de la Mare, Roberts, Behn, and the like. I have often suspected that those who challenge poetry written especially for children are a bit too far away from the young child's mind and imagination. Much depends, of course, on the child, his background, and on whether or not his parents have read to him from an early age. (One can tell from a child's writing, in minutes, if he has had this advantage.)

One must throw out the "cute" poetry for children and try to establish criteria for judging the excellence of poetry, bearing in mind that certain criteria applied to fantasy, realistic fiction, and other forms of literature, apply to poetry as well.

Again, Robert Frost's words, "a poem goes from delight to wisdom." The delight is to be stressed, whether it is the delight of Edward Lear's nonsensical "The Jumblies":

> Far and few, far and few,
>   Are the lands where the Jumblies live:
> Their heads are green, and their hands are blue;
>   And they went to sea in a sieve.

or the beauty of Emily Dickinson's sun rising "a ribbon at a time," or Shelley's widow bird, who

> . . . sate mourning for her love
> Upon a wintry bough;
> The frozen wind crept on above,
> The freezing stream below.

Delight is of prime importance, and the poem must reach the child if delight is to be met. Always will the wisdom follow, whether it is the stretching of the imagination, the discovery of self and the self's intuitive knowledge, the essential stillness of the soul, or its unbounded joy and happiness. And the wisdom must vary from child to child. What will add dimensions to one person's life will not necessarily affect another's.

The degree to which the reader is provoked to find the part, the fraction that is missing or not understood, is another measure of a poem's worth. It may be the simplest image, the fewest words. I cannot forget the delight on the face of a fourth grader in our class the day we read Marie Louise Allen's poem of winter, where "bushes look like popcorn balls." Of course, she seemed to say, I knew it all along, but I never heard it said. Now I shall see bushes differently in the winter. Imagine the offshoots of the discovery, the "finding," should the child look at bushes in summer, in fall, and let her imagination run free. Perhaps she will even extend the comparisons, the imaginings and findings to trees, to flowers. She has found something meaningful to her.

A third criteria, the one most important to me, is applied to all types of literature, but it is least understood in poetry. It is best stated by the postulate, Let the Reader Make the Ultimate Judgment. For something as personal, as emotional as poetry, this sounds rather like a political declaration, a philosophical statement. Yet how often does the poet, completely captivated by his own visions, leave no room for the reader's imagination. In stanza after stanza, the writer must make his point, must hammer it in, superimposing his adult vision so that the child's is all but stifled.

Mae Durham, in the University of California symposium, pointed out that there are three types of writing. The first is poor, for the writer does all of the reader's feeling and thinking for him. In fair writing, the second type, the writer extends more generosity to the intelligence of his audience, but still insists on proving his premise. In the third category — that to which we ascribe excellence — however, the writer gives the reader time to think, time to feel.

Compare three poems describing the common experience of a child watching the rain interrupt his play. The first is a turn-of-the-century bit in ten stanzas, in which Little Ned, "angry" and frowning at the "hateful rain," is observed and chided by the poet:

> It grieves me much, my child, to see
> Such temper as you show;

and reminds him that

> ... He who sends the rain
> To bless the fading flowers
> Sees every naughty look with pain.

and admonishes him further to temper his anger and to remember the blessings of the rain. This extreme example of didactic verse, right down to a rosebush hanging its head, Ned's "splendid fun" spoiled, and the ensuing sermon, is odious to any child.

The second poem, published in the fifties, shows another boy watching the rain, in five stanzas. He wonders what he will do, for he has napped, eaten, watched his sister dressing dolls, watched the cats cleaning themselves, watched the clouds parting, the wind changing; and as the poem ends, he informs us that he will soon be outside again. Although there is no sermon, the poet has limited the imagination of the child reading; the child will have very little "finding" to do here.

The third poem is:

> Rain, rain, go away,
> Come again another day.
> Little Johnny wants to play.

Now this is only Mother Goose; but it gives the essence, the core of what the other poems tried to say; and more importantly, it allows the child the joy of putting himself into the poem. It gives full range to his feelings, his thoughts: why he dislikes the rain; what is going on about him; what he will do when the rain is over and he can play. Here is no limitation of observed detail, no walls, sisters, cats, or fading flowers. Is not this the stillness, is it not the unsaid, the room for imagination?

Of course, Mother Goose will not do for a child beyond the early years. Here is a poem by W. B. Yeats that was shared with sixth, seventh, and eighth graders:

> THE CAT AND THE MOON
> The cat went here and there
> And the moon spun round like a top,
> And the nearest kin of the moon,
> The creeping cat, looked up.
> Black Minnaloushe stared at the moon,
> For, wander and wail as he would,
> The pure cold light in the sky
> Troubled his animal blood.
> Minnaloushe runs in the grass
> Lifting his delicate feet.
> Do you dance, Minnaloushe, do you dance?
> When two close kindred meet,
> What better than call a dance?
> Maybe the moon may learn,
> Tired of that courtly fashion,
> A new dance turn.
> Minnaloushe creeps through the grass
> From moonlit place to place,
> The sacred moon overhead
> Has taken a new phase.
> Does Minnaloushe know that his pupils
> Will pass from change to change,
> And that from round to crescent,
> From crescent to round they range?
> Minnaloushe creeps through the grass
> Alone, important and wise,
> And lifts to the changing moon
> His changing eyes.

When the class was asked to comment on the poem, there was a long silence. Finally, one girl volunteered that she could not understand it, and she lapsed into thought. Another remarked that it made her feel lonesome; another felt "scared."

But a fourth ventured that "the cat and the moon are alike." And a fifth said, "I never thought of a cat like *that*."

This is the joy — the discovery, the very reason why children are given poetry. There is no All-About book on cats, nor encyclopedia article, nor picture book on any fanciful cat that can ever do what the Yeats poem does. For the child it is just the beginning; for the adult who discovers Yeats's meaning, it is a different poem. However we receive it, it is the "ah" and the "oh," the stillness, the "now" of it all, the intuitive, the imaginative, the not-yet-fathomed.

Still, one should never make the mistake of coercing children into poetry because it is good for them. Children can be presented with poetry; they can be guided to it. But they should never be forced to read it. Poetry is not facts with which to pass a test. It is not a feat of memory with which to astound parents and friends.

Poetry is not the rose with a name, a color — a spot in the garden, an arrangement in a vase; not the food the rose is fed nor the dust with which it is sprayed to keep bugs away. It is the scent. And no amount of explanation, no amount of cajoling or discussion or teaching can equal the joy a child will find, should he stoop to smell the rose himself.

From *The Horn Book* for August, 1964

WHERE ARE WE GOING WITH POETRY FOR CHILDREN?

By Patrick J. Groff

THOSE CONCERNED with poetry for children are faced today with several perplexities about this form of literature. Among these are the basic problems of defining the term, poetry for children, and finding the best way to attract children to poetry. If we are to develop children's esteem for poetry, we are inescapably influenced by these two considerations.

A survey of the writing on poetry for children over the past ten years convinces one that the first question has no dearth of answers. There appears to be no reluctance on the part of different writers to rush in with various opinions; and often each new response appears more grand and splendiferous than the last.

We are continually pressed to accept definitions of poetry that are based on emotional reactions. For example, Myra Cohn Livingston, a children's poet, believes that

Poetry is after all a personal thing; its meaning to each human being is private. It invades the innermost thoughts; it clings to and bolsters the inner life. It is not something to be rationalized or explained. . . .

(Happily, the last view is not accepted everywhere. If it were, the result would be the reduced employment of thousands of English teachers.) Often the emotional approach is carried forward in a train of excessive language. Lindley Stiles, the long-time dean of education at the University of Wisconsin, recently gave one of these effusive paeans to poetry. According to this sometime poet, "Without poetry, learning becomes pedantic and life becomes existence merely, devoid of ideals and inspiration." And he further declares that "the poet has the greatest sensitivity, analytical ability, wisdom of interpretation, and skill with ideas, imagery, and language." His overly dramatic defense of poetry cannot but be seen as an intentional downgrading of prose literature and therefore must be both unfair and unwarranted. Worst of all, the very idea that poetry has such high-class distinctions acts to frighten away the middle-brow adult on whom the child depends for his literature.

Others have claimed that poetry has many psychological values for children. It is not unusual to hear it said that poetry for children allows them to experience life in a deeper sense, acts as an antidote for violence, recreates the emotions, passes on wisdom, stimulates the imagination, enhances the appreciation of nature, stirs the emotions, develops a feeling for beauty, develops an awareness of the spiritual elements of life, is a source of courage, provides for relaxation.

Poetry may very well do some of these things on the occasions when a poem and a child hit it off. Nevertheless, few, if any, of these definitions of the uses of poetry give us any significant clues as to the characteristics that make it distinct from prose literature. Every objective implicit in each of the definitions could be accomplished just as well, or perhaps better, with prose. Little, if any, evidence shows that poetry accomplishes for the child the host of things commonly attributed to it. Available is more than a little thinking to support the belief that if children's literature were able to do these things, they would be done much more effectively with the sustained effect a child gets from a novel than with the transitory images he gains from a poem.

Others profess what I consider a false bewilderment, as did the late Eleanor Farjeon:

> What is Poetry? Who knows?
> Not a rose, but the scent of the rose;
>
> . . . .
>
> Not myself, but what makes me
> See, hear, and feel something that prose
> Cannot: And what it is, who knows?*

*From "Poetry" from *Poems for Children,* J. B. Lippincott Company.

The need for such artificial humility about poetry on Miss Farjeon's part seems uncalled for. She must have known very well what was good poetry for children, or she could not have written so much of it. Those who are seeking after some way to find the standards of poetry are nonplused by such elusiveness.

On the other hand, Flora Arnstein argues that poetry is quite simple. In her words, it is an uncomplicated record of experiences and, therefore, should be readily and completely understandable. "Boiled down to its essence, it is merely a reconstruction of an experience. And, here is the point, all poetry is just that: the presentation, in words, of experience...." The example she uses to demonstrate the thesis is "The Pasture" by Robert Frost, the meaning of which is very apparent:

> I'm going out to clean the pasture spring;
> I'll only stop to rake the leaves away
> . . . .
> I sha'n't be gone long. — You come too.

Mrs. Arnstein's unsophisticated definition of any kind of poetry, including that written for children, should not be accepted, however, since the objections to it are many. Our senses often deceive and distort experience. May Swenson, for instance, has remarked on the crudeness of our experience:

> Hold a dandelion and look at the sun.
> Two spheres are side by side.
> Each has a yellow ruff.
>
> Eye, you tell a lie,
> That Near is Large, that Far is Small.
> There must be other deceits.*

A simplistic definition of poetry is wrong. Poetry must surely go beyond the flat surface of experience and physical phenomena.

---

*"Hold a dandelion" was included in "The Poet as Anti-Specialist," *Saturday Review*, January 30, 1965. It appears in Miss Swenson's essay "The Experience of Poetry in a Scientific Age" in *Poets on Poetry*, edited by Howard Nemerov.

There seems to be a more precise definition of poetry that not only can remove it from the never-never land of mysticism set up by Eleanor Farjeon and others, but also will allow a working definition of it so that one will not be afraid to form judgments about what is and what is not poetry. Especially we need this to rid ourselves of such illogical statements as: "What is poetry for one person is not poetry for another." There is an explanation of poetry that will disentangle the confusion.

The definition is apprehensible and to the point: poetry for children is writing that (in addition to using, in most cases, the mechanics of poetry) transcends the literal meaning of expository writing. It is not the kind of writing that appears in newspapers and popular media or the kind of writing that is found in classroom textbooks. It is writing that goes beyond the immediately obvious. Poetry, then, consists of those aspects of writing that cannot be readily explained, unless one has some knowledge of what is going on. In contrast to that which is readily and completely understandable to all, poetry is often ambiguous.

"The Pasture," tested against this definition is revealed as a poem only in the mechanical sense. True, it has some poetic features: a certain cadence, rhyme, and some slight inversion of sentence pattern — "And wait to watch the water clear, I may." (The word order seems used largely to satisfy a rhyme scheme, "away-may.") The poem does have a refrain, and even a colloquial word, "sha'n't" (if colloquialisms are poetic). But these are all a part of the mechanics of poetry. To identify a poem on the basis of such elements is too easy. For example, a child recently said when asked what a poem was, "It's lines that are all capitalized and even on the left side, and all squiggily on the right." Another said, "Poetry is what rhymes." Obviously, to define poetry merely in terms of its mechanical features does not take much perception or maturity.

In another sense, "The Pasture" is not exceptional poetry because with startlingly few changes the poem could be made into a paragraph of prose. To show this, drop the first refrain in the poem and put the third line into a regular pattern.

Compare the result with "Afternoon on a Hill," by Edna St. Vincent Millay:

> I will be the gladdest thing
> Under the sun!
> I will touch a hundred flowers
> And not pick one.
>
> . . . .
>
> And when lights begin to show
> Up from the town,
> I will mark which must be mine
> And then start down.

Try as one might, one cannot reduce the poem to prose as can so easily be done with "The Pasture." One mark of poetry, then, is that it is not translatable into prose.

Here I want to stress that the use of original combinations of words is probably the easiest, the best, and the most obvious way to write poetry that transcends the literal and goes beyond a complete or obvious meaning. Consequently, in poetry a word has much more meaning than a word in prose. In the former the emphasis is connotative rather than denotative. Words possess suggested significances apart from their explicit and recognized meanings. It is the guessing element that requires the reader to go below the surface of words, to plumb their literal meanings. Figurative language most often provides the guessing element. A poem without metaphor, simile, hyperbole, personification, metonymy must compensate for the loss of these poetic devices in some other way. Sometimes it is in the use of words of a certain tone, for in poetry the language, not the subject, is of utmost importance. Ultimately, as Archibald MacLeish says, "A poem should not mean, but be." Its subject is not presented by means of language. Rather the reverse is true: language is presented with the aid of its subject matter. In "The Pasture" the emphasis on subject denies the poem much status as poetry.

It may seem paradoxical after the foregoing to say that the best way to attract children to poetry (our second major problem) is to pay the closest attention to the subject matter of poems chosen for them. This does not contradict the premise of the importance of language, however. Unless a poem says something to a child, tells him a story, titillates his ego, strikes up a happy recollection, bumps his funny bone — in other words, delights him — he will not be attracted to poetry, regardless of the language it uses. Many have known the agony of going through highly-thought-of anthologies of children's verse-poetry to find them full of "my dears" and lyrical odes to fairies and nature. Most of this whimsey and sentimentality is due to false notions about children held by misguided adults. The child of today is not attracted to archness, coyness, or mere prettiness. While it may be true that some very conventional modern girls might still like poetry such as that by Rose Fyleman, the reaction from the modern boy will be without doubt something like "Stop! You're putting me on!" Therefore, let us give a decent but definite burial to such bathos as:

> I wish I were a bumble bee
> So merry, blithe and gay,
> To buzz and hum from flower to flower
> All on a summer's day.
>
> I wish I were a butterfly
> Upon a buttercup.
> I'd flutter down the woodland paths
> And then I'd flutter up.
>
> I wish I were — but then, oh dear!
> A sudden thought strikes me:
> For if I were a butterfly,
> I could not be a bee.
>
> I'd love to be a bumble bee
> All summer time, and so
> I'm glad I'm not a butterfly
> To flutter to and fro.*

If we find such poems in present anthologies, let us ignore them in the hope they will wither away. Or better yet, replace them with poems of real life in an honest world like the one portrayed by Gwendolyn Brooks:

---

*"A Thought" by James Reeves, not intended for serious publication. From *Teaching Poetry*, Heinemann Educational Books Ltd., 1958.

> These buildings are too close to me.
> I'd like to PUSH away.
> I'd like to live in the country
> And spread my arms all day.*

Despite an agreement to spare the modern child "sissy" or "flighty" poetry, there nevertheless remain two schools of thought as to how to select poetry for him. One of these decries the use of poetry especially written for children. Its most pertinent argument is that one cannot present well a poem that he cannot read with some enjoyment. There is little doubt that much of the poetry written especially for children offends an adult's intelligence. The other side strongly supports the work of children's poets who write little or not at all for adults, and contends that children need special consideration. The battle seems to be worth fighting, regardless of the side one is on, for if we have only children's poetry, we run the risk of beginning with something less than the best. Surely, we should not believe that the young child can be gradually led to excellence through acquaintance with poems of lesser quality. The achievement of excellence is seldom accomplished in this way. Start with the best must be the maxim. On the other hand, one commits a capital offense by believing that it makes little difference where the poetry that children read and hear is chosen from. This opinion leads to the choice of the overly abstruse, the ancient, or the "cute." A selection from the first two categories may surely be poetry, but children are often overwhelmed by the strange vocabulary, antiquated subject matter, and rusty language. The last inevitably misses the mark of poetry that we have set up here.

When working with the youngest it is important, therefore, to keep in mind two criteria for the selection of poetry. The first is that the subject matter delight children. The second is that the language actually be poetic. The younger the children are, the more important is the former. As they grow older, language assumes primary importance. Moreover, the process of selection seems one of only two variables, the second being accepting children as they are. Consequently, the variables

---

*Four lines from "Rudolph Is Tired of the City" from *Bronzeville Boys and Girls* by Gwendolyn Brooks.

appear to be, first, the poems to be used and, second, the means used to attract children to them.

In schools, still another controversy has centered around how to attract children to poetry. First is the "hands-off" approach to poetry. Its advocates make no place for memorization, study, or activity connected with the use of poetry. Poetry is introduced in an entirely incidental way. "Forget any obligation to appreciate poetry or to indulge in any critical appraisal of it" expresses the feeling of this group. Teachers who have this opinion really would not touch poetry with a ten-foot pole, even though they continually say that poetry must be "caught not taught." The stand apparently stems from a negative reaction to the unfortunate days of forced memorization, analytic scanning of meter, and the testing of the content of poems. If the feeling of "hands-off" has done any good, it has been through the removal of some of the unfortunate practices in the use of poetry.

What the "hands-off" policy has not done, unfortunately (if a cliché is permitted), is to fish out the poetry baby before the dirty water of forced memorization and other disagreeable practices is flung away. Too, as courses of poetry are successively dropped as a result of this overreaction, it has been felt increasingly that poetry is too precious and fragile a literary commodity to be handled in the way other writings are. What seems left in the schools are sporadic readings by teachers or an occasional reading of a poem by children out of the basal reader. Poetry, a high literary form, apparently holds at present the lowest priority of utility in the language program.

While the actual teaching of poetry in elementary schools has largely disappeared (but not in other English-speaking countries, one would gladly hasten to add), a most curious practice has taken its place — teaching children to write poetry before they have had opportunities to truly learn about it. (See, for example, the suggestions in Nina Walter's book, *Let Them Write Poetry*, or those in Flora Arnstein's *Poetry in the Elementary Classroom*.) Staggering the imagination are suggestions of how children can be taught to write poetry, the most demanding of all literary forms, before they have learned to understand what it is, to react to it, and to distinguish it from prose, before they have learned to appreciate either prose or poetry. The growth of this practice is explained by the unfortunate belief, which schools perpetuate, that any writing put together in a certain distinguishable form can thereby be called poetry. Hence the flood of execrable doggerel that goes under the name "creative writing."

While all is not lost, to arrest the seeming downward plunge of the status of poetry and to forestall the misunderstanding, suspicion, and, finally, dislike for poetry so common in children by the time they reach the ages of ten or eleven, a drastic reversal of directions in the use of poetry for children is called for. First, we should emphasize the few "new" (if not young) poets for children who have pushed the art forward from the days of Walter de la Mare and Rachel Field. The new poetry is found in the social realism of Gwendolyn Brooks, the unpretentious warmth of Eve Merriam, the exhaustive imagery of Mary O'Neill, the gentle persuasion of Harry Behn, and in the urbane versatility of James Reeves (the single Briton of this group). Second, we should renew the teaching of poetry as such so that an understanding of it can be used as the basis upon which to build trust and appreciation of poetry as children grow older. Finally, we need to encourage publishers to look for children's poetry where it naturally emerges. We have seen that the commissioned book of poems for children by the established adult poet has been much less the success than was hoped for. For as Christopher Morley said, "poetry . . . does not often visit groups of citizens sitting down to be literary together."

From *The Horn Book* for August, 1966

FLIGHT PLAN FOR THE WINGED FOAL

By Dorothy E. Ames

LIKE BEDROCK, the fundamental truths endure: ". . . that all men are created equal; that they are endowed by their Creator with certain inalienable rights." In the trusting naïveté of childhood we first hear these words. They become part of our heritage of faith and pride in the principles of our nation. Still clinging to their basic spirit, in later life we have learned to edit the script. We insert "in opportunity" after "equal." Then, if we are teachers our lives become focused upon safeguarding the inalienability of our children's right to the abundant life.

Is this a proper introduction for a discussion of the uses of poetry and verse in the primary grades? After reading Annis Duff's *Bequest of Wings* I believe that it is. I propose to look at the place of poetry in *my* primary classroom with the children whom *I* know. They live in a rural Maine township. Seven miles away is a small mill town. Their parents are farmers, farm laborers, or mill workers; some combine farm work and mill work.

A check of school records for my class of thirty-one second graders last year shows two pupils whose parents had university education; one whose parents both had Bible college training; in eight cases either one or both parents had finished high school. The remaining twenty youngsters were children of people whose education had stopped after a brief try at high school, after the eighth grade, or, not infrequently, even earlier.

If one were able to get a statistical check on the most frequent wish of parents for their children, I imagine that the tally would run heavily to some version of "I want my child to have a better chance than I had." Chance at *what* we must leave unstated. Values vary, but each parent, if he could, would bear gifts. Ironically, one most precious gift, easily available and within almost every parent's power to bestow, too often lies ignored. This is the gift which Annis Duff describes in her book.

For her children the gifts were lavish. A daughter and a son were richly endowed with all the singing words that a highly literate mother and father could pour forth as freely and naturally as rain and sunshine nurture a growing plant. From infancy their ears were tuned to the cadence of verse, ranging from nursery rhymes to measured magic from *The Tempest*. Yet nothing was strained; nothing was forced. Language in its loveliest forms was the natural accompaniment to the Duff children's living.

And what of *my* children? What of Milton, bearing a name proud in English letters? He comes to school unwashed. Of the many holes in his dirty T-shirt one is strategically located for Milton to contemplate his navel. Most mornings his eyes are dull. (Television? certainly; bathroom? no.)

"You know what, Mrs. Ames? Last night Nathan he climbed up where Mumma keeps her pikked shears and cut a big hole outa the blanket. She sure whaled him good."

"You know what? Me'n Linwood seen this here big old trout layin' on the rocks by the brook. He sure stunk. Whadya suppose coulda happened?"

"You know what? (ah, the eyes are shining) I've gotta big junk of frog eggs all stuck together tight. I put 'em in this here old can with water in it. They'll turn into pollywogs, I betcha. Linwood ain't got none."

That is my Milton. His classmates range up the scale in privilege. None but brother Linwood quite touches Milton's nadir, but the gradation is gradual all the way up to Alton, loved, scrubbed, alert, and eager, well acquainted with balanced meals, bathtub, and bookshelves.

The first mandate of both poets and poetry lovers, namely, that poems are best when they are sung, spoken, or read aloud, is easily followed in the primary grades. There is no alternative. Reading has not yet progressed far enough for poems to be met on the printed page. A few of the youngsters entering our rural first grade may have known books of poetry in their mothers' hands, but for most of them what little verse they have heard has come from the memory of parents, grandparents, or older sisters.

Their repertoires are meager. "Jack and Jill," "Jack Be Nimble," and "Humpty Dumpty" seem to be the most familiar of the Mother Goose rhymes. Some of the children can recite several others; many know the opening lines of quite a few, but haven't had enough repeated contact with the verses to be able to carry them through to the end.

Here then is the starting point, if we are to take the children where they are. Time for rhymes, whether casually worked in while we wait, all washed, for the call to lunch or more formally planned as part of our opening exercises or for a change of pace after number work, is enthusiastically shared. Sometimes teacher starts the chorus; more often, in response to "Who knows another poem?," eager hands shoot up and light voices lead the way for "Little Bo-Peep" or "One, Two, Buckle My Shoe."

Sidney has a speech defect. If he can manage it, his favorite method of communication is to grab my arm and point at what he wants. When that doesn't bring results, I hear something like "Wah boo kay." It took a while to be able to interpret accurately, but now we get along famously. "You want a blue crayon?" He smiles, pleased with my understanding, and repeats, perhaps this time getting the "l" into "blue" or the "on" after "kay."

What does Sidney do while we say "Goosey, Goosey, Gander"? He says it too. He enjoys the rhythm, I know, for Sidney beats time with nodding head or waving hand, and I think that this group articulation is helping him gradually approach a more normal speech pattern. Everyone is saying it. He knows the words. He joins in, relaxed and happy. Instead of avoiding speech he is voluntarily practicing it.

Nursery rhymes, of course, are just a starting point. A teacher who enjoys verse herself, who can see the pictures in the words, and who can let the thought ride the waves rather than letting the waves engulf the thought, finds in little children an audience to warm the heart. There is no dearth of lively verses, rollicking verses, funny poems, story poems.

These are the ones to choose for the getting-acquainted part of the year. The delicate, sensory images can wait their turn. How about trying Vachel Lindsay's "The Little Turtle"[1] for size?

> There was a little turtle.
> He lived in a box.
> He swam in a puddle.
> He climbed on the rocks.
> He snapped at a mosquito.
> He snapped at a flea.
> He snapped at a minnow.
> And he snapped at me.
> He caught the mosquito.
> He caught the flea.
> He caught the minnow.
> But he didn't catch me.

Milton liked that right away. My stock went up with him. He said, "Read it again." (Milton sits near to me. Things seem to work better that way.) And so I read it again, and *we* read it a third time. Yes, the third time the readers are *we*, for a whispered, smiling "You say it too" shows that this simple, rhythmic pattern has made the story theirs already.

Sometimes the poems are tossed out for no particular reason. It just seems like a good time to hear a poem. Often, however, the apt verse comes to mind to follow some classroom event. Our basic reader has the "Johnny Cake" version of the beloved folk tale. When we have read it and have raced around the room acting it out, Christina Rossetti adds an extra fillip to the fun:

> Mix a pancake,
> Stir a pancake,
> Pop it in the pan;
> Fry the pancake,
> Toss the pancake,—
> Catch it if you can.[2]

This one goes on the board. There are no hard words here. The second grade knows all about *-an* words, *-ake* words, *-op* words, and *-y* words. *Toss* may be new, but it's high time to recognize *catch*. Can you put two small words together to

1. From *Johnny Appleseed* by Vachel Lindsay (The Macmillan Co., 1949).
2. From *Sing-Song* by Christina Rossetti (The Macmillan Co., 1924).

make a long one? Of course you can. What's hard about *pancake* when you know both parts of it already? It's easy to read; it's fun to read!

We like to keep our noise in and the hall noises out. Sooner or later comes the time for William Rands' gusty bit of parental indignation:

> Godfrey Gordon Gustavus Gore —
> No doubt you have heard the name before —
> Was a boy who never would shut a door!
>
> The wind might whistle, the wind might roar,
> And teeth be aching and throats be sore,
> But still he never would shut the door.
>
> His father would beg, his mother implore,
> " Godfrey Gordon Gustavus Gore,
> We really *do* wish you would shut the door!" . . .

This is a relatively long poem, going on for five more stanzas which carry the threat to send him off to Singapore on a raft made of a shutter. He promises to remember . . .

> "You will?" said his parents; " then keep on shore!
> But mind you do! For the plague is sore
> Of a fellow that never will shut the door,
> Godfrey Gordon Gustavus Gore!"[3]

Christopher Robin may have been very young and later no more than six, but he's none too young for our seven- and eight-year-olds to play with. I like to begin on Milne with "James James Morison Morison Weatherby George Dupree," more formally known as "Disobedience." Anyone who thinks that children don't like to memorize poetry should try saying this a few times. The first stanza seems to stick fast after only the first hearing. The rest of it is taken away from you before you would believe it possible. This has often been our poem for the end of the day when boots and jackets and mittens are on and it isn't quite time for the buses yet. Here we are all gathered round, eyes shining, mouths dancing, "You must never go down to the end of the town if you don't go down with ME! Good-by, Mrs. Ames, see you tomorrow!"

3. From *Time for Poetry* by May Hill Arbuthnot (Scott, Foresman and Co., 1951).

"Tomorrow and tomorrow and tomorrow creeps in this petty pace. . . ." If that becomes the doleful chant of the primary teacher, she has herself to blame. The dull classroom, the restlessly inattentive classroom, the tense THIS-YOU-MUST-LEARN classroom, and even the overtly defiant classroom are not entirely relics of the unenlightened past. We all have our lapses, our unshining hours. There is no panacea. Rather, there can be a well-stocked mental and emotional cupboard of varied preventives and remedies. Not the least of these is the teacher's use of verse.

So you won't be able to hear all three reading groups before noon unless you keep pounding along? Is Bertha's blithe disregard for the difference between *what* and *that* making you a bit edgy? Are you wondering when Kenneth's plastic ruler will fly off its pencil twirling-post and hit someone back there in the eye? Are you unnerved that Linwood's devotion to picking the scab off his arm is greater than his devotion to his number paper? Perhaps it's time to forget that last reading group for a while, lest sound turn to fury. A ten-minute break with Laura Richards' "The Monkeys and the Crocodile" from *Tirra Lirra* — no, we're studying neither monkeys nor crocodiles — may be all that is needed to revitalize both you and them.

A good laugh together is helpful, of course. There is more to it than that, however. The funny story with its vivid word-pictures of those teasing monkey children and their tragicomic come-down came out of a *book!* Teacher *read* it! Maybe there's something to this reading business after all. Maybe it's worth looking hard to see whether the word is *what* or *that*. Prose reading naturally can carry the same implications; but the swing of the music, the rhyme, and the compactness of verse selections make them ideal for quick therapy.

"But poetry," we can hear the earnest pedagogue complain, "should give the child beauty. Aren't you going to use any of the lovely descriptive nature poems?"

Wordsworth's "I Wandered Lonely as a Cloud" was spread before my own unperceptive eyes when I was no more ready for it than a kitten is for an eight-inch catfish. There is nothing wrong with the catfish. The old cat knows how to handle it and finds it delectable. But the kitten will starve with the same fine food before it. There are, however, two words in the Wordsworth poem which I wish to pounce on now: "INWARD EYE!" Those daffodils which overpowered and, let's face it, disgusted me thoroughly so many years ago "flash upon that *inward eye* which is the bliss of solitude." I want my pupils to use, cherish, and nurture the magic "inward eye."

The child has imagination. Let no one doubt that. The very reason that you can't get through to Patsy on four from nine being five when she already knows that four and five make nine may very well be that her "inward eye" is seeing the four new pairs of socks, all different colors, that Mother brought home from town for her last night. Claude's "inward eye" is seeing the neat plastic boat that he's going to buy with the money from the pop bottles he knows he can take back to the store. He lost his place in the reader as soon as that word "bottles" appeared in the paragraph.

How can we capitalize on the child's natural gift of imagination? Let us be very careful in choosing our descriptive poems for youngsters. The "bliss of solitude" means nothing in those words. Milne does it better with "Halfway down the stairs/ Is a stair/ Where I sit...."

Then come on outdoors with Milne.

> Where am I going? I don't quite know,
> Down to the stream where the king-cups grow,
> Up on the hill where the pine trees blow —
> Anywhere, anywhere. I don't know.
>
> Where am I going? The clouds sail by,
> Little ones, baby ones, over the sky.
> Where am I going? The shadows pass,
> Little ones, baby ones, over the grass.
>
> If you were a cloud, and sailed up there,
> You'd sail on water as blue as air,
> And you'd see me here in the fields and say:
> "Doesn't the sky look green today?"[4]

· · · · ·

[4]. From "Spring Morning" from the book *When We Were Very Young* by A. A. Milne.

That is kitten-size fare for mind pictures. Of course! He's calling the fields the sky, so he says it looks green.

Consider what Rachel Field does for the "inward eye" in her poem "The Little Rose Tree" —

> Every rose on the little tree
> Is making a different face at me!
>
> Some look surprised when I pass by,
> And others droop, but they are shy.
>
> These two whose heads together press
> Tell secrets I could never guess.
>
> Some have their heads thrown back to sing,
> And all the buds are listening.
>
> I wonder if the gardener knows,
> Or if he calls each just a rose?[5]

Being introduced to lines such as these, quietly and lovingly, by a teacher whom the child has come to trust for reading something that is worth hearing may well make all the difference between an eye that sees and a blind one. Need we say that the seeing eye and the inward eye must be the teacher's first? If not, she had better let poetry alone. Rushing pellmell through metric lines — this must be good because it's in the anthology — without taking time to *see the pictures* yourself as you read is the surest way to kill. Conversely, the reader, though she may have no aspirations of her own to create verse, truly shares the writer's creativity when she interprets his work with honesty, insight, and enjoyment.

Little by little the child's power to enjoy the more elusive, more difficult, and more rewarding experiences with poetry can be enlarged. With a sound foundation of ear attuned to music and mind receptive to imagery, the child will be ready for whatever his later school years may offer.

What should be said about the bugaboo of killing poetry by over-analysis and too much explaining? In our efforts to

5. From *Poems* by Rachel Field.

avoid the sort of things which James Thurber scarifies in his sketch "Here Lies Miss Groby" we may be in some danger of going to the opposite extreme. I well remember my first experience with Browning in high school. "My Last Duchess" had been assigned. I had "read" it. I was a conscientious student. I thought that I had done my job thoroughly. Then in class my teacher unlocked the poem. She explained. Those compressed lines, those subtle hints, those meaning-packed but half-expressed suggestions of innocent gaiety running afoul of urbane cruelty came alive for me. In that one class period I learned how to get inside a Browning poem. The catfish were mine from then on! Bless her! I'm so glad she hadn't been warned not to spoil a poem by explaining it. We don't forego salt because too much salt may ruin the roast.

Another bugaboo that I am inclined to meet with partial reservation is the shunning of any verse that appears to have a didactic tinge. While it is true that poetry is not approached primarily to teach a lesson, nevertheless, the fact that a lesson may be imbedded in a good poem is no reason for avoiding the poem. I have found young children thoroughly responsive to Emerson's "Fable" (The Mountain and the Squirrel) with its penetrating conclusion:

> "Talents differ; all is well and wisely put;
> If I cannot carry forests on my back,
> Neither can you crack a nut."

This does not mean that I hold a brief for the singing commercial of the moralist who supposes that the precept couched in meter and rhyme thereby becomes a poem and will be absorbed painlessly.

Allied to this matter of the true poem which may doubly serve by teaching is the question of deliberately presenting a bit of verse wherein the rhyme may help to pin down some needed phase of language usage. If it be a sin, I plead guilty to having composed each of the following verses to combat the "me and Joe went fishing" type of case confusion which seemed to introduce every experience told in our "sharing" time.

THE SNOWPLOW

We heard it chugging, so Billy and I
Ran to the road when the plow came by.
It pushed the snowdrifts way off to one side,
Shaved off the road, made it clean and wide.
The plow roared closer. I gave a big shout.
Up went a drift, and I yelled, "Look out!"
The man in the snowplow leaned over to see
Two blinking snowmen made from Billy and me.

HELLO UP THERE

Daddy and I saw a bird in a tree.
I think that the bird saw Daddy and me,
Because when Daddy and I came by,
We looked at the bird and called out, "Hi!"
And the bird called back to Daddy and me
His funny hello of "Chee, chee, chee!"

I consider that type of verse a legitimate and useful teaching device. Easily learned, the lines provide an accessible touchstone for correct usage in a trouble spot. Always being careful not to force rhymes or labor a point, a teacher can turn the love of rhythm to the children's advantage in many similar ways. When they have reached the dictation stage in writing, for example, a simple stanza using *-ight* words in rhyme may clinch the spelling pattern in their minds forever. A word of warning is in order here, however. Avoid run-on lines in verses which you wish young children to copy. Let sentence capitalization be firmly engrained before confusing the issue with the fact that lines of poetry are conventionally started with big letters.

Ordinarily, hearing poems and saying poems is a matter for just our classroom. Occasionally, however, we are called on to perform. Christmas brought a second-grade venture into choral speaking before the school assembly.

I had watched my kitten at home having a glorious time batting a low-hanging ornament off the Christmas tree and around the floor, and my class had become fond of "Willie," the black and white and yellow cat in their reading book. The two coalesced into:

> Willie pick himself a star
> From the Christmas tree.
> Hanging from a lower limb,
> Could that star be meant for him?
> Happy kitten he.
>
> Willie said, "The house is warm,
> Bright and glittery.
> Minding what the angels sang,
> See, my people even hang
> Playthings just for me."

With eyes a-sparkle they said their poem together while the smallest boy in the class, transformed to a black and white and yellow cat, batted the star from the cardboard tree which all had helped to make and decorate.

Pegasus, the old myth tells us, with a blow of his hoof caused the fountain of the Muses to spring from Mount Helicon. Can we bring the children to Pegasus — the horse with wings, swift and soaring, lovely in motion, to be mounted with skill and ridden with joy? Let him at first be a gay, gliding foal trying easy ascents for the young riders. Let them grow with him until the "bequest of wings" be fully realized.

From *The Horn Book* for April, 1961

V

FANTASY, YESTERDAY AND TODAY

One cannot measure, on first reading, the significance of the great fairy tales. Their very gaiety, high imagination and nonsense belie the years that have gone into their creation. They wear those years of growing so lightly they would seem to be the pleasure (not the work) of moments. . . . It even took many years for the master of the fairy tale, Hans Christian Andersen himself, to discover the "art form" of the children's fairy tale. But into those years went much living and growing and gathering treasure so that when the time came, the mouth could speak "out of the abundance of the heart".

From "Out of the Abundance",
editorial by Ruth Hill Viguers

Articles

DEALINGS WITH THE FAIRIES, AN APPRECIATION OF GEORGE MAC DONALD *by Jane Douglass*

DAILY MAGIC *by Edward Eager*

DOCTOR DOLITTLE: HIS LIFE AND WORKS *by Helen Dean Fish*

NEWS FROM NARNIA *by Lillian H. Smith*

A LETTER FROM C. S. LEWIS *by James E. Higgins*

PAUL FENIMORE COOPER AND "TAL" *by Louis C. Jones*

THE FLAT-HEELED MUSE *by Lloyd Alexander*

"OUT OF THE ABUNDANCE", EDITORIAL
by Ruth Hill Viguers

DEALINGS WITH THE FAIRIES

An Appreciation of George MacDonald
By Jane Douglass

"CORAGE God Mend Al," an anagram made from his name, would be a fitting title for a memoir of George MacDonald. Superb phantasiast that he is, it is this quality of soul that pervades his books for both children and adults. And of the many facets of his work — and there are many, for he was poet, novelist, essayist, and preacher — it is as a writer for children that he will be most honored and loved. Nothing, I am sure, would have gratified him more; and it is these stories, so perfectly illustrated by Arthur Hughes, *Dealings with the Fairies, At the Back of the North Wind,* the "Princess" books, and *Phantastes,* that represent his greatest achievement. Janet Adam Smith, in her excellent book, *Children's Illustrated Books,* has this to say about the collaboration of George MacDonald and Arthur Hughes:

> As Tenniel entered perfectly into Carroll's imagination, so did Arthur Hughes into George MacDonald's. MacDonald's books are marked by a loving understanding of children, a sense of magic, and a very firm grasp of right and wrong. We find all these qualities repeated in Hughes. . . . MacDonald's books appeal at different levels; by the interest of the stories, by the sentiment behind the stories, by the deeper meaning. Hughes' pictures also appeal at different levels. They perfectly illustrate the action but leave behind a memory of something never actually put into words. They satisfy children; they charm and trouble grownups.

It is generally agreed that when George MacDonald's stories began to appear in *Good Words for the Young,*[*] Arthur Hughes found a truly congenial subject. Both the writer and

---

[*] *Good Words for the Young,* published monthly, was edited by Norman Macleod from 1869-1870; by George MacDonald, 1870-1872. Bound volumes of this famous periodical are in outstanding collections in the United States, including the New York Public Library, the Houghton Library at Harvard, and the Library of the Florida State University at Tallahassee.

the artist respected as well as loved children and never played down to them. This collaboration started in 1867 with the enchanting *Dealings with the Fairies*. The perennial favorite, "The Light Princess," with five illustrations, is the first story in it. A perfect copy of the first edition of this book, with its subtitle, "Where More Is Meant than Meets the Ear," is in the Rare Book Division of the New York Public Library. It is barely five inches square, but it is beautifully made and the leaves are embossed in gold that still glitters when the dust is wiped away, although it was printed nearly one hundred years ago.

The dedication says:

My children:
    You know I do not tell you stories as some papas do. Therefore, I give you a book of stories. You have read them all except the last. But you have not seen Mr. Hughes' drawings before. If plenty of children like this volume, you shall have another soon.
                                        Your Papa

Plenty of children did and still do. One wonders what became of the little girl to whom this copy in the New York Library was given, so long ago, "with love, from the author." How she must have enjoyed its contents: "The Light Princess," "The Giant's Heart," "The Shadows," "Cross Purposes," and "The Golden Key." Here are fairy tales to meet many moods and tastes, the two most famous being "The Light Princess" and "The Golden Key." "The Light Princess" was a favorite of the MacDonald children, and in the Houghton Library at Harvard one may see the parchment scroll from which MacDonald read it aloud to them and later to his English classes at Bedford College. "The Golden Key," chosen as the title for a recent study of George MacDonald, is considered by the late John Malcolm Bulloch of Aberdeen to be MacDonald's greatest story. Of it he wrote in his *Bibliography of George MacDonald*, "Its balance, its movement, its colour enables it to challenge, in mere craftsmanship, any story of its length."

In 1924, in London, under the editorship of George MacDonald's son, Greville MacDonald, *Dealings with the Fairies* was again published under the title, *The Fairy Tales of George MacDonald*, the illustrations reproduced from the original pen-and-ink drawings by Arthur Hughes. Dr. MacDonald, himself a writer of stories and books for children, contributed a delightful and inspiring preface. In addition to the five stories in the first book, there are two more — "Photogen and Nycteris" (Day Boy and Night Girl) and the famous "Carasoyn." "Carasoyn" is the story so loved by Angela Thirkell and mentioned by her along with *Phantastes* in her novel, *County Chronicle*. It is highly regrettable that this beautiful book, *The Fairy Tales of George MacDonald*, seems to be disappearing from the shelves of our public libraries. That George MacDonald told or read these stories to his children in no way detracts from the thought that a really fine writer for children is a true poet subjected to the sternest discipline. This is indeed the case as Rumer Godden reveals in her stories and suggested in her recent lectures in the United States.

In 1870, in addition to other work, George MacDonald undertook the editorship of the magazine *Good Words for the Young*. For this magazine he had written, in 1869, a best-seller, as dear to child lovers as to children. This was *At the Back of the North Wind*, and its inspired illustrations were by Arthur Hughes. The secret of the enduring appeal of this book is its two-world consciousness and the simplicity and restraint with which it is written. Quietly, but with great depth of feeling, it tells the story of Diamond, the cab horse, and another Diamond, the little boy who lived over a coach house in London. But it is more than the tale of a boy's love for his horse. The child, Diamond, is visited by a lovely and mysterious Lady, who takes him on many adventures over land and sea, and, finally, to the Back of the North Wind. The story was published, as a book, with the Hughes illustrations, in London in 1871-72. Since then it has had many printings. The old and more artistic editions are hard to come by. As no one will part with them, they rarely turn up in the second-hand shops. Every few years it seems to challenge an illustrator; it is still read and loved, still bought by the average reader, still sought by the collector. To the imaginative, thoughtful child and to some grownups, there is more in *At the Back of the North Wind* than a story of other days in London. This is the poetic side, assuring us that Death is a Beginning, not an Ending, that it is indeed the richer life to be found at the back of the north wind.

Of *The Princess and the Goblin*, the first of the "Princess" books, George MacDonald said, "I know it is as good work of the kind as I can do, and I think it may be the most complete thing I have done — Perhaps I could find a market for this sort of thing in America." It is to our credit that he did. Soon after it came out in *Good Words for the Young*, it was published as a book in 1872. Happily, the illustrations for both were by Arthur Hughes. The story of Irene, the lonely little Princess, the mighty King, her father, and Curdie, the brave boy who worked in the mines, is too well known to need repeating. But the most penetrating interpretation of it should be told. It is by G. K. Chesterton, who wrote, in his Introduction to Greville MacDonald's *George MacDonald and His Wife*:

> Of all the stories I have ever read, including even all the novels of the same novelist, *The Princess and the Goblin* remains the most real, the most realistic; in the exact phrase, the most like life. What I mean is this: It describes a little Princess living in a castle in the mountains, which is perpetually undermined, so to speak, by subterranean demons who sometimes come up through the cellars. She climbs the castle stairways to the Nursery or to the other rooms, but now and again the stairs do not lead to the usual landings, but to a new room she has never seen before and cannot generally find again. Here a good great-grandmother, who is a sort of Fairy Godmother, is perpetually spinning, and speaking words of understanding and encouragement. When I was a child, I felt the whole thing was happening in a real human house, not essentially unlike my own, which also had staircases, and rooms, cellars. . . . Since I first read it, some five alternating philosophies of the Universe have come to our Colleges out of Germany, blowing through the world like an East wind. . . . But for me that castle is still standing in the mountains and the light in the tower is not put out.

And J. F. Harvey Darton, in his authoritative study, *Children's Books in England*, published by the Cambridge University Press in 1932 (revised edition, with an Introduction by Kathleen Lines, 1958) agrees, in part, with Mr. Chesterton and, wholeheartedly, with imaginative children, in praise of this poetic and fascinating story. He says, "More than any prose-storyteller for children of that period, George MacDonald brought serious imagination into the fabric of his tale."

A well-known editor of children's books, discussing with me *The Princess and the Goblin*, said that even as a small girl, as fascinated as she was with the events in the story, she found it tremendously reassuring that the silver thread led the children home. Greville MacDonald, illustrating this fairy-teaching and its acceptance by children, in a footnote to Chapter VII of the aforementioned biography of his parents, quotes these words from his friend, Miss Rose Goodwin:

> Nothing could happen that could make my first introduction to him [MacDonald] pass from my memory. Such a poignant ecstatic experience, at such an age (I was only six years old), was too profound, too thrilling for time to do other than deepen the impression. It chanced . . . that I got hold of an old *Good Words for the Young*, the number containing that part of *The Princess and the Goblin* beginning with the chapter entitled "That Night Week." You will remember how it describes the little Princess, terrified by the goblin creature, running up the hillside and finding heavenly refuge at last in her lovely grandmother's beautiful room. Those starry, vanishing walls! That fire of roses! The mysterious lamp that could shine through impenetrable stone! I had been reading steadily since I was four. I knew Grimm, Andersen, Lewis Carroll, etc., but never, never had I read *anything* approaching this!

In 1873, *Good Words for the Young* became *Good Things* and continued through 1877. George MacDonald's "A Double Story," another well-loved fairy tale, appeared in its pages in 1873 and was reprinted in the United States in *Wide Awake*, a popular children's magazine published in Boston in the 1880's.

Anne Carroll Moore, in *My Roads to Childhood*, describes the power of George MacDonald to interpret and dramatize the spiritual experience of childhood. Such high praise does not mean that MacDonald was lacking in humor. His fairy tales are full of characters, sad and gay, wicked and good; and it is regrettable that too little is said of his sense of fun. Best of all, they are as full of hope as rainbows. Nor do they belong to one period, as delightful as it is to taste the flavor of the old days, which is undoubtedly there. Time is not important to children: they look backward as well as forward. To label George MacDonald's children's books as old-fashioned is as unfair as it is to assume that children are interested entirely in comics, how-to-do-it, or scientific and factual books. Children are interested in all sorts of things and respond to what is available. Just as they often reveal a great deal of taste in books and pictures, so will they absorb the trivial and mediocre. The sensitive librarian will tell you that in spite of changing times and fashion, fairy tales are still among the most popular books in the children's room.

"Should children be led to love fairy tales?" is a question often asked nowadays. Long ago, writing to his friend, Thomas Poole, Coleridge had this to say on the subject, "I know all that has been said against it; but I have found my faith in the affirmative. I know no other way of giving the mind a love of the great and the whole." This George MacDonald certainly did beginning with his first fairy tale and continuing through them all. Indeed, in them he seems to come "full circle" for *Phantastes* was his first prose work. Written in 1858, it was widely pirated. It is best known in England in the handsome edition illustrated by Arthur Hughes, published in 1905. This is the edition so loved by Marjorie Bowen and described in her moving book, *The Debate Continues*; the favorite, too, of Angela Thirkell, who in so many books refers to the abiding influence of MacDonald. It is unfortunate that *Phantastes* is so little known in the United States.

On the title page of *Phantastes* are the words:

> In sooth, my masters, this is no door.
> Yet is it a little window, that looketh upon a great world.

Phantastes is a fairy tale, but it is far more. Nor was it written for children, although they can appreciate the exquisite illustrations by Arthur Hughes and many of the poems and quotations. Whether read as a fairy story or a romance, or, as C. S. Lewis and W. H. Auden suggest, as the superb expression of the mythopoeic imagination, there is a time to truly enjoy it. When one is most impressionable, when the imagination is most keen, the heart most susceptible, and the mind most eager and retentive — that is the moment to read *Phantastes*. It is exciting to trace the influence of this book upon C. S. Lewis. It was the little Everyman's edition of *Phantastes* that so captivated him and of which he writes in *Surprised by Joy*. Heading for a glorious week-end of reading in the country, on a railway station bookstall he found and bought a copy of *Phantastes*.

> That evening [writes Mr. Lewis] I began to read my new book. The woodland journeyings in that story, the ghostly enemies, the ladies both good and evil, were close enough to my habitual imagery to lure me on without the perception of a change. It is as if I were carried sleeping across the frontier, or as if I had died in the old country and could never remember how I came alive in the new. For in one sense the new country was exactly like the old. I met there all that had already charmed me in Malory, Spenser, Morris, and Yeats. But in another sense all was changed. I did not yet know (and I was long in learning) the name of the new quality, the bright shadow, that rested on the travels of Anados. I do now. It was Holiness. For the first time the voice of the sirens sounded like the voice of my mother or my nurse.... It was as though the voice which had called to me from the world's end were now speaking at my side. It was with me in the room, or in my own body, or behind me ... never had the wind of Joy blowing through any story been less separable from the story itself.... I found the light shining on those woods and cottages, and then on my own past life, and on the quiet room where I sat, and on my old teacher where he nodded above his little *Tacitus*.... Up till now each visitation of Joy had left the common world momentarily a desert. ... But now I saw the bright shadow coming out of the book into the real world and resting there, transforming all common things and yet itself unchanged. Or, more accurately, I saw the common things drawn into the bright shadow. *Unde hoc mihi?* In the depth of my disgraces, in the then invincible ignorance of my intellect, all this was given me without asking, even without consent. That night my imagination was, in a certain sense, baptized; the rest of me, not unnaturally, took longer. I had not the faintest notion what I had let myself in for by buying *Phantastes*.

Phantastes is the story of the journey through Fairy Land of the youth, Anados, and his development there. On the night of his twenty-first birthday, he sets out to find his ideal and comes home rejoicing that he has lost his shadow — the maleficent part of him that vulgarizes what it touches, or, as George

MacDonald describes it, "that crushes the flowers upon which it lies." The title is derived from a poem by Phineas Fletcher called "The Purple Island," published in 1633, which tells us that there are Three Great Councillors that rule the Castle of the Mind. They are Judgment, Imagination, and Memory. The second, Imagination, or Phantastes, is the most precious. If Anados fails to reach the country he sets out to discover, he gets close enough to it to believe in it. It is a spiritual pilgrimage out of this world of impoverishing possessions and restlessness into the Fairy Kingdom of Heaven. Once having stepped with Anados from his bed into the flowering wood — into the truer land of faerie and imagery — we can never quite leave it.

From *The Horn Book* for August, 1961

DAILY MAGIC

By Edward Eager

IT is customary, in writing of E. Nesbit, to begin by telling how one first read her stories in *The Strand Magazine*, either devouring the installments one by one as they appeared, or perhaps even better, coming upon them unexpectedly in old bound volumes in some grandmotherly attic.

This did not happen to me. My childhood occurred too late for the original Nesbit era, and too soon for the revival sponsored in this country by William Rose Benét, Christopher Morley, May Lamberton Becker, Earle Walbridge and others (not to mention the firm of Coward-McCann, which earned everlasting honor by beginning to reissue her books in 1929, and has continued to do so ever since).

I was dimly aware of the renewal of interest in Nesbit in the early thirties, but since I was then entering my own early twenties, with no thought of ever again having anything to do with the world of children's books, it all seemed very remote.

It was not till 1947 that I became a second-generation Nesbitian when I discovered a second-hand copy of *Wet Magic*, while casting about for books to read to my son. I have not got over the effects of that discovery yet, nor, I hope, will I ever.

Probably the sincerest compliment I could pay her is already paid in the fact that my own books for children could not even have existed if it were not for her influence. And I am always careful to acknowledge this indebtedness in each of my stories; so that any child who likes my books and doesn't know hers may be led back to the master of us all.

For just as Beatrix Potter is the genius of the picture book, so I believe E. Nesbit to be the one truly "great" writer for the ten-, eleven- and twelve-year-old. (I don't count Lewis Carroll, as in my experience the age when one stops being terrified by, and begins loving, *Alice* is about thirteen and a half. And Kenneth Grahame, whose *The Golden Age* had an undoubted influence on the Nesbit style, is an author to wait for, too, I think. As for Mrs. Ewing, so sadly forgotten of late, she is best come upon a bit earlier, except for *Mary's Meadow*, which might almost have been written by E. Nesbit herself.)

How to describe the Nesbit charm for those who don't yet know it? Better for them to stop reading this article and read the books themselves. I have read all I could find of those that matter (she wrote countless potboilers that are not worth searching for). And I have read the excellent biography by Doris Langley Moore, never published in this country but still obtainable, I believe, from England.

From this book the real Edith Nesbit Bland emerges lifesize and unforgettable, stubborn, charming, wrongheaded, parading in flowing gowns, scattering ashes from her omnipresent cigarette. One finds her plunging ardently into Fabian socialism, handling unconventionally but with childlike directness the problems presented by a philandering husband (a whole novel could be written about her marriage with Hubert Bland). Later one grows impatient, watching her waste valuable time and energy trying to prove that Bacon wrote Shakespeare.

Then there is the charming interlude of what might be called her intellectual flirtation with H. G. Wells. Wells, whom she admired immeasurably (he is the "great reformer" in chapter twelve of *The Story of the Amulet*), had read some of her writing, decided (incomprehensibly) she was a man, and named her Ernest in his mind, a nickname that was to remain through their friendship. One day, after they had met, he appeared at Well Hall unexpectedly, bag and baggage, announcing, "Ernest, I've come to stay." E. Nesbit was delighted. In the words of Mrs. Langley Moore, "nothing could have gratified her more than this frank confidence in her Bohemianism." And of course we see plainly that nothing could have. It was such an ungrown-up thing to do. So unconventional an arrival must have gone straight to the heart of the child Edith, still very much alive somewhere inside the fascinating, unconventional Mrs. Bland.

Elsewhere in the book we are told that E. Nesbit resented the time taken up by her children's stories, and yearned to be free of them in order to devote herself to writing novels and poetry. We may be forgiven for not believing it. Maybe Mrs. Bland felt like that, or pretended to, but not E. Nesbit. Naturally, moving in the circle that she did, among all those witty people doing and saying such grown-up things, she must have known times when she pined for recognition on an adult plane. Recognition, and the very much needed money that went with it, were always important to her.

But her books for children were never the mere potboilers she claimed they were. Every page shines with the delight the writer took in fashioning it, and this is a thing that cannot be faked. I know. In truth it is her "adult" writing that bears a synthetic stamp. Her poems and novels are mere self-conscious attitudinizing, the little girl playing "lady" in borrowed clothes, and all of them have long been forgotten. It was when the child in her spoke out directly to other children that she achieved greatness.

I do not mean to equate genius with arrested mental or emotional development. But there are lucky people who never lose the gift of seeing the world as a child sees it, a magic place where anything can happen next minute, and delightful and unexpected things constantly do. Of such, among those of us who try to write for children, is the kingdom of Heaven. And in that kingdom E. Nesbit stands with the archangels.

Of course there are other people who plainly have never known what it is like to be a child at all, who would suppress fairy tales and tell children "nothing that is not true." (I once knew a lady who denied her children Santa Claus, till they rebelled and forced her to relent. And when one year she so far relaxed as to say that he had been there and brought *one* of the presents, her little girl cried, "And did he wear a red coat and a white beard?" "No," said the lady, stubbornly progressive to the end. "He wore a business suit!")

Tragically, toward the end of E. Nesbit's life, the fantasy-haters were in vogue (again)! One of the saddest chapters in Doris Langley Moore's book is the one that tells of her sending stories to publishers, only to have them returned with the comment that there was no longer any demand for "her sort of books."

The thought of these lost, unpublished Nesbits is enough to make the reader weep. "Bitter unavailing tears" indeed! It is true that the books of her later years are not so strong as her first work, but who knows? She might have found a second wind and finished in a burst of triumph, like Verdi. And if not, even second-rate E. Nesbit is better than no E. Nesbit at all. Which is my justification for having dared to write second-rate E. Nesbit myself.

Still, even without these forgotten manuscripts (what one would give to know even the titles!) there remain in print today, on one side or the other of the Atlantic, fifteen books. And fifteen books of such golden quality are a priceless treasure for any child.

First in any listing of E. Nesbit's works always must come the three books dealing with the Bastable children, delectably titled *The Treasure Seekers, The Wouldbegoods* and *The New Treasure Seekers*. (There is a fourth book, *Oswald Bastable and Others*, obtainable in England, which contains four additional Bastable adventures, as well as eleven other short pieces.)

Who could forget the Bastables, particularly the noble Oswald? One sees them as perpetual pilgrims, marching forever down the road with peas in their shoes and a brave plan in mind to save the family fortunes, stopping by the way to dam the stream (and later cause a nearly-disastrous flood), forgetting in their zeal the cricket ball left lodged in a roof-gutter (which still later is to cause a flood of another kind).

And yet, so short are the memories of critics that one frequently sees the Bastable books listed as fantasies, or among "magic stories." They are of course nothing of the kind, but belong firmly in the realistic tradition of heroic naughtiness, or naughty heroics. And surely of all the naughty children in literature, none were ever so heroic as they, nor any heroes so (unintentionally, of course) very naughty!

Nevertheless, in spite of all the fun, in spite of the unforgettable, endearing Oswald, I question whether the Bastable stories are the best introduction to E. Nesbit today, at least for American children. Because they are realistic books, the details seem more dated, the "Britishness" more marked, than in the Nesbit magic stories. The things these children do are too different from the things children do today for them to qualify as "easy reading." Thus the very elements which make these books unique may be the elements which stand in the way of their acceptance.

If there is resistance to E. Nesbit on the part of some American children in these days, I think it may well be because they encounter the Bastable stories first. Certainly every child should know the Bastables, but if on first exposure he doesn't see their charm, let him meet E. Nesbit instead in the world of fantasy, where background counts for less and once the story gets going, all is gas and gaiters. Then, if he is a right-minded child, he will be won to her forever, and Oswald and his brothers and sisters can follow later.

Before passing on to the Nesbit magic stories, there are two more "realistic" books, one of which must be ordered from England, to be mentioned briefly. *Five of Us and Madeline* is a collection of E. Nesbit's last stories, published after her death and edited by her daughter, Rosamund Sharp. Ten of the stories introduce a new family modeled on Bastable lines, and very nice, too. And "the fell Madeline," pale and mousy and sniffing and cowardly, yet capable of great moments when hard pressed, is a personage to remember. Interestingly, this is the first book illustrated by Nora S. Unwin. The drawings were done when she was still a girl in her teens and, frankly, their interest is purely historic.

Of *The Railway Children* it is the accepted thing to say that it is too sentimental, and perhaps it is, though the sentiment is never false and often touching. And if the story is unbelievable, still the things that happen to Roberta and Peter and Phyllis are just the things that any child would know *ought* to happen to a family that moves to a house near the railway tracks. Yes, *The Railway Children* deserves wider circulation.

With *The Wonderful Garden* one comes close to the very best of E. Nesbit, yet it is a book hard to define. Is it "real"? Is it fantasy? It is either or both. Here is a book in which every event *could* have a prosy, dull, boring, logical explanation. Or there could be magic at work, and of course the children in the book, Caroline and Charlotte and Charles, know that there is. This "magic or not?" formula is one oddly challenging and tempting to the writer, and devilish hard to bring off. I know, because I've just finished trying it, myself. E. Nesbit handles it with consummate skill, to make an almost perfect book. *The Wonderful Garden*, with its incidental and fascinating flower-magic lore, is a book peculiarly attractive to the adult reader, and for this reason I would hesitate before pressing it over-enthusiastically on any non-Nesbit-inoculated child. Again, let him meet her first in the purely "magic" books. Then he will demand all the rest.

Of these magic books there are eight, and of these eight two, *The Magic City* and *Wet Magic*, are late works and, authorities agree, inferior to her best writing. Perhaps. But who could forget Philip waking in the night and walking over the bridge and into the city he has built himself, of blocks and books and bric-a-brac? Who could forget those engaging dachshunds, the cowardly Brenda and the heroic Max? Who could forget the languishing mermaid in *Wet Magic* ("We die in captivity!") and, later, the battle of the books, with its picture (by H. R. Millar, of course) of Boadicea vanquishing Mrs. Markham and the Queen of the Amazons dealing with Miss Murdstone? (Here again, however, adult appreciation may be different from a child's.)

We are left with a golden half-dozen. There are the "five children" books (*Five Children and It*, *The Phoenix and the Carpet* and *The Story of the Amulet*). There are the Arden stories (*The House of Arden* and *Harding's Luck*). And, shining proudly by itself, there is *The Enchanted Castle*.

Who can choose among them? Who can describe perfection? Given only one choice, I would take *The Enchanted Castle* for *my* desert island, but Doris Langley Moore would not agree, though Roger Lancelyn Green (in *Tellers of Tales*, Edmund Ward, England) feels as I do.

But why make comparisons? Read them all. Step up, step up and meet the Psammead and the Mouldiwarp (and the Mouldierwarp and the Mouldiestwarp). Learn how to make Ugly-Wuglies (and *then* see what happens)! Find out how it feels to own a magic carpet *and* a phoenix at the same time. And what takes place when the magic carpet begins to wear out and develops a hole in the middle? Explore the lost kingdom of Atlantis. Go seeking for the real head of the house of Arden and follow the adventures that begin when a crippled boy in a London slum plants strange seeds in his back garden.

And always remember that magic has a mind of its own and will thwart you if it can. So that if you wish, for example, to be invisible and the magic ring you happen to have on you is geared to twenty-four hour cycles (or twenty-one, or fourteen, or seven; you never can tell with magic), invisible you will remain till the time is up. Or four yards high, as was poor Mabel's fate on one historic occasion. And think of the complications, as you go about your daily round.

For if there is one thing that makes E. Nesbit's magic books more enchanting than any others, it is not that they are funny, or exciting, or beautifully written, or full of wonderfully alive and endearing children, all of which they are. It is the *dailiness* of the magic.

Here is no land of dragons and ogres or Mock Turtles and Tin Woodmen. The world of E. Nesbit (except for some elaborate and debatable business with magic clouds toward the end of *The House of Arden*) is the ordinary or garden world we all know, with just the right pinch of magic added. So that after you finish reading one of her stories you feel it could all happen to *you*, any day now, round any corner.

The next time you pick up what you think is a nickel in the street, make sure it *is* a nickel and not a magic talisman. And don't go scrabbling about in sandpits unless you want your fingers to encounter a furry form and your startled ears to hear the voice of a Psammead begging to be allowed to sleep undisturbed for another thousand years.

But of course you *do* want your fingers and your ears to encounter just that; all right-minded people do.

The next best thing to having it actually happen to you is to read about it in the books of E. Nesbit.

From *The Horn Book* for October, 1958

DOCTOR DOLITTLE:
HIS LIFE AND WORKS

By Helen Dean Fish

IT seems quite suitable that the title of an article on Hugh Lofting's imaginative character, Doctor Dolittle, should follow the familiar formula of a biography of a great man of the real world. For Doctor Dolittle lives, as truly as any man whose portrait has been painted, and his "work" is, in its way, as important as that of any prelate or potentate.

That is, if one considers it important to create and make real for children a dream of complete understanding and complete helpfulness between men and animals. Hugh Lofting was possessed by a great ideal of world peace and understanding, and deep in his characterization of Doctor Dolittle and in the Doctor's relations with his animal friends lies what Hugh Lofting had to say on this subject. It is a simple message and a very old one. It could transform this old world: *do to others* (*every* other, man and beast) *as you would like to have them do to you.*

Doctor Dolittle is beloved by children, whether they are conscious of the reason or not, because he can be depended upon to follow this golden rule. It is his kindness that continually leads him into adventures in which he meets danger and excitement. And he always comes out victorious because he is not only courageous but ingenious. Thereby he is the sort of hero with whom children will go through thick and thin.

Doctor Dolittle is a good man for children to know because he stands for kindliness, patience and reliability, mixed with delightful humor, energy and gaiety, a combination rarely met and hard to beat. The creation of this character is described by the author: "It was during the Great War and my children at home wanted letters from me — and they wanted them with illustrations rather than without. There seemed very little of interest to write to youngsters from the Front: the news was either too horrible or too dull. And it was all censored. One thing, however, that kept forcing itself more and more on my attention was the very considerable part the animals were playing in the World War and that as time went on they, too, seemed to become Fatalists. They took their chances with the rest of us. But their fate was far different from the men's. However seriously a soldier was wounded, his life was not despaired of; all the resources of a surgery highly developed by the war were brought to his aid. A seriously wounded horse was put out by a timely bullet.

"This did not seem quite fair. If we made the animals take the same chances as we did ourselves, why did we not give them similar attention when wounded? But obviously to develop a horse-surgery as that of our Casualty Clearing Stations would necessitate a knowledge of horse language.

"That was the beginning of the idea: an eccentric country physician with a bent for natural history and a great love of pets, who finally decides to give up his human practice for the more difficult, more sincere and, for him, more attractive therapy of the animal kingdom. He is challenged by the difficulty of the work — for obviously it requires a much cleverer brain to become a good animal doctor (who must first acquire all animal languages and physiologies) than it does to take care of the mere human hypochondriac.

"This was a new plot for my narrative letter for the children. It delighted them and at my wife's suggestion, I decided to put the letters in book form for other boys and girls."

Doctor Dolittle became a beloved character to Hugh Lofting's two children and little Colin even adopted the name. The precious letters came home to America with the family in the autumn of 1919. Of this voyage the poet and novelist Cecil Roberts recently wrote a reminiscence:

"Crossing the Atlantic I had a neighbor in my deck chair. Every evening about six he said he had to disappear to read a bedtime story to Doctor Dolittle. I enquired who Doctor Dolittle might be and he said it was his little son. The next day a snubnosed boy appeared on deck with his mother and thus I made the acquaintance of the original Doctor Dolittle.

Later Hugh Lofting at my request showed me some of his manuscript and he wondered if it would make a book. I was at once struck by the quality of the stories and, enthusiastic about their publication, recommended him to my publisher, Mr. Stokes. I never saw Hugh Lofting again but when his first Dolittle book came out, he sent me a copy with a charming inscription."

The reception of *The Story of Doctor Dolittle* in 1920 — on both sides of the Atlantic — is well known. The little doctor of the animals was instantaneously and universally beloved and the reason why his appeal continued, unabated, through volume after volume for the next thirteen years was because he possessed all the vitality, completeness and variety of a truly great human character. All that Doctor Dolittle does and says exerts charm for his young readers, just as a rare and beloved personal friend never fails to claim a child's allegiance and response.

As to Doctor Dolittle's "life and work" — he was, at the opening of *The Story of Doctor Dolittle*, a regular country practitioner, though very partial to animals as patients. Then came the episode of the crocodile and the linoleum and his sister's ultimatum — either the crocodile must leave or she will go and get married. It was a great decision, made quietly and with who knows what inner satisfaction, when Doctor Dolittle said, "All right. *Go* and get married."

After that Doctor Dolittle became the great doctor of the animals. His journey to Africa to cure the monkeys of an epidemic established his fame the world around.

In *The Voyages of Doctor Dolittle*, the Newbery Medal book, he went to Spidermonkey Island on a great exploration. In *Doctor Dolittle's Post Office* — Africa again — he organized a mail service for the birds and animals. Incidentally, the backgrounds of Doctor Dolittle's foreign travels are the lands which Hugh Lofting knew from his early years of travel as an engineer, before World War I.

Doctor Dolittle's Circus took the Doctor back to England as manager of a highly successful country circus in which the wonderful Pushmi-pullyu was the leading feature. In *Doctor Dolittle's Zoo* he went into show business in England, with kindness to animals as his first rule, and *Doctor Dolittle's Caravan* took him further in the entertainment field with an animal orchestra and a canary opera. *Doctor Dolittle's Garden* showed him at home at Puddleby, studying insects and developing his Dog's Lodging House and Museum in his garden. In *Doctor Dolittle in the Moon* he explored that distant body, which he reached by means of a giant moth, and the following book, *Doctor Dolittle's Return*, records his welcome back to Puddleby. This book, published in 1933, was the last until *Doctor Dolittle and the Secret Lake*. But Hugh Lofting remained true to his child audience in his work on the new book, and Doctor Dolittle lived on in the hearts of his readers.

Hugh Lofting always said that the letters he received from children about Doctor Dolittle were a great inspiration to him. Though he received very many, he could always tell which were written as part of a lesson in school and which were from the heart, written because some child friend of Doctor Dolittle simply had to write to Hugh Lofting about him. When such a letter came, Mr. Lofting dropped anything he was engaged upon — his breakfast or catching a train — and answered the letter. Some delightful child friendships evolved from this. The children's letters frequently contained suggestions for new adventures for Doctor Dolittle, offers of collaboration and queries about details of the Doctor's life that showed the writers believed in him as a real person whose acquaintance they shared with Hugh Lofting.

It was this sort of inspiration, combined perhaps with his marriage to Josephine Fricker, the removal of his home to California and the arrival of a new son in 1936, that led Hugh Lofting to begin the great story of Doctor Dolittle's new voyage to Africa to rescue the giant turtle, Mudface, who survived the Flood. It took him a dozen years to complete text and drawings, though part of the text and a number of the drawings were printed in a Dolittle syndicated feature in the *New York Herald-Tribune* in 1923.

The turtle Mudface is already familiar to readers of *Doctor Dolittle's Post Office*, who will remember, toward the end of that book, a mysterious letter brought to the Doctor by the Swallow Mail when he arrived at Fantippo after the adventure at the pearl fisheries. It was written clumsily in mud and contained an invitation to come to visit the writer as the oldest weather prophet in the world. He claimed to be the turtle who prophesied the Flood. "If you will come to see me," the letter ran, "I will teach you a lot about weather. And I will tell you the story of the Flood, which I saw with my own eyes from the deck of Noah's Ark. P.S. I am a turtle."

This was a challenge Doctor Dolittle could not resist. Led by a giant snake, he went to Lake Junganyika in the heart of the jungliest part of Africa — the Secret Lake, visited by no man since the Flood. Mudface's thrilling tale took two weeks to tell. After hearing it, Doctor Dolittle prescribed for the turtle's gout, and with the help of the birds and animals, built him an island to live on, out of reach of the water, and left him in his new home.

The new book, *Doctor Dolittle and the Secret Lake*, relates the adventure of the Doctor's return to Africa several years later to find and rescue his friend the turtle who has been buried by an earthquake. He hears and records again, with the help of Tommy Stubbins, the story of the Flood. It is a dramatic and exciting tale and readers of all ages who have been privileged to read the manuscript before publication have hailed it with the old enthusiasm. Children who read the first Dolittle story in 1920 are now twenty-eight years older — many of them parents of young Dolittle lovers. There is a treat in store for many a family who will enjoy reading aloud the new Dolittle book, parents and children together. For that is a characteristic of Hugh Lofting's books — and a part of Doctor Dolittle's "work" — that he speaks a common language to readers young and old. Hugh Lofting believed that a good story should be good for a reader of any age; that it was his job as author to write so simply and entertainingly that a child could understand all he had to say, even when meeting unfamiliar words and expressions. He resented the word "juvenile" applied to a book, thinking it quite as silly as a classification of "seniles" would be.

Christened Hugh John Lofting, he was born of Irish-English parentage in Maidenhead, Berkshire, England, on January 14, 1886. As a small boy he loved animals and all things of nature and kept a combination zoo and natural history museum in his mother's linen closet — until discovered. Like a proper English boy, at the age of eight he went away to school. At Mount St. Mary's, a Jesuit school in Chesterfield, Derbyshire, he learned Latin and Greek, and decided to become a civil engineer in order to see the world. He loved mountain climbing and fishing as a boy and throughout his life.

In 1904, at sixteen, he came to America to attend Massachusetts Institute of Technology and returned to England the following year for further study at the London Polytechnic, after which his career as a civil engineer began. He prospected in Canada in 1908, worked with the Lagos Railway in West Africa and with the Railways of Havana in Cuba for the next four years, thus achieving his boyhood ambition.

In 1912 he returned to America, married Flora Small, and tried his hand at writing articles and short stories until World War I came along. It was for his two children, Elizabeth and Colin, that he wrote the first Dolittle letters when he served as Captain in the Irish Guards in Flanders and France. He was wounded and invalided out in 1917.

The Loftings returned to America in 1919 and settled at Madison, Connecticut. Hugh Lofting served in the British Ministry of Information in New York and in 1920, with *The Story of Doctor Dolittle*, began his career of writing for children. He enjoyed very much talking to children and spent much time visiting schools, libraries and clubs.

Mrs. Lofting died in 1927 and his second wife very shortly after marriage in the influenza epidemic of 1928. In 1935 Hugh Lofting married Josephine Fricker, of Toronto, and moved to Topanga, California, where his son Christopher was born. His health had been uncertain for the last few years, but he worked as steadily as possible on *Doctor Dolittle and the Secret Lake*, which, happily, he finished before his death at his Santa Monica home on September 27, 1947.

Hugh Lofting's friend, Sir Hugh Walpole, did not read *The Story of Doctor Dolittle* until 1922 when he picked the book up in the Hampshire Bookshop during a visit to Smith College. He wrote the author a letter about it, so delightful that it was made into an introduction to the tenth printing. It claimed the book as "a work of genius — the first real children's classic since *Alice*," and predicted that Doctor Dolittle would go down the centuries "as a kind of Pied Piper with thousands of children at his heels."

Doctor Dolittle is everyone's friend and everyone's reading. There are Dolittle lovers all over the world — for the stories have been translated into nine languages — and Dolittle lovers everywhere understand certain things. They know, for instance, that every animal is an individual; they are likely to be a little more patient and politer than other people — especially to animals. And they share a dream of peace in all the world that may come some day if children will learn to practice Doctor Dolittle's particular brand of lovingkindness and friendliness.

Doctor Dolittle is an anchor to windward in a world increasingly difficult for children. He invites his reader into an imaginative world that is secure and delightful and that contrasts reassuringly with the confusion of a day spent in listening to the radio, seeing a movie or television, or "reading" the comics. Doctor Dolittle is always entertaining and exciting, but he is a person who gives a sense of dependability in a noisy and uncertain world. To quote Miss E. H. Colwell in an appraisal of Hugh Lofting in *The Junior Bookshelf*, "Whatever the danger, Doctor Dolittle remains calm and however awkward the situation he always retains his top hat and little bag."

From *The Horn Book* for October, 1948

NEWS FROM NARNIA
By Lillian H. Smith

"LISTEN," said the Doctor. "All you have heard about Old Narnia is true. It is not the land of men. It is the country of Aslan, the country of the Waking Trees and Visible Naiads, of Fauns and Satyrs, of Dwarfs and Giants, of the gods and the Centaurs, of Talking Beasts."

The world called Narnia is the world that C. S. Lewis has created in seven stories for children; each story has a beginning, a middle, and an end, and each may be read independently of the others. Yet in these seven books, taken as a whole, we see a complete story with a beginning, a middle, and an end, in much the same way that we see, first, single stars in the sky, and then see them as a constellation which takes on a pattern our eyes can follow and recognize.

Narnia is not in our world nor in our universe. Narnia has its own sun and moon and stars, its own time. Yet the landscape is a familiar one, a green and pleasant land of woods and glades, valleys and mountains, rivers and sea. The trees, shrubs, and flowers, many birds and animals, are those we know in our own world. Even the unfamiliar, the strange and fabulous ones, are in old stories we have heard and read.

Narnia's history is brief, as we reckon time in our world, though in Narnian time it covers many thousands of years. It began when "Sherlock Holmes was still living in Baker Street and the Bastables were looking for treasure in the Lewisham Road." In London, too, lived Polly and Digory, who were looking for adventure. It was Digory's Uncle Andrew, a dabbler in magic, who sent Polly and Digory out of our world and into a world of darkness, which was Narnia waiting to be born.

Digory was "the sort of person who wants to know everything" and his curiosity brought great trouble to Narnia later on. For the children had visited a dying world before coming to Narnia, and because Digory could not resist the desire to know what would happen, he broke the spell that bound an evil witch to the dying world of Charn. When the children are drawn into a new world, the witch, though against their will, comes too. And so evil enters Narnia before it is five hours old.

As the children stand in the nothingness of this new, dark and empty world, they hear a voice singing, and with the song suddenly there were stars overhead. Soon, the sky on the eastern horizon turned from dark to gray, then from pink to gold, and just as the voice swelled to the mightiest and most glorious sound, the sun arose and the Singer himself stood facing the rising sun. "It was a Lion."

The Lion's song of creation changes as he paces the waste land, and, as Polly said, "when you listened to his song you heard the things he was making up: when you looked round you, you saw them" — "all things bright and beautiful, all creatures great and small." Narnia is born.

But, since evil has already entered Narnia through the curiosity of two human children, the Lion, who is called Aslan, decrees that "As Adam's race has done the harm, Adam's race shall help to heal it."

Digory and Polly are sent over the Western Wild and mountains of ice, to a walled garden with gates of gold. Here, Aslan tells them, must be gathered the apple whose seeds will be Narnia's safeguard against the witch in the years ahead. And this was the first of the comings and goings between Narnia and our own world as it is told in *The Magician's Nephew*.

All our news of Narnia comes from the various human children who find themselves there whenever evil times fall on the land. Centuries of peace and plenty pass unrecorded until four other children, in the story of *The Lion, the Witch and the Wardrobe*, find all of Narnia wrapped in a blanket of snow and ice. Under the witch's spell, it is "always winter and never Christmas." The children and the Narnians are pitted against the witch, who calls to her aid all the "abominations": Ghouls, Boggles, Ogres, Minotaurs, Cruels, Hags, and Spectres. But Aslan, the Lion, has been seen in Narnia, and with his coming the spell of evil over the land weakens, and signs of spring are followed by budding trees and rushing brooks as the children, with the talking beaver as their guide, journey to meet Aslan at the great Stone Table where the battle against the witch will be decided.

Although not the first story in Narnian chronology, *The Lion, the Witch and the Wardrobe* was the first to be published, and is, I think, the first for children themselves to read. For, from the moment Lucy opens the wardrobe, steps inside to explore, and is suddenly standing in the middle of a winter forest with snow crunching underfoot, the adventure is a magnet that draws the reader deeper and deeper into the life of Narnia and into concern for all that happens there. At the same time, the reader is aware that there is more to the story than what meets the eye, phrases that set young minds and hearts pondering, overtones that set up rhythms heard not only in this book, but in all the stories as they appeared year after year until the last two, *The Magician's Nephew* and *The Last Battle*. In these the children's questions are answered and the full harmony is heard and intuitively grasped at last.

Each story has its own landscape — or seascape. For C. S. Lewis, the face of nature, its changing moods and seasons whether seen in windswept wastes or in a small mossy glade where hawthorn is in bloom, has its part in his developing theme, in shaping the sequence of events and in giving reality to the reader's imaginings as he accompanies the characters of the story on their adventures in the magical land of Narnia.

The characters themselves, apart from the human children who come there as visitors, reflect the author's mature and scholarly interest in mythology and medieval romances. They reflect and communicate his abiding love for the Old Things which belong, perhaps, to a golden age, backwards in time, when men and birds and beasts spoke to each other in common language, a fabulous age which, it may be, lived on in myth and fairy tale as a kind of race memory of another, more innocent, world.

It is Trufflehunter, the badger, whose sense of race hints at the prehistoric antiquity of animal traits, the unchanging persistent tenacity with which they pursue their own ends.

"You Dwarfs," says Trufflehunter, "are as forgetful and changeable as the Humans themselves. I'm a beast, I am, and a Badger what's more. We don't change. We hold on."

Among the other characters who live on in memory after we have closed the books is that valiant Chief Mouse, Reepicheep, whose code of chivalry would seem to have been learned at King Arthur's Round Table, for "his mind was full of forlorn hopes, death or glory charges and last stands." He is one of the company who sails in the *Dawn Treader* "towards Aslan's land and the morning and the eastern end of the world," and, after the last battle of all the battles, he is found at the open gates of Aslan's country to bid his friends welcome.

And there is Puddleglum, the Marsh-wiggle, who takes so dim a view of every prospect, but who is the faithful, hardy guide in the children's quest for the lost Prince Rilian. Says Puddleglum: "Now a job like this — a journey up north just as winter's beginning, looking for a Prince that probably isn't there, by way of a ruined city that no one has ever seen — will be just the thing. If that doesn't steady a chap, I don't know what will." When the Prince is found, in the underworld of the witch, and when she uses her black arts to persuade the children that only the underworld exists and that Narnia is only a myth, it is Puddleglum who stamps out the flame whose evil fumes bewilder and confuse their minds and hearts. It is Puddleglum who throws the challenge to the witch: "Suppose we *have* only dreamed, or made up, all those things — trees and grass and sun and moon and stars and Aslan himself. Suppose we have. Then all I can say is that, in that case, the made-up things seem a good deal more important than the real ones. . . . I'm on Aslan's side even if there isn't any Aslan to lead it. I'm going to live as like a Narnian as I can even if there isn't any Narnia."

And so we come to Aslan, the Lion, who is the heart and the periphery of these stories and their reason for being: Aslan, whose pervasive influence is felt at all times, in all places, whether visible or invisible in the world of Narnia. He says to the children "remember, remember, remember the signs. . . . Here on the mountain I have spoken to you clearly: I will not often do so down in Narnia. Here on the mountain, the air is clear and your mind is clear; as you drop down into Narnia, the air will thicken. Take great care that it does not confuse your mind."

We may call these books fairy tales or allegories or parables, but there is no mistake about the significance of what C. S. Lewis has to say to the trusting, believing, seeking heart of childhood. But C. S. Lewis knows well that if children are to hear what it is he has to say to them, they must first find delight in the story he tells. And so the fresh and vigorous winds of his imagination carry his readers exuberantly through strange and wild adventures, adventures that, half consciously, they come to recognize are those of a spiritual journey toward the heart of reality. This is the final quality, I think, of C. S. Lewis' writing about the country of Narnia; that above and beneath and beyond the events of the story itself there is something to which the children can lay hold: belief in the essential truth of their own imaginings.

From *The Horn Book* for October, 1963

A LETTER FROM C. S. LEWIS

By *James E. Higgins*

C. S. LEWIS CONSIDERED himself to be something less than an expert in the field of children's books. In a letter to me dated July 31, 1962, he wrote: "... my knowledge of children's literature is really very limited. ... My own range is about exhausted by Macdonald, Tolkien, E. Nesbit, and Kenneth Grahame." Yet it was this lack of expertness, as he wished to call it, which allowed Lewis to bring a new breath of freshness to the field. Not since Paul Hazard's *Books, Children and Men* (Horn Book, Inc.) had so distinguished a man of letters left such an indelible mark upon the pages of the history and criticism of children's books. For the children of today and tomorrow, Lewis has left *The Lion, the Witch and the Wardrobe* and his other books of Narnia, while for the adults who in any way influence the reading habits of children, he has left not only these books but also critical comment that is rich with imagination, wisdom, and integrity.

I believe that a second letter I received from Professor Lewis, in which he answered questions I put to him concerning writing for children, is a valuable contribution to this legacy, for although a few of his answers can be found elsewhere,* there are comments, particularly those concerning his habits of composition while writing "juveniles," which, to my knowledge, he writes down here for the first time.

It is for this reason that I would like first to share this letter, and then to comment on his answers.

---

*Readers who wish to know more about Lewis' reasons for turning to the fairy tale, which he discusses under the fifth point in the letter, are directed to two articles written by Lewis on the subject: "On Three Ways of Writing for Children," *The Horn Book*, October, 1963, and "Sometimes Fairy Stories May Say Best What's to be Said," *New York Times Children's Book Review*, November 18, 1956.

Magdalene College, Cambridge
2 December 1962

Dear Mr. Higgins:

1. Surely I never questioned the "legitimacy" of mythopoeia — only the propriety of classifying the art which it belonged to as "Literature."
2. The Narnian books are not as much allegory as supposal. "Suppose there were a Narnian world and it, like ours, needed redemption. What kind of incarnation and Passion might Christ be supposed to undergo *there?*"
3. Only after Aslan came into the story — on His own; I never called Him — did I remember the scriptural "Lion of Judah."
4. No. I never met Chesterton. I suppose the same affinity which made me like him made us both like Macdonald.
5. I turned to fairy tales because that seemed the form which certain ideas and images in my mind seemed to demand; as a man might turn to fugues because the musical phrases in his head seemed to be "good fugue subjects."
6. When I wrote *The Lion* I had no notion of writing the others.
7. Writing "juveniles" certainly modified my habits of composition. Thus (*a*) it imposed a strict limit on vocabulary (*b*) excluded erotic love (*c*) cut down reflective and analytical passages (*d*) led me to produce chapters of nearly equal length, for convenience in reading aloud. All these restrictions did me great good — like writing in a strict metre.

Yes. I get wonderful letters from children in U. S. A. and elsewhere.

Yours sincerely,
C. S. Lewis

The first comment is a further clarification of a statement made by Lewis in the preface to *George Macdonald: An Anthology*. He raises the problem that confronts the literary critic as he deals with myth. In describing Macdonald's work, Lewis states:

> ... the texture of his writing as a whole is undistinguished, at times fumbling.... What he does best is fantasy — fantasy that hovers between the allegorical and the mythopoeic. And this ... he does better than any man. The critical problem with which we are confronted is whether this art — the art of myth-making — is a species of the literary art. The objection to so classifying it is that the Myth does not essentially exist in *words* at all!

Openly acknowledging the problem that Macdonald's prose presents to the literary critic, Lewis, nevertheless, implies that the impact of the genuine literary experience is not to be measured only by the author's facility with language or by the reader's ability to appreciate style. He holds that the *stuff* of the story is equally important in this regard and that it is well to remember that the author of integrity must continually root this stuff out from deep within himself. It is George Macdonald, the *man* who is the author, whom Lewis acknowledges as his master.

It is also in this connection that I was led to ask Lewis if he had ever met G. K. Chesterton, because both of these modern sophisticates, whose lives and works bear striking resemblances, were deeply affected by one or more of Macdonald's works; Lewis especially by *Phantastes* and Chesterton by *The Princess and the Goblin*. As men of letters, Chesterton and Lewis far surpassed Macdonald in literary skill and artistry, but their indebtedness to him goes much deeper than craftsmanship. They found a power and a depth in the fairyland of George Macdonald that enabled each of them to advance from the shadows of doubt to the peace that is found with religious conviction.

Even as a boy, Lewis had read fanciful tales created by writers who had much more sophistication than Macdonald, but in the works of Macdonald, he found a quality which he did not find in the others. Lewis sometimes calls this quality goodness and at other times holiness. He also identifies this as the art of myth-making — the art of partially lifting the veil from one of the mysteries of life through the medium of story.

This leads to a consideration of the second comment made by Lewis in his letter. When I first read *The Lion, the Witch and the Wardrobe* it troubled me, for I constantly made allegorical comparisons which were inappropriate for a good reading of the story. I read into the story an evangelism that was not there; I made out-of-the-story comparisons that were invalid. It disappointed Lewis that so many adults supposed that he had written the Narnia books because he felt they were the best means of reducing his Christian apologetics to a form fit for child consumption; in fact, the stories only appear this way to adults because they do indeed spring from, as Lewis put it, "the habitual furniture of the author's mind."

After reading *The Lion, the Witch and the Wardrobe* to several different groups of children and noting their response, I was less convinced that Lewis had intended an allegorical design. I came to think of it as more myth than allegory, and this is how I worded my second question to him.

It is interesting to note that, in his answer, Lewis avoids both terms and uses the word supposal. Note too that he underlines the word *there* to stress that he never expects his readers to be constantly making allegorical comparisons between Earth and Narnia. That the readers will have to make comparisons between their own world and the imaginative world of the book is obvious, but the stories of Narnia, in this sense, are more like science fiction than allegory.

The theme of the Narnia books is redemption. It is a religious theme, but, at the same time, a theme stripped bare of the familiar religious symbols which anchor it to Earth. Lewis reasons that Earth may be only one of the places in God's vast universe that is in need of redemption. *Suppose* there are other places. Other worlds. His is a story of Narnians, but told in descriptive terms that Earthlings might understand.

Lewis does not ask his readers to search for meaning, and there is no promised deepening of appreciation for those who do. The reader is merely asked to open the eyes of his heart so that he can truly respond to the sufferings and joys of Aslan the Lion. And this the child can do perhaps far better than the adult. And this is the reason why The Chronicles of Narnia are children's books, no matter who may read them.

Consider too what Lewis says of Aslan in his letter: "I never called Him." The image of a magnificent Lion pushed its way into the imagination of the author without ever having been beckoned, just as God had so rudely come back into the life of young Clive Lewis without invitation. The Lion of Narnia is not meant to overstep the boundaries of the story so that he may stand in comparison with the Lion of Judah. Lewis realized that a story works best within its own confines, having, as it does, its own unique mode of instruction. He knew from experience that a reader could be joyously surprised by God within a work of fiction. Had it not happened to him?

The sixth comment simply explains how Narnia came into

existence. In *The Lion, the Witch and the Wardrobe*, Narnia is the setting for the story, but it is not yet a world with a beginning and a history, because Lewis had not yet thought of it as a world with a beginning and an end, but only as a story with a beginning and an end of its own. When he says that he had no notion of writing the others, Lewis is referring to the six books that would follow. At this point in his writing, he faced the same situation that his friend Tolkien had faced while writing *The Hobbit*. Lewis, like Tolkien, suddenly found himself immersed in a mythological world of his own making, but strangely enough a world of which he knew very little concerning its origin. His own curiosity prodded him to discover imaginatively the beginnings of Narnia and then to trace its history to the time of Armageddon, for without his permission the story of Narnia had swept over the confining margins of a single book.

Lewis concludes the letter by listing four ways in which he modified his habits of composition.

"It imposed a strict limit on vocabulary."

In children's books that are worthy of consideration as literature, the words are the instruments of the story. They may be little words or big words, difficult words or easy words, monosyllabic words or polysyllabic words, words with silent e's or hard c's. Their existence is justified when they are words that make a positive contribution to the artistic telling of a story appropriate for children.

The choice of words is always in the hand of the writer, and his decisions concerning the choice of words are artistic considerations. The telling of a story is always of prime importance. Words are selected for whatever they may lend to the narration. Such selection is very different from the choices of a writer who works within the confines of a publisher's controlled vocabulary list based upon "scientific" analysis.

The writer of fiction for children must be constantly working to create vivid images, for imagery carries the story off the flat surface of the printed page and onto the dimensional screen of the reader's inner eye. Some writers, in reaching for the easy word, find only the general word, which, at its best, only explains a thing or an action but never brings it to life. Lewis is aware of his young readers' limited acquaintance with words, and he consciously limits his vocabulary, but he never passes up the concrete or specific merely for the sake of familiarity. For instance, the Narnian ship *Dawn Treader* is one with a fore and an aft, not a front and a back. It has a forecastle and a galley, a port and a starboard, a poop deck and a tiller. It is not Lewis' intention to instruct children on the subject of ships (though they may learn about them); he wants them to take an exciting voyage aboard one. There is a world of difference between the two.

"Excluded erotic love."

"My goodness! But of course!" a reader is inclined to exclaim. It is significant, however, that Lewis feels pressed to mention this exclusion; the reason being that the pervading theme of all his books is love — divine love and the human love which necessarily springs from the divine. This is not the spongy emotion which self-indulgent man sometimes invents for his own pleasure. It is the hard, painful, overwhelming love for which man has been grasping from the beginning of time. It is the love which was given life when a voice burst out of the heavens one day to lay not a request but a commandment upon the head of man: "Thou shalt love. . . ."

Lewis asserts that divine love is the force which commits man to the good life. It is the love that, once found, captures the imagination and reduces the meaning of life to terms so simple that both child and man can respond in turn. It is the love which leads a man of such high learning as Lewis back to the simple faith of childhood.

It is a love that is found everywhere: in the eyes of an enemy or in the smile of a friend, in the smoke of a city or in the delicate hand of a statue, in the cry of poverty or in the sigh of contentment, in the crash of the gale or in the hush of the zephyr. It is found everywhere, even in the telling of a children's story.

"Cut down reflective and analytical passages."

It is worth noting that Lewis does not use the word exclude when referring to reflective and analytical passages. He does, in fact, include much more of this kind of writing than most writers for children are willing to do. Readers often come away from the Narnia books, as they do from Saint-Exupéry's *Little Prince*, feeling somehow that there were two stories unfolding and that they observed one and participated in the other.

Lewis does not, however, pull up the reins of narrative to make insertions; the reflective passages run beneath the surface of narration. The tide of story always pulls strongest, and the undercurrent will only be felt by those readers who have the ability and the inclination to plunge beneath the surface from time to time, allowing the undertow to move them in another direction.

There are some child readers today who will find any reflective passage not to their liking because such a passage is usually accompanied by the voice of the author. One must remember that Lewis had strong ties with the past. He was admittedly not a student of contemporary children's books. The kind of stories he created were stories that still would have pleased him as a child reader. And Lewis' childhood, one should also remember, was still in the era of the book, the time when stories were not yet being told through the rapid sensory media of mass communication. Too, the stories Lewis tells reach even further back, to the era before the book, when tales were communicated, for the most part, through the human voice.

Lewis tells his story to a listening audience. This is the best way he knows of telling a story, and surely many readers still find special delight in a story told this way. There is no denying, however, that for every reader who has a receptive ear for this technique, there will be at least one, and perhaps more, for whom it will not strike a pleasing chord, especially among those whose reading inventory is rather limited. One also suspects, in this regard, that children in the United States, whose literature is not quite so strongly linked with the past, find this more often a problem than do children in Great Britain.

Most children today are virtually ignorant of the delights of oral narration. Their experience with stories is almost totally confined to print or the pictorial. It is only natural then that many of them should expect a story whose author is voiceless.

Whenever these children feel the presence of the author, they look upon it as an intrusion. They will be less tolerant of the narrative techniques employed in many of the classics, unless they are first helped to discover the pleasures of the spoken word.

The problem leads us to Lewis' final modification: "Led me to produce chapters of nearly equal length, for convenience in reading aloud."

This statement by Lewis illustrates a very important point to be remembered about literature: children are engaged in literary experiences long before they can read; and for a lifetime after they have learned to read, adults may still enjoy some stories best when they are heard through the human voice. There is a great deal of magic that accompanies a story well told or read aloud that a silent reading fails to capture. The distinction between literature and reading is one which needs further consideration from those adults actively engaged in bringing children and books together.

Lewis fashions his children's story in the tradition of the ancient storyteller. He uses the magic of sound to spin his web of wonder and fancy. He hears his story just as poets like Vachel Lindsay and Robert Frost hear their verse. And then when he transcribes what he hears into print, he discovers that sound has influenced his choice of words, it has affected his rhythms and patterns, it has determined his use of punctuation. Indeed, it has invaded every facet of his style, even down to such a seemingly insignificant consideration as chapter length.

In examining the work of C. S. Lewis, one would be hard pressed to find a man who better represents the integrity which a children's author ought to bring to his work. He was not a student of child behavior nor did he ponder for any length of time the subject of children's likes and dislikes in books. Lewis turned to the children's story, more specifically to the tale of "supposal," because it was the art form that best suited the subject of his story; he then became actively engaged in overcoming the unique demands of the form itself.

From *The Horn Book* for October, 1966

PAUL FENIMORE COOPER AND *TAL*

By Louis C. Jones

PAUL FENIMORE COOPER is a tall, dark, restless man with an itching foot that seldom lets him settle down for long, even in the famous village of Cooperstown, New York, which his great-great-grandfather, William Cooper, founded and his great-grandfather, James Fenimore Cooper, made known throughout the world. He has seen the odd and out-of-the-way places, the corners where the tourists do not gather. Last year it was the Straits of Magellan, in 1923 it was Albania; betwixt and between there have been other, no less interesting spots, but it was the Albanian trip that made *Tal* and *Tricks of Women and Other Albanian Tales* possible.

In 1923 the world was even less aware of Albania than it is today, when we remember the gallant defense by the rugged mountaineers of that little land against the legions of Mussolini. The highways were mountain trails, the principal communities villages of little stone houses with red tile roofs. There was practically no written Albanian language, and the spoken language of the north was meaningless to those who lived in the south. It was a land where the empire of the Turkish sultans had met and married the culture of the Balkans, where Greek and Roman Catholic worshipped around the corner from the mosque. It was, it seemed to Paul Fenimore Cooper, the proper place for a couple of young fellows to take a walking trip. And that is what he and a friend of his did, guided by an ancient Albanian and his little, foot-wise pack donkey.

The land caught Cooper's imagination. It had the fantastic qualities of Coleridge's Xanadu, and long after he had returned to America the memories of its people and its mountain passes, its curious mixture of Orient and Occident haunted him. His characteristic intellectual curiosity caused him to undertake that most difficult task of learning, under the tutelage of the distinguished scholar of language, N. B. Jopson, the southern Albanian language. He read the two collections of Albanian folk tales taken down from the lips of the people by Auguste Dozon and Holger Pedersen, for the literary monuments of the Albanian people were entirely in their folklore.

Around 1926 Cooper set about writing a novel; it was to be brittle, sophisticated. He worked hard at it, but something was wrong and it wouldn't jell. As an antidote he began writing fantastic fairy tales about a never-never land called. Troom, a wise old man who seemed in the author's mind's eye to be not unlike his Albanian guide, and the old man had a donkey. There was something of the folklore of Albania, something of its fantastic mountain land, but there was also in the stories much of the young man who was doing the writing. One day his mother, a most wise and gracious lady, picked up from his desk one of these tales about the old man, Noom-Zor-Noom, and his talking donkey, Millitinkle. After she had read it she persuaded her son that here lay his real genius and that in the high art of the juvenile lay greater values than in the somewhat sophisticated novel. This was the encouragement Cooper needed and *Tal* grew from isolated stories to a unified work of art. It is perhaps worthy of note that he wrote the stories rapidly, completing a story every two days, and after they were written he created the framework in which they are set.

Tal has the quality of familiar ways; ways as ancient and beloved by the childhood of the world as the fairy lore to which it has listened for thousands of years. Golden-haired Tal is a king's son who has been stolen from the kingdom of Troom and whose father has, for eight years, been seeking the storyteller who can please the Golden Door, the speaking door which will tell the whereabouts of the child. Noom-Zor-Noom is one of the contesting storytellers and the friend who not only causes the Golden Door to speak, but brings the boy back to his parents. Less familiar are other aspects of the story: the fine madness of the details, like the tavern kept by a horse, the sardonic humor of the talking Millitinkle, the travel on a streak of lightning, to mention a few where there are hundreds. And while the framework is indebted to the folk-tale tradition, the details and patterns within the framework are highly individual and creatively vital. The stories are those which the old man, Noom-Zor-Noom, has written on a block of black crystal, and which he finds occasions to read as he and the boy Tal and the donkey Millitinkle journey through weird and wonderful lands on the way to Troom. *Tal* comes of a strange lineage, kin to the folk tales of Albania, but also kin to the *Arabian Nights*, the adventures of Munchausen, the trickster japes of Tyll Eulenspiegel and his Turkish cousin, Hodja, and the travel books Cooper read as a boy. But especially it reflects the creative abilities of its author, abilities which place the book on the same shelf with *The Wind in the Willows* and *Alice*.

None can write the history of a book, for it has a prenatal history in the life, mind and spirit of the author and it has an afterlife in the minds of those who read it and remake it into their own experiences. We know, for example, that numberless children in Harlem named their cats Millitinkle and that children in the Neurological Institute in New York put on a puppet show based on *Tal*. We know that hundreds of children's libraries in the land have loaned the book and patched and repaired and rebound it until it is hardly recognizable. Twenty years after its publication it is impossible to buy a copy (I have tried, I know) and it is equally impossible to quiet its reputation. Why some publisher hasn't brought out a new edition with attractive and sympathetic illustrations, I do not understand. I believe that a new generation has the right to make its acquaintance and be caught in its cobweb of enthralling fantasy.

Tricks of Women and Other Albanian Tales was published in 1928, the year before *Tal*. These are not children's stories, but translations of the Albanian folk tales which Dozon and Pedersen had published. Few readers in America could vouch for the accuracy of the tales as translations (certainly not I), but they have the ring of validity as folklore. They are told simply, clearly, with a sure sense of word selection. Many of these are the universal stories of our Western heritage, including a Potiphar's wife and a Cinderella; others are less well known, but all of them have the smooth, well-worn quality that comes of having been told and retold through a thousand years. The barbarism is so muted that it seems right and appropriate and beyond the normal laws of life. But also the fantasy is so interwoven with the barbarism that they form warp and woof.

It is in the quality of their fantasy that *Tal* and *Tricks of Women* are blood brothers. They stir the mind out of its pedestrian rut and send it soaring. If this isn't one of the primary functions of all literature, then I have spent a lifetime misunderstanding literature.

Note: Tal and *Tricks of Women and Other Albanian Tales* were published by William Morrow & Company.

From *The Horn Book* for January, 1950

THE FLAT-HEELED MUSE

By Lloyd Alexander

THE MUSE IN CHARGE OF FANTASY wears good, sensible shoes. No foam-born Aphrodite, she vaguely resembles my old piano teacher, who was keen on metronomes. She does not carry a soothing lyre for inspiration, but is more likely to shake you roughly awake at four in the morning and rattle a sheaf of subtle, sneaky questions under your nose. And you had better answer them. The Muse will stand for no nonsense (that is, non-sense). Her geometries are no more Euclidean than Einstein's, but they are equally rigorous.

I was aware of the problems and disciplines of fantasy, but in a left-handed sort of way; because there is a difference between knowing and doing. Until I met the Muse in Charge of Fantasy personally, I had no hint of what a virago she could be.

Our first encounter was relatively cordial and came in the course of working on a book called *Time Cat*. I suspect I learn more from writing books than readers very likely learn from reading them, and I realize now that *Time Cat* is an example of a fantasy perhaps more realistic than otherwise. Basically, only one fantastic premise moved the story: that Gareth, a black cat, could take the young boy Jason into nine historical periods. The premise included some built-in and plausible hedges. Boy and cat could talk together during their journeys — but only when no one else was around to overhear them; after their return home they could no longer speak to each other, at least not in words. They enjoyed no supernatural protection or privilege; what happened to them, happened — indeed, if Gareth met with a fatal accident, Jason would be forever marooned in the past. They weren't allowed to interfere with or change the course of history, or do anything

Copyright © 1965 by Lloyd Alexander. By permission of the author.

contrary to laws of the physical world and their personal capacities. Jason was a boy and Gareth was a cat.

Within those boundaries, the problem became one of straightforward historical research, with some investigation into how cats were regarded in various eras. Ichigo, the boy emperor in the Japanese adventure, really existed. His wanting to dress kittens in kimonos was valid; there was an extravagant preciousness in the Japanese court of that epoch, and historical records state that such things happened. In other adventures, only slight accommodations made it acceptable for Jason and Gareth to be where they were, doing what they were doing.

The creation of a fantasy that starts from the ground up is something else again. Melancholy men, they say, are the most incisive humorists; by the same token, writers of fantasy must be, within their own frame of work, hardheaded realists. What appears gossamer is, underneath, solid as prestressed concrete. What seems so free in fantasy is often inventiveness of detail rather than complicated substructure. Elaboration — not improvisation.

And the closer a self-contained imaginary world draws to a recognizably real one (Tolkien's Middle Earth instead of Carroll's Wonderland) the more likely its pleasant meadows are to conceal unsuspected deadfalls and man-traps. The writer is wise if he explores it thoroughly and eliminates them. His world must be all of a piece, with careful and consistent handling of background, implements, and characters.

I began discovering the importance of consistency as a result of some of the research for *Time Cat*, originally planned to include an adventure in ancient Wales. Surely everyone cherishes a secret, private world from the days of childhood. Mine was Camelot, and Arthur's Round Table, Malory, and the *Mabinogion*. The Welsh research brought it all back to me. Feeling like a man who has by accident stumbled into an enchanted cavern lost since boyhood, both terrified and awestruck, I realized I would have to explore further. Perhaps I had been waiting to do so all these years, and some kind of moment had come. In any case, I replaced the Welsh episode with an Irish one and later turned all my attention not to the beautiful land of Wales I knew in reality, but an older, darker one.

My first intention was to base a fantasy on some of the tales in the *Mabinogion*, and I started research accordingly. However, I soon found myself delving deeper and deeper into the legends' origins and significance: searching for what exactly I didn't know — to the despair even of the librarians, who must be among the most patient people on earth. A historical-realistic approach did not work. Unlike the Irish and Norse, the Welsh mythology has been irreparably tampered with, like so many pictures, old and new, cut apart and pasted every which way.

Sifting the material, hoping to find whatever I was groping for, I accumulated box after box of file cards covered with notes, names, relationships, and I learned them cold. With great pains I began constructing a kind of family tree or genealogical chart of mythical heroes. (Eventually I found one in a book, already done for me. Not the first book, but the fifteenth!) Nothing suited my purposes.

At that point, the Muse in Charge of Fantasy, seductive in extremely filmy garments, sidled into my work room. "Not making much headway, are you? How would it be," she murmured huskily, "if you invented your own mythology? Isn't that what you *really* want to do?"

She vanished. I was not to see her again in her aspect as temptress, but only as taskmistress. For she was right.

Abandoning all I had collected, I began once more, planning what eventually became *The Book of Three*. My previous labor had not been entirely in vain; it had given me roots, suggestions, possibilities. In addition, I was now free to do as I pleased. Or so I thought.

True enough, the writer of fantasy can start with whatever premises he chooses (actually, the uncomplicated ones work best). In the algebra of fantasy, A times B doesn't have to equal B times A. But, once established, the equation must hold throughout the story. You may set your own ground rules and, in the beginning, decree as many laws as you like — though in practice the fewer departures from the "real" world the better. A not-very-serious breach and the fantasy world explodes just as surely as if a very real hydrogen bomb had been dropped on it. With inconsistency (so usual in the real world), the machinery moving the tale grinds and screeches; the characters cease to be imaginary and become simply unreal. Truth drains out of them. Admittedly, certain questions have to be begged, such as "How did all these people get here in the first place?" But they are like the axioms of geometry, questioned only by metaphysicians.

Once committed to his imaginary kingdom, the writer is not a monarch but a subject. Characters must appear plausible in their own setting, and the writer must go along with their inner logic. Happenings should have logical implications. Details should be tested for consistency. Shall animals speak? If so, do *all* animals speak? If not, then which — and how? Above all, why? Is it essential to the story, or lamely cute? Are there enchantments? How powerful? If an enchanter can perform such-and-such, can he not also do so-and-so? These were a few of the more obvious questions raised by the Muse, now disguised behind steel-rimmed spectacles. Others were less straightforward.

"This person, Prince Gwydion," she said, "I presume, is meant to be a heroic figure. But what I should like to know is this," she added in an irritating, pedantic voice. "How is he different from an ordinary human being?"

I replied that I was prepared to establish that Gwydion, though not invincible, had a somewhat longer life span, greater strength and physical endurance. If he had powers of enchantment, these were to be limited in logical ways. I admitted, too, that he would nonetheless get hungry, thirsty, and tired.

"All very well," she said. "But is that the essential? Is he a human being with only a little more capacity? You must tell me how he is truly and rationally different."

I had begun to sweat. "He — he knows more? Experience?" I choked. "He sees the meaning of things. Wisdom."

"I shall accept that," she said. "See that you keep it in mind."

On another occasion, I had planned to include a mysterious and menacing portent in the shape of a dark cloud. The Muse, an early riser, prodded me awake sometime well before dawn.

"I've been meaning to speak with you about that cloud," she said. "You like it, don't you? You think it's dramatic. But I was wondering if this had occurred to you: you only want a few of your people to see the cloud, is that not correct? Yet you have already established a number of other characters in the vicinity who will see it, too. An event like that? They'll do nothing but talk about it for most of the story. Or," she purred, as she always does before she pounces, "did you have something like closed-circuit television in mind?"

She clumped off in her sensible brogans while I flung myself from bed and ripped up all my work of the night before. The cloud was cut out.

Her subsequent interrogations were no gentler. Perhaps I should have foreseen all her questions and spared myself much revision. In defense, I can only say that I must often put something on paper and test the idea in practice. I did, gradually, grow more aware of pitfalls and learned to distinguish the telltale signs of mare's-nests.

The less fantastic it is, the stronger fantasy becomes. The writer can painfully bark his shins on too many pieces of magical furniture. Enchanted swords, wielded incautiously, cut both ways. But the limits imposed on characters and implements must be more than simply arbitrary. What does not happen should be as valid as what does. In *The Once and Future King*, for example, Merlyn knows what will happen in the future; he knows the consequences of Arthur's encounter with Queen Morgause. Why doesn't he speak out in warning? It is not good enough to say, "Well, that would spoil the story." Merlyn cannot interfere with destiny; but how does T. H. White show this in *specific* detail? By having Merlyn grow backwards through time. Confused in his memories, he cannot recollect whether he has already told Arthur or was going to tell him. No more is needed. The rationale is economical and beautiful, fitting and enriching Merlyn's personality.

Insistence on plausibility and rationality can work for the writer, not against him. In developing his characters, he is obliged to go deeper instead of wider. And, as in all literature, characters are what ultimately count. The writer of fantasy may have a slight edge on the realistic novelist, who must present his characters within the confines of actuality. Fantasy, too, uses homely detail, but at the same time goes right to the core of a character, to extract the essence, the very taste of an individual personality. This may be one of the things that makes good fantasy so convincing. The essence is poetic truth.

The distillation process, unfortunately, is unknown and must be classed as a Great Art or a Major Enchantment. If a recipe existed, it could be reproduced; and it is not reproducible. We can only see the results. Or hear them. Of Kenneth Grahame — and the same applies to all great fantasists — A. A. Milne writes: "When characters have been created as solidly ... they speak ever after in their own voices."

These voices speak directly to us. Like music, poetry, or dreams, fantasy goes straight to the heart of the matter. The experience of a realistic work seldom approaches the experience of fantasy. We may sail on the *Hispaniola* and perform deeds of derring-do. But only in fantasy can we journey through Middle Earth, where the fate of an entire world lies in the hands of a hobbit.

Fantasy presents the world as it should be. But "should be" does not mean that the realms of fantasy are Lands of Cockaigne where roasted chickens fly into mouths effortlessly opened. Sometimes heartbreaking, but never hopeless, the fantasy world as it "should be" is one in which good is ultimately stronger than evil, where courage, justice, love, and mercy actually function. Thus, it may often appear quite different from our own. In the long run, perhaps not. Fantasy does not promise Utopia. But if we listen carefully, it may tell us what we someday may be capable of achieving.

From *The Horn Book* for April, 1965

"OUT OF THE ABUNDANCE"

BIOGRAPHERS of E. Nesbit invariably note the fact that she was well in her forties before she began writing her "magic" books — those which children and adults on both sides of the Atlantic continue to love, and which have touched off the imaginations of such writers as C. S. Lewis, Edward Eager and Dan Wickenden. Yet it is possible that, even had the economic circumstances of her life been different, she would not have been ready any earlier to write *Five Children and It* and *The Enchanted Castle*. Those first forty years were a time of storing up treasure: a childhood full of change, but happy nevertheless; a marriage which challenged all her courage and gallantry but gave her deep love as well; children through whom she knew both intense sorrow and great joy; warm friendships, and companionships with stimulating minds and personalities; years of writing, writing, writing, learning the skills which would be put to their full use when she found the proper vehicle for her talents.

The great fairy tales have with few exceptions (*Alice in Wonderland* is one of them) been written by people in their forties or later: people like Kenneth Grahame, William Henry Hudson and Antoine de Saint Exupéry who did many things besides write; people such as Hans Christian Andersen, George MacDonald (he was a grandfather before he wrote his first fairy tale), James Barrie, Walter de la Mare, Selma Lagerlöf, Ella Young, C. S. Lewis, to name but a few, who wrote many other things before they wrote their fairy tales.

One cannot measure, on first reading, the significance of the great fairy tales. Their very gaiety, high imagination and nonsense belie the years that have gone into their creation. They wear those years of growing so lightly they would seem to be the pleasure (not work) of moments.

C. S. Lewis has spoken of the children's story, particularly the fairy tale, as the "art form" which is right for the things he has wanted to say. Few people have ever expected to gain either prestige or wealth from the writing of children's stories, and it is not surprising that the writer longing for recognition has looked for it as a poet or novelist or playwright, not as a writer for children. It even took many years for the master of the fairy tale, Hans Christian Andersen himself, to discover the "art form" of the children's fairy tale. But into those years went much living and growing and gathering treasure so that when the time came, the mouth could speak "out of the abundance of the heart." R. H. V.

From *The Horn Book* for October, 1958.

VI

PEOPLE AND PLACES

"The pleasant peaceful days. Do you remember..." wrote Beatrix Potter Heelis from war-torn England in 1941. I remember well, and one day in particular.

* * * * *

It was past time to leave and as we went down the path again, the sun burst forth and shed a golden evening over the garden. And I knew that in this one day I had found Mrs. Tiggy-Winkle only to lose her as the hours passed. In her place was a dear friend.

From "A Visit to Mrs. Tiggy-Winkle"
by Elizabeth H. Stevens

Articles

A VISIT TO MRS. TIGGY-WINKLE *by Elizabeth H. Stevens*

A VISIT WITH PATRICIA LYNCH *by Hilda van Stockum*

WALTER DE LA MARE *by Pamela Bianco*

PERRIN'S WALK *by Harry Behn*

ILLUSTRATING "THE WIND IN THE WILLOWS"
by Ernest H. Shepard

THE RIVER SEVERN AGAIN *by Arthur S. Gregor*

OF A PEACOCK AND A WILD GOOSE *by Margery Evernden*

A PRESENT FOR ALICE *by Margaret Reardon*

A VISIT TO MRS. TIGGY-WINKLE
By Elizabeth H. Stevens

"THE pleasant peaceful days. Do you remember . . ." wrote Beatrix Potter Heelis from war-torn England in 1941. I remember well, and one day in particular. It was in 1930 that I first met Mrs. Heelis. My aunt and I were staying in the English Lake country near the little hamlet of Sawrey. Auntie had met and made friends with Mrs. Heelis on a previous visit, and now that she was again in the neighbourhood the usual courtesies were exchanged. Upon one such occasion arrangements were made for an afternoon's expedition into the remote countryside to the west of Sawrey. Mrs. Heelis, who knew every inch of this area, was to be our guide. Auntie would provide the picnic, and I, the young niece, would drive the car.

Auntie and I set forth just after lunch to fetch our courier at her house, Castle Cottage. We left our car in a lane on the edge of Sawrey, though to be sure, Sawrey is so small it is all edge. We walked up a path bordered by a low box hedge and were transported into the world of Tom Kitten. Here was the very garden into which he and his sisters, dressed in their best, had been sent with instructions to "walk on your hind legs" and "keep your frocks clean." The low hedge enclosed flowers of every color and variety. In this yard there was no grass. It was all flower beds intersected by a few paths. Stock, hollyhocks, snapdragons, roses and violas, forget-me-nots and mignonette, all blooming simultaneously and all vividly bright, as flowers in that damp climate usually are. There is no need to plan an English garden for a succession of bloom. Everything blooms at once and stays blooming, it would seem, all summer. The effect was enchanting.

We neared a long low house or cottage with an inviting front door. I had Tom so much on my mind that I half expected to be greeted by an "affronted" Tabitha Twitchit welcoming us to a teaparty whose "dignity and repose" were destined to be disturbed by "extraordinary noises overhead." But no one at all appeared at the door and, turning to locate a curious clopping noise coming from the end of the house, we beheld someone who, in truth, seemed to be not Tabitha but Mrs. Tiggy-Winkle. The resemblance was startling even though the garb of Mrs. Heelis, for she it was, and Tiggy differed. In place of a pink-and-white striped dress and mob cap, she wore voluminous grisly homespun. On her head was a wide hat of rusty black, straw I believe, in deference to the so-called summer weather. I found myself wanting to look underneath this hat to see if the "little person had prickles." On her feet were the cloppiting clogs, an excellent idea in the Lake Country whose earth varies from damp to squishy. Her shape was round and low and a little bent, and peering from under the hat were the brightest eyes I have ever seen, at once shy and keen, earthy and humorous. We stepped to meet our hostess and for a moment it was all I could do not to greet her with the affection and demonstration due Mrs. Tiggy. I had come expecting to be impressed with a famous author and here I was feeling I had found that writer's own creation. But when I withdrew my image and saw her as she really was, I faced a person quite as appealing as any character in her books.

My sudden and unexpected feelings of warmth made me as shy as she. Auntie, however, never at a loss, kept the conversation rolling and without entering the house we went back to the car and got down to the business of the day.

It occurred to no one that the weather was inclement for a tour or a picnic tea. The skies were, as usual, rainy or at least misty. The cold was, as usual, penetrating, and the dampness was, as usual, all pervading. But after a while cold damp feet and cold damp hands and cold damp clothes coming out of a cold damp cupboard become the order of the day, enhancing the cozy comfort of a pot of tea, a glass of sherry, and a fire in the grate.

No time to think of such comforts now. Away we lurched over miles of hill and dale in what must be the most unfrequented parts of the Lake District. We bumped down muddy lanes to dead ends, backed up again, climbed rocky hills and stopped every few miles while our guide chatted with farmers about their sheep. Raising and perfecting the Hardwick strain was one of her greatest interests.

In all ways she seemed a true country woman. As we drove along, our conversation was of farmers, old customs, country fairs and sheep. We also heard homely bits about farmers' wives, babies, and marriageable daughters. In every way she seemed indigenous, and it was hard to remember that she had been raised a daughter of well-to-do parents in far-away London.

Until tea time not one word was spoken of her books, and we felt that was the way she wanted it.

She told us that her homespun clothing was made from the wool of her own sheep and woven by a neighbor. By now we were wishing we, too, were dressed in something as stout and as warm.

The countryside looked exactly as pictured in *Jemima Puddle-Duck:* bare hills, a cluster of trees here and there, stone walls, foxgloves, and mist.

To reach Buttermere which, despite its homey name, is a bleak and lonely lake, we drove over the Honister Pass. No doubt this is now a paved road but then it was a narrow tortuous way surfaced with loose gravel, pebbles, and rocks. On one side of the road rose a steep hill, and on the other the land dropped off to a valley hundreds of feet below. We climbed and slipped and climbed again over the dreadful stones and were just reaching the summit when a bus mounted the crest and careened down toward us. A scream of brakes was followed by a tense silence while each driver estimated the situation. Reversing for miles was impossible, so there was nothing left to do but cautiously work our way past each other, with never an inch to spare. We hugged the hillside and expected each moment to be scraped by the bus or to hear it crash over the ledge. I trust I looked more intrepid than I felt. There was never a word of protest from my companions, but I believe they knew this was a tight spot, for ten years later Mrs. Heelis wrote to ask if I remembered wriggling a large car past a bus on a narrow pass near Buttermere. She added that it was my aunt's faith in my skill as a chauffeuse which emboldened her to keep her seat.

After we had come through this experience alive and unharmed, it seemed time to pause and refresh ourselves. Under a nearby tree, backed to a stone wall with a view of Buttermere at our feet, we found ourselves somewhat protected from the drizzle. We unpacked Auntie's picnic basket. Thank God for England's primus. We may lead her in some mechanical marvels but we have no portable stove to compete with this. Soon the kettle was boiling, the teapot scalded and the tea brewed. To keep the pot properly warm it was covered with a quilted cozy made of Liberty silk. We sat on raincoats and sliced bread with a Georgian silver knife, cutting it very thin, spreading it with fresh butter and wild strawberry jam. The scene was delectable to my American eyes — a perfect example of the rites of the British Empire being preserved at all times and in all circumstances. I felt the need of capturing this moment and screwed up my nerve to ask rather casually if anyone thought it would be a good idea for me to take a picture. I did not have to be told that Mrs. H. was camera shy, and I dreaded the answer. Perhaps it was my hesitancy that made her rise to the occasion and enthusiastically endorse the proposal. I snapped Auntie, Mrs. Heelis and the teapot between.

When she saw the picture later she was much amused and suggested that there should have been a third person around the caldron! But I did not think either of them looked like a witch.

Tea broke down whatever social barriers remained, and on our way home conversation was entirely spontaneous.

We stopped at Newlands, the setting for *Mrs. Tiggy-Winkle*, and walked up the path taken by Lucy "until Littletown was right away down below" and we could have "dropped a pebble down the chimney."

This visit made it possible for us to talk about the nursery books, though only casually to be sure, for they belonged to the past and Mrs. Heelis really wanted them kept there. That we could talk about them at all was perhaps because she felt that we had now identified her with a happy life of sheep raising and marriage and could look into her past without trying to divorce her in our minds from the present, where she quite definitely wanted to stay.

Was it for this same reason that she displayed that diffidence for which she was famed? Indeed she was considered a recluse by the summer residents in that region. I believe she adopted this role for self-protection, fearing that if she were too accessible literary scalp hunters would force her from the part in life she most wanted to play, respected leader in the world of sheep and fell.

Years later I realized that the books were products of unhappy years and I understood still more why she did not want them to be the center around which her life revolved.

The only reference she ever made to us implying that the years before her marriage had been bleak was a comment made to Auntie whom she met one day on a street in Ambleside. To Auntie's remark that she was sorry to hear that her mother, Mrs. Potter, had been unwell, Mrs. Heelis replied, "Yes, she has been quite ill — a disagreeable old woman."

She told us that she had bought the original Peter Rabbit in Covent Garden and brought him home to her parents' Victorian household tucked away in a paper bag. He was kept in her schoolroom retreat and eventually died from eating too many peppermint candies.

She deplored having become sympathetic to rabbits when, each morning, she beheld the destruction in her garden.

After more miles of peregrinations, we returned to Castle Cottage and were invited in to warm ourselves before returning to our hotel. On entering the front door we came directly into a rather long low room. A coal fire burned in a grate at one end and almost the entire room was taken up with an oval table. To move about you had to squeeze around it. There was another similar room forming the front of the house and from this a small stone passage led to butteries or larders or whatever such dank little rooms are called.

But the main room was cheery and welcoming. A few lovely old pieces of furniture were wedged in about the table and when we sat down to chat it was on chairs drawn up to the table.

A glass of sherry helped re-establish our circulation and as it darkened outside it seemed brighter and brighter within.

Mr. Heelis, the Ambleside lawyer with whom Mrs. H. had eloped at an age usually considered advanced for that procedure, greeted us with true country courtesy. Mutual respect and affection were apparent in their attitude each to the other.

While Auntie and Mr. Heelis sat at one side of the table discussing topics of local interest, Mrs. H. went to a cupboard and took out a little package covered with tissue. By the firelight she laid back the paper with elaborate and loving care and revealed a damask napkin, yellowed with age. In the corner was embroidered a "C" with a crest above. I believe it was one of her most treasured possessions, and one which I understand has not been located since her death. It is supposed this was a napkin belonging to Charles Edward Stuart. People in this region think either that it was left when he came through on his triumphant drive southward in 1745, or that it was forgotten by a distraught little band beating a retreat north, soon afterward, destined for Culloden and defeat. Prince Charlie was alive to Mrs. Heelis as he is to all Scots in the Highlands today. What is the magic of personality that it can survive two hundred years, undimmed and glowing?

"One more thing," whispered Mrs. H. as she returned this package to the dresser and, producing a folder, laid it on our side of the table. In it were the original paintings for *Squirrel Nutkin*. The precision and charm of these exquisitely delicate water colors were a revelation. I had long known and loved each little picture in my own copy at home but no plate, even in the early editions, does justice to the original. The picture of the squirrels paddling out in single file to Owl Island, every bushy tail spread out for a sail, was worth a trip to the Lakes to see.

In Hill Top Farm, just across from Castle Cottage, the original illustrations of almost all the books are now displayed. This farmhouse itself was Mrs. Heelis' first Lakeland home and is the setting for *Tom Kitten, Roly-Poly Pudding* and *Samuel Whiskers*. The kitchen and stair landing evoke memories to everyone familiar with the books, just as the countryside about is hauntingly nostalgic to all who have absorbed much of it in extreme youth, when impressions are vivid.

It was past time to leave and as we went down the path again, the sun burst forth and shed a golden evening over the garden. And I knew that in this one day I had found Mrs. Tiggy-Winkle only to lose her as the hours passed. In her place was a dear friend.

From *The Horn Book* for April, 1958

A VISIT WITH PATRICIA LYNCH

By Hilda van Stockum

FROM her books we already knew Patricia Lynch (or Mrs. R. M. Fox, as she is called in private life) as a sensitive person with quiet humor and poetic imagination. Meeting her confirmed and amplified this impression. There is an intensely joyous atmosphere in the house of Mr. and Mrs. Fox. You reach it by bus from Nelson's Pillar through the oldest, northern part of Dublin in the direction of Clontarf, where Brian Boru waged his famous battle. Between Patricia's house and Clontarf lies the famous Thor's Wood, so named by the Danes. There also is the "crow wood" which appears in her book *Long Ears*.

The Foxes' house is small and modern and has a garden full of flowers and vegetables. The house itself is divided neatly into two studies — Patricia's and R. M.'s. (R. M. has about nine books to his credit; Patricia, double that number.) Patricia's study is the more severe and looks more like work! Visitors are received in R. M.'s, which has a businesslike table, comfortable chairs, a sofa and a fire.

One immediately gets the impression that here are two very busy and very happy people who live in perfect companionship and retain a lively interest in each other's work. There is an innocent merriment, a lighthearted goodness about them which makes one feel that one has strayed into a little paradise hidden away behind the boulders and storms of our turbulent and uncertain age. There is also a slightly fairy quality about the Foxes, so that each time I visit them I am surprised that they are still there, that the house has not suddenly vanished into thin air, taking them away to some unreachable "Tir-na-nog."

Yet they are both very down-to-earth people, full of common sense. I get the impression that Patricia is the more active and disciplined. There is a look on Mr. Fox's face that reminds me of a schoolboy who likes to play hookey occasionally. He tells me that it is Patricia who does most of the gardening. His version is that Patricia slugs away in the garden, comes in when she is exhausted and sits down and writes a book to rest herself.

He recounted to me his experience on one of the few occasions when he took the spade in hand. He was writing a book on the Irish rebellion and having great trouble with the nib of his fountain pen. It wouldn't write. In disgust he threw it down and went into the garden to dig. The first thing he dug up was a gold nib. It lay gleaming on the black earth. He picked it up and tried it on his pen. It was a perfect fit. He finished the book with it. All of which confirms what I said about the fairy quality of the place. But, as Mr. Fox says, he needs a *literary* motive to send him into the garden! Patricia, on the contrary, is never "literary." He testifies to the fact that she is an excellent cook. She can make rabbit taste like chicken and she is especially good at homemade wines — elderberry and black currant, and rhubarb wine which tastes like champagne.

She loves birds and has a pet robin that sings to her. Mr. Fox says that she holds conversations with it and she herself admits that the robin gives her ideas for stories. But, like Robert Louis Stevenson, she gets most of her ideas from dreams. She can dream serially and continue the story night after night. *The Grey Goose of Kilnevin* was a dream and she has kept the dream-like cadences in her prose, so that the reader feels that he is dreaming the story himself! It was serialized in the *Irish Press* and she continued it as she dreamt it. Once when a holiday necessitated some advance copy, the paper sent her a cryptic telegram asking for "more goose, please!"

The Turf-cutter's Donkey was first published as a serial in the *Irish Press* under the title *The Turf-cutter's Children*. A friend of Patricia's had a servant who used to read it as straight reporting and once when the turf-cutter's children were in trouble the servant came running to her mistress, saying,

"You know, ma'am, there's terrible things happening in the country and nobody seems to be doing anything about them!"

Soon after *The King of the Tinkers* came out, Patricia was looking at a display of the book at a shop in O'Connell Street. Two farmers' wives came along and she overheard the following conversation:

"I'm going to get a book for the boy."

"Well, there you are, buy that."

"Oh no, that's about the tinkers. I'll not have anything about tinkers in *my* home."

"Arra, don't be foolish! That book shows them up for what they are and sure isn't it time the truth was told about them? Come on in now and you'll have no more trouble with that boy."

It is quite true that children love Patricia's stories. My own children are very fond of them and of Patricia. Once when I exclaimed that I had more good friends than I deserved, Elisabeth, aged seven, said, "Well, give me one of them then." "Which one do you want?" said I. "Patricia Lynch!" she answered promptly.

At the first Irish Book Fair in Dublin Patricia autographed numbers of her books (some worn so ragged that the children were ashamed to show them); and she talked about imagination in children's literature. The next day a leader came out in the *Irish Times* saying that imagination was no longer much in demand; that the present generation wanted facts and seemed much too practical to read fairy stories. There was an instantaneous protest from the public. Letters came pouring in to the editor to tell him how wrong he was — letters often written by the children themselves and sometimes by the parents, testifying to the popularity of Patricia's books and to the number of times they had been read.

Grownups from as far away as Canada write to thank her for her stories of Ireland. In 1950 she received a certificate of service to literature from the Eugene Field Society. Her *Dark Sailor of Youghal* was chosen as one of twenty children's books for the UNESCO International Traveling Exhibition; and Cardinal Hayes' Committee of Literature in New York selected *The Grey Goose of Kilnevin* as one of the hundred best books of the year for young and old Catholics.

Patricia comes from Cork, which gave many famous names

to literature — Sean O'Faolain, Lennox Robinson, Daniel Corkery, T. C. Murray, Frank O'Connor. They have in the main a realistic approach while Patricia combines her realism with a strong element of the fantastic, thereby continuing an ancient vein in Irish writing. She is as patriotic as the other writers; she used to bring food and books to the Irish rebels who were imprisoned after the Easter rising. And she is as concerned as anyone for the future of Ireland, but she feels that realism need not be negative, that the good is more real than the evil and that there is plenty of it to write about. She likes to put down anything that occurs to her regardless of "whether the children will understand it." "Let them have books they can grow into," she pleads.

In *A Storyteller's Childhood* she has written about her own early youth and her sojourn with an Irish Shanaghy. She began to write poems when she was nine. Her first was about a dearly beloved cat who had been taken away to Egypt where her father lived. (He edited a paper in Cairo.) When the cat died she wrote the poem to relieve her feelings. She entered literary competitions in several boys' papers which she read. Her earliest successes were with poems and then she won a first prize of three guineas for the story of a daffodil. Other competitors had talked *about* the daffodil, but Patricia wrote from the point of view of the plant itself. She described the feelings of the bulb when it went into the soil and its delight when pushing its green tips above the earth. It was a foreshadowing of a later success which is due mainly, I think, to her imaginative participation in the life of all created things.

I like to think of the child Patricia. When looking at the intensely alive, twinkling brown eyes in her reserved and rather quiet face I picture her as a small, slight child in whom a natural dignity and reluctance to show her feelings hid a passionate nature. There is little of the critic in Patricia; one still feels the child — tasting, experiencing, accepting life rather than judging it.

When she was only sixteen she became a free-lance journalist and interviewed many interesting people. (She remembers especially visiting E. Nesbit.) In between interviews she wrote her first children's story, *The Cobbler's Apprentice*.

For this she received the silver medal at the Tailtain Festival in Dublin. This was an ancient Irish festival in honor of the warrior queen Tailta who won a battle from a neighboring chieftain and bargained for as much land as her cloak would cover. Unfastening her Tara brooch she spread the cloak on the ground and it magically expanded until there was space enough on which to build a town. It was called Tailtown and festivals were held there with prizes for sports and poetry. The custom was revived in Dublin in 1924 but has since been dropped again.

The success of *The Cobbler's Apprentice* led to Patricia's next book, for the children of the editor of the *Irish Press* were so fond of it that he selected her to write the youth's serial in his paper.

Her method of writing is amazing in its simplicity. She sits down and writes and whatever she writes is good. It is as if she were made of literature and merely had to cut off chunks of it! Her youth in the country, among the beauties of Ireland — its uncertain, dreamy weather, the kindness of its peasants, the haunting tragedy of its history and folklore — has permeated her stories. To read them is to be, yourself, a child there. And if you know Irish children, with their obstinate adherence to little, well-known facts, coupled with an expectation of unlimited magic, you realize that the same qualities are to be found in her books. She has immensely enriched children's literature and has given it a unique contribution. It seems right and fitting that free Eire should have in her an apostle to bring the love of Ireland into countless foreign homes. And her gentle philosophy, her awareness of the unseen, her stressing of simple ideals should be good medicine for children brought up in countries less fortunate than the Ireland of Patricia Lynch.

From *The Horn Book* for October, 1953

WALTER DE LA MARE

By Pamela Bianco

WHEN, in February 1919, I sailed from England to America with my father, a friend gave me as a farewell gift the collected poems of Walter de la Mare, in two volumes, with "For Pamela, in lieu of rosemary" written upon the flyleaf of volume one. No inscription could have been more appropriate, for on page 179 of volume one was a poem, four lines of which have ever since served as a return ticket to my childhood, so vividly do they recall a particular period of it. They are:

> An apple, a child, dust,
> When falls the evening rain,
> Wild brier's spicèd leaves,
> Breathe memories again.[*]

I have only to read those four lines, and I am twelve years old again and living in San Remo, where wild brier roses bordered the dusty roads above the sea. It was the spring of 1919. One day I received a letter from my father who was then in London arranging an exhibition of my drawings which was to be held at the Leicester Galleries in May. He wrote:

"I have just sent Mummie a beautiful book of poetry entitled *Peacock Pie* by a great English poet called Walter de la Mare. His verses are very very beautiful. Mr. Heinemann very much wants him to write some verses to go with your drawings of children so as to make up together a fine book. Unfortunately Mr. de la Mare is at present away from London and has not seen any of your drawings, but he'll probably be back in May, and after he has seen your work I feel hopeful that he may be willing to write something. He wrote me a very nice letter the other day, regretting that the drawings cannot be sent to him (you see they are being mounted for the exhibition). Would you like to read one of his poems?"

---

[*] From *Collected Poems 1901-1918* by Walter de la Mare. Copyright, 1920, by Henry Holt and Company.

There followed, in my father's handwriting "The Truants," and when I read it I lost my heart to Walter de la Mare.

In August 1919 my father came to San Remo, bringing with him the carbon copy of a set of miraculous poems which Walter de la Mare had just written. I felt very proud when he told me that William Heinemann was going to publish them that winter, together with some of my drawings, in a book to be entitled *Flora*.

My father also brought with him from London *The Songs of Childhood* and, as a gift to me from Walter de la Mare, *The Three Mulla-Mulgars*. I thought this book was the most beautiful one that I had ever read.

During the remainder of that summer we lived under the spell of Walter de la Mare's poetry and could think and talk of little else. Every day my father would read aloud to us from *Peacock Pie* or from *The Songs of Childhood*, for wherever we went we always took one or the other volume with us. The custom of reading Walter de la Mare's poetry aloud, begun by my father during that memorable summer, was to continue for many years.

In November 1919 my parents, my brother Cecco, and I were going to England to live and I looked forward eagerly to meeting Walter de la Mare. Before leaving Italy I received a letter from the poet, written on grey paper in a delicately lovely and somewhat hieroglyphic handwriting. I treasured that letter and I have kept it so very carefully during these long past years that it still looks as if it had been written only a few days ago.

We arrived in London on a November evening, and the next morning my father went to Anerley to pay his respects to Walter de la Mare. He was accompanied by Cecco. They returned with a tea and supper invitation from the poet and his wife, for the following Sunday.

When Sunday afternoon came and the four of us were on our way to Anerley at last, I began, all of a sudden, to feel dreadfully shy. We left from a London station with a high glass ceiling. On one of the station walls was a large red and grey advertisement which one could not help noticing, try as one might. It bore a drawing of an armoured knight, and beside him, written in enormous letters, was the following poem:

> When knights were bold,
> They all wore armour.
> When nights are cold,
> Wear Swann's pyjama.

I thought it was dreadful to have to read such a poem while on my way to meet Walter de la Mare. If poetry were to be read at all on such an occasion, I reasoned, surely only the very best should be permitted. Nevertheless, there the poem was; and eventually the reading of it took its place in my mind as one of the rituals connected with our trips to and from the poet's home.

When we stepped out of the station in Anerley, snow was beginning to fall. I remember that we walked along brick pavements and that many of the gardens we passed had hedges with little bright red berries. Presently we came to 14 Thornsett Road, the house in which Walter de la Mare lived. At our knock the front door opened immediately; and there to welcome us, in the gathering dusk, were the poet and his wife, their son Dick, and their beautiful dark-eyed daughter, Florence. Although Dick and Florence were only a few years older than I, they both seemed grown up to me. Mrs. de la Mare was a lovely person, of very great charm and warmth.

After removing our wraps, we went into the drawing room where a cheerful log fire was blazing. Still feeling shy, I sat upon a cushion at one side of the fireplace and gazed upward at Walter de la Mare. He looked exactly as I thought a poet should, and both in appearance and in manner lived entirely up to my dreams. He was dressed that day in a navy blue suit; his eyes and hair were dark brown, he had a beautiful classic face which bore an expression of great nobility, and his approach was gentle and warm-hearted.

To my surprise, the first thing Walter de la Mare did, after we all were seated, was to pass a yellow cigarette tin to my parents, asking them whether they cared for "gaspers"; and upon their each taking one, he did the same and proceeded to smoke it, exactly as any other man might.

I turned from Walter de la Mare to gaze instead at what I thought was a brown velvet cushion in one of the armchairs. Suddenly it moved, and to my amazement I discovered that it wasn't a cushion after all, but a rabbit — one of the most enormous rabbits I had ever seen. Mrs. de la Mare told us that his name was Rupert. She then related how upon one occasion Rupert had been brought to death's door by a severe chill. All hope for his recovery had long been abandoned, when somebody thought of wrapping him in one of the poet's woolen undershirts and placing him in a warm oven. This was done. After a short sleep Rupert awoke — miraculously cured.

Presently Jenny and Colin, the two younger de la Mare children, returned from a coasting expedition, and we all had tea. Fifteen-year-old Jenny had a charming personality and was lovely to look at. After tea, Florence brought forth her album and asked me if I would draw a flipmouse in it, a flipmouse being a magic creature of her own invention, namely, a mouse with wings. Resting the album on the piano top, I drew upon one of its pages a flipmouse stealing fruit from an épergne in which he was seated. Then Cecco and I went into the dining room to help Jenny and Colin lay the supper table.

During supper the four of us sat together at a table beside the bay window, while the grownups sat at a long table in the middle of the room. Occasionally we would join in the grownup conversation; and upon Jenny's suddenly challenging a statement made by her father, the poet turned to her and said, "Not only am I old enough to be your father — I am also old enough to be *my own* father, so I ought to know what I am talking about!"

That night, as we returned home tired and happy, my mother told us how she had long been secretly troubled because Walter de la Mare was named Walter — a name she had never particularly cared for — and what a relief it had been to her to discover that the poet's wife always addressed him as "Jack" instead.

During the next fifteen months, several unforgettable evenings were spent with the de la Mares in Anerley. Then America became our home, and a great many years were to go by before I was to see the poet again. Every once in a while we would write to one another. Walter de la Mare's letters were gem-like in content.

Late in 1951 I wrote a letter to Walter de la Mare, telling him that I was going to Bad Godesberg in the spring to stay with Cecco and that on my way to Germany I would stop in England to pay him a visit.

By return post I received a letter from the poet in which he expressed the hope that I might be in England in April because that was the month in which he was born.

It was an April evening when I stepped ashore in England and a day or so later, just before his seventy-ninth birthday, I had tea once more with Walter de la Mare. When I saw him again my first feeling was one of amazement at how young he was — it seemed as if the long years had never been.

After tea we spoke of old times and of three dear people, no longer upon this earth, who had been present during those long ago Sunday evenings in Anerley.

In Walter de la Mare's beautiful home in Twickenham there reigned a feeling of peace and timelessness. So much so that, after I had taken leave of him with a promise to return if possible on my way back to America, it was a great shock to find myself back in the everyday world again.

I went to Germany and thence to Italy. In Florence I began two letters to Walter de la Mare, which were never finished. I then wrote and finished a third letter, telling him how sorry I was that due to a change in sailing plans I would not be able to stop in England on my way home after all, as I had so looked forward to doing. The poet wrote me a sad and very beautiful letter in reply.

That was the last letter I was to receive from Walter de la Mare. Some months after I returned home there came a note from a friend of his, saying that the poet had not been well, and that he had reluctantly agreed not to write any letters although he still read them. This news greatly saddened me and from that day on, fearing that my letters might tire the poet, I wrote only short messages to him.

The death of Walter de la Mare, in June 1956, came as a sorrowful shock, for, although I knew that he had been ill for a very long time, somehow, in the back of my mind, there existed the thought that when I next returned to England he would still be there.

I cherish the memory of Walter de la Mare. I realize that my life has been infinitely richer because of him, and I consider it a blessing and a privilege to have been one of his friends.

I had so hoped that I might see him again, but it was not possible. Instead I am now one of the countless who mourn this very great poet — and I wish that the past might return.

From *The Horn Book* for June, 1957

PERRIN'S WALK

By Harry Behn

"Last spring I spent one whole beautiful day with Eleanor Farjeon and that evening wrote this impression of the timelessness that glows about her, and about her cottage at the end of Perrin's Walk, Hampstead. Just beyond her garden the city vanishes and one expects to see Perrin himself go by out to his pasture."

For Eleanor Farjeon

This way the shepherd goes, past cottages
That still are there, past tumbled triumphal arches
Of roses over gateways, trudging slowly
Mildly by to his flock in the morning early,
Pausing now to consider a leafy bed
Of ripe and ruddy fruit among the straw.
Sampling a berry as an Olympian
Tasting ambrosia, he finds it good.

Flicking away its small green star, he marvels
On so much sweetness, marvels on difference
Which now he weighs against a purple grape
Crushed on his tongue, finding it also good
But somber in its savor, dark and holy
Blood of an ancient god in a gray old vine.

And Perrin nods to an acquaintance winging
Out of the woods into an orchard tree
To sing, and he whistles his own shepherd's trill,
Catching in reply a scattering
Of snowy petals about him as a child
Out of the apple boughs drops light as a mayfly,
Dancing away in sunlight into the air.
And he remembers her as he had known her

Ages ago when she was mossy-old
And shaggy-wise, complete and sound and round
As an oak's acorn, a cool mysterious tree
Shading the earth within her. And he marvels
On innocence and ripeness, on the fullness
Of difference and sameness in one seed.

This way the shepherd goes, beneath a weaving
Breath of wind as past the sun a cloud
Slides trailing a shadow swiftly over woods,
Over an orchard and a barley field,
Over a pool flashing an instant white,
Tinting the white fleeces an instant blue.
And he marvels on the wind that is never still
In leaves or grass, in sky or humming bells.

Trudging mildly by in the morning early,
Sound and round as earth itself, he marvels
On one day's variable wonder, aware
Of the infinite around him, finding it good —
Sun, earth and music stirring to the strange
And shadowy, immortal touch of change.

From *The Horn Book* for April 1962

Revised March, 1968

ILLUSTRATING "THE WIND IN THE WILLOWS"

By Ernest H. Shepard

"THERE are certain books that should never be illustrated" is true in many senses, and I had felt that *The Wind in the Willows* was one of these. Perhaps if it had not already been done, I should not have given way to the desire to do it myself, but it so happened that when the opportunity was offered me, I seized upon it gladly.

The characters that Kenneth Grahame chose for his story — the little animals from the woods, the fields, and the waters of England — and which he portrayed with such sympathy and understanding showed, to me, how clearly he had seen into the mind of a child. Indeed, they had grown from the letters and stories he used to write from time to time to amuse his own child.

Mother Earth has a lot to offer to those who try to understand her and to know the ways of the little people who live, who burrow, who scratch, and store, and who climb and swim; whose short lives are spent in the hunt for a livelihood, be it worms or beetles, nuts or fish. Like us human folk they are forever busy — Mole, the field worker, the digger; Rat, the perfect waterman, wise about currents, eddies and what not; Badger, big and stout, uncouth but oh! how dependable, a champion of the smaller folk; and Toad, the impossible and lovable, never out of a scrape and never ceasing to boast. These are not caricatures, they are the real thing, brought to life by a man who loved them and all that they stand for, and it was he who told me where they lived and where to find them.

Kenneth Grahame was an old man when I went to see him. Not sure about this new illustrator of his book, he listened patiently while I told him what I hoped to do. Then he said, "I love these little people, be kind to them." Just that; but sitting forward in his chair, resting upon the arms, his fine handsome head turned aside, looking like some ancient Viking, warming, he told me of the river near by, of the meadows where Mole broke ground that spring morning, of the banks where Rat had his house, of the pools where Otter hid, and of Wild Wood way up on the hill above the river, a fearsome place but for the sanctuary of Badger's home and of Toad Hall. He would like, he said, to go with me to show me the river bank that he knew so well, ". . . but now I cannot walk so far and you must find your way alone."

So I left him and, guided by his instructions, I spent a happy autumn afternoon with my sketch book. It was easy to imagine it all, sitting by the river bank or following the wake of little bubbles that told me that Rat was not far away. Across the water lay the flat meadows and somewhere there I knew that Mole was, even now, making ready his bed for the winter, to wait for the first breath of spring — and again beyond, on the rising ground, the great expanse of Wild Wood with Badger laying in his winter stores. Toad, I imagined, would be snoring in post-prandial ease in his armchair away down stream at Toad Hall. I poked and pried along the river bank to find where was Rat's boat house, and where Mole had crossed the water to join him, and, as I listened to the river noises, the little plops and ripples that mean so much to the small people, I could almost fancy that I could see a tiny boat pulled up among the reeds.

Dusk was settling, down on the water, with a rising mist, but, above, the late sun was shining on the wood — a faint afterglow of autumn glory, when I turned homewards, treading carefully just in case something was underfoot.

I was to meet Kenneth Grahame once again. I went to his home and was able to show him some of the results of my work. Though critical, he seemed pleased and, chuckling, said, "I'm glad you've made them real." We seemed to share a secret pleasure in knowing that the pictures were of the river spots where the little people lived.

This is the story that I can tell of how it came about that I was to play my part in helping to bring *The Wind in the Willows* a little nearer to the reader. If I had not met Kenneth

Grahame I should never have had the temerity to embark on the work, but he gave me encouragement that no one else could have given me, and I wish that he could have lived to see the finished work, whatever his verdict would have been.

One more word — way down the river, on the hill beyond Marlow, among the lovely woods, is the home where the bells of Marlow Church come pealing across the valley, and where, on a winter's night, strange little footprints might be seen on the snow — funny little hoofprints meandering, perhaps unsteadily. Could it be Bertie and his friends, I wonder.

From *The Horn Book* for April, 1954

THE RIVER SEVERN AGAIN
By Arthur S. Gregor

> *In order to know what we have come from and to what we tend. . . . From Darwin's 1837 notebook.*

I CROSSED THE WELSH BRIDGE and walked along the River Severn toward the center of the town of Shrewsbury. I had just come down from The Mount, the house in which Charles Robert Darwin had been born, following the road along which he had so often run on his way to school.

The house in which he lived until his twenty-second year, when he went off on his journey around the world, stands on the top of a gentle hill overlooking the river and the town. A formidable, unimaginative red-brick building three stories high, it is surrounded by formal lawns, gardens, and old trees. (The little tulip tree that Darwin brought back from his *Beagle* voyage has done very well; its sturdy branches rise above the chimney pots on the roof.)

The high-ceilinged rooms within the house are stiff and impersonal as though intended to impress his physician father's patients rather than insure the comfort of his family. It must have been extremely difficult to keep such a house warm during the long damp midland winter, and I could understand the elation of Charles and the other children on those rare occasions when their father permitted them a fire in their rooms. How different The Mount is from the friendly, unpretentious house at Down in which Charles Darwin raised his own family, a home in which everything was accessible to small children.

Dr. Darwin, however, could not have chosen a better site for his home. From an upper floor I could see the River Severn, lined with thick bushes, snaking back and forth through the green-timbered Shropshire hills; the town below in the center of the saucer-shaped valley; and, rising clearly above the housetops, the spires of the building where Charles Darwin once so reluctantly had gone to school.

I had come up from London on unfinished business. There were questions about the life of Charles Darwin whose answers eluded me, questions about the influences that had helped to mold him. Perhaps I would find a clue here in Shrewsbury. At all events I would look upon what he had seen through a small boy's eyes long ago. I walked slowly into town along the bank of the Severn, taking in the unexpected sunshine. Young people were picnicking on the shore and small boys were boating in the river. It was a fine warm spring afternoon after weeks of cold and rain.

Near the railroad station I took the street to the right and came to a large courtyard behind which loomed a massive blackened old Tudor building, formerly the Shrewsbury Grammar School, now the Shrewsbury Public Library. I glanced at a bearded figure seated on a high pedestal and entered through an arched portal that led into an inner court. Toward the end of the last century the school had moved out of town and the library had come to take its place, but the building has remained very much as it was during Darwin's student days.

I climbed the stairway to a long high-beamed gabled room lined with dark varnished wooden panels into which generations of Shrewsbury Grammar School boys, as far back as the early sixteenth century, had carved their initials. I looked out of the west window to the town below and the surrounding countryside. This had been Darwin's school from the ages of nine to sixteen. He must have often sat here and looked out of this window, his eye caught by the sight of the familiar outline of the red-brick house rising out of the trees across the Severn.

Severe treatment, proclaimed the celebrated headmaster Dr. Samuel Butler, builds character. And Dr. Butler was going to build character whether the boys liked it or not. No nonsense about fancy foods; only spoiled them! Skimmed milk and dried toast for breakfast! Milk, bread, cheese, and water or small beer for supper! Boys who persisted in feeling hungry after such repasts could always daydream about the roast goose that had appeared at table at Michaelmas and the pork pie at Christmas. Then there was always tea, coffee, and buttercakes for those who could afford to purchase these delicacies out of their allowance. Although Dr. Butler felt the practice softened up his boys, he graciously extended to anxious parents the privilege of sending baskets of prepared meats to supplement the daily menu.

The school food was so bad that at one time the entire school rebelled. At a prearranged signal the boys rose from the table without touching a morsel and departed. When Dr. Butler attempted to punish the ringleaders, all the students went on strike and returned only after their parents had intervened.

There were other "extras" at Shrewsbury besides the tea, coffee, and buttercakes. The mathematics instructor charged a special fee for lessons and so did the writing master. A single bed was also charged as an extra.

Charles slept in a long, narrow room that accommodated approximately twenty-five boys with a single window at the long end. The school had no bathing facilities for the boys, and all his life Charles was to remember the foul odor that greeted him when he awakened on a damp winter morning. Although there was no means of heating the dormitory even on the coldest day, Dr. Butler provided only one blanket for each boy. Once Dr. Darwin complained and asked for an additional blanket for Charles, who had just returned to school after having been seriously ill with scarlet fever. Dr. Butler replied by suggesting that Charles had probably been spoiled by the luxuries of home.

Food, blankets, and other creature comforts did not loom large in Dr. Butler's eyes. The boys were in school to study, not to have every whim indulged. The study of Latin and Greek was the one thing worth living for, and anything that took time away from this sacred pursuit was discouraged, especially sports. Football was fit only for butcher boys and boating was prohibited altogether. But the gentle Severn was only a few yards from the west wall of the school and the boys took their chances. To escape detection they would throw their coats over their heads whenever they spied a master on shore. They did not often escape.

Violating the rules was no light matter. Flogging was the order of the day for most infractions, the whipping being administered by the headmaster himself. Dr. Butler flogged so frequently and so well that, even in an age when physical punishment was the customary method of discipline, the school developed among the citizens of Shrewsbury a special reputation for brutality. Boys whose crimes were not flagrant enough to merit flogging were imprisoned for a period of several hours in a small closet in Dr. Butler's study called the "Black Hole." Sometimes the headmaster, beset by more pressing affairs, overlooked his captives and kept them confined all night long. Their classmates, however, fortunately remembered and kept up their spirits with smuggled refreshments.

Worse than the pain and humiliation Dr. Butler inflicted upon his students was the example he set them. Using him and his faculty as their models, the boys took to bullying each other. Younger boys were stripped to the waist, forced to kneel before their beds, and then beaten with birch rods by the older boys.

Shrewsbury was no worse than any other English secondary school. In fact, in the thirty-eight years Butler presided over Shrewsbury it became one of the most famous public schools, a reputation it has preserved to this day. Some boys, undoubtedly, were able to take the cruelty of the masters and the bullying of their classmates, especially those who won the favor and protection of their teachers because they excelled in "the one study worth living for."

But what about a boy like Charles Darwin who could not conform to the demands of his masters and who lived for things other than Latin and Greek, such as collecting minerals and shells or dabbling in chemistry? Dr. Butler may have been pompous and despotic, but he took his job with utter seriousness. He simply could not comprehend such a boy. Yet he had to pound the classics into his head, sinner and idler though he might be. How? Shame him — drag him up before the entire school in chapel and denounce him: "Here's a boy, plays around with his gases and the rest of his rubbish and works at nothing useful." The room roared with laughter. Charles had acquired a nickname that would cling to him for the rest of his school career, "Gas."

Quick to pick their cue from the headmaster, the teachers echoed his judgment: "An ordinary boy. No promise at all; no promise at all." The verdict reverberated through the stone corridors and reached the dormitories. Years later a former classmate had this to say, "Charles Darwin? Dull and apathetic!"

I imagined the boy looking up from his Latin verses to watch the sun go down over the western hill.

Run home after supper? He knew he could get back before the gates were closed for the night. He was a fast and powerful runner. But they would scowl at him. "What are you doing here?" Caroline would find fault and his father would lecture. No welcome there. Home so near and yet so far away. Most of the other boys came from great distances and they were often homesick. His home was only a brisk run along the river's edge and up the hill, and he was homesick too. It might just as well be in a foreign land. He tried to console himself by thinking of his mother, but all he could stir up was a vague memory of how her deathbed had looked. He quickly put it by.

He had one refuge to which he could flee. Within the private world of his hobbies he was his own master, free of the judgment and disapproval of others. Here he was in charge; he ordered, he arranged. His beetles did not criticize. In school there were none of the compensations for him that came to the students who pleased their masters — the recognition and the awards. But along the river's edge or under an old tree, magnificent prizes lay waiting that would be Charles Darwin's alone, his discovery, his achievement.

He could not help absorbing the judgment of his teachers and his parent: "What are you good for, Charles Darwin? What are you good for? Not very much!" To some extent their estimate of his worth became his also. In later life, long after he had become one of the great men of his world, he never ceased wondering that he had turned out so well, as though it were all a mistake, and he would wake from a dream, again in chapel and again the butt of Dr. Butler's ridicule. The tragic thread that runs through his life was woven during the Shrewsbury years. His shyness, his withdrawal from society, and, perhaps, his long and mysterious illness had their beginnings in those early years when he so desperately needed the acceptance and encouragement that were so completely denied.

Sitting there in his old classroom, I seemed to understand that look of questioning, brooding sadness that haunts the portraits of his mature years. I went downstairs into the darkening courtyard and looked up at the figure on the pedestal. It was Darwin: Charles Darwin in his venerable old age, the shaggy brows, the magnificent beard, the gentle, kindly eyes. There he sat looking over the country of his unhappy boyhood — the little town, the winding River Severn, and the green Shropshire hills beyond. Despite the humiliation he endured, the dire predictions, and the complete lack of recognition of his worth, he became one of the greatest scientists that ever lived, Shrewsbury School's most famous son.

From *The Horn Book* for October, 1966

OF A PEACOCK AND A WILD GOOSE

By Margery Evernden

TWENTY YEARS have passed since the death of Selma Lagerlöf, but at the entrance to her manor house in Värmland there still lives a peacock so magnificent that the visitor must pause to wonder that one bird can bear such a length of gilded and turquoise tail.

The visitor must wonder, too, at the presence of so exotic a creature in this secluded Swedish valley.

The peacock is, however, no accident. The desire to see for herself a bird of paradise, kept long ago by Captain Stromberg upon his good ship *Jakob*, once gave a small, lame Värmland girl the will to walk again. For the frail child that tottering progress down a ship's companionway, with the cabin boy to urge her on, was the first of many journeys and the first of many triumphs. After all the journeys and all the triumphs she did not forget the fabulous bird.

Another bird, product of her own imagination — a wild goose bearing on his back the tiny figure of Nils Holgersson — brought to Sweden's most renowned author both her greatest fame and the fulfillment of her dearest personal dream. To the wild goose and his passenger, naughty Nils, Selma Lagerlöf owed the preservation of her childhood home, beloved Mårbacka.

The story began on a November day in 1858 when Selma was born, the fourth of the five children of Lieutenant Erik Gustaf Lagerlöf and his wife Louisa. Life in a fine Värmland home a century ago was rich in tradition and good fellowship — rich, too, in more tangible assets. Iron works flourished in the countryside, and the blue hills not far away produced the finest forests in all Scandinavia.

But Selma learned early that life even in her lovely valley had serious problems. There was not only the terrible pain in her leg. There was, also, at Mårbacka increasing financial trouble. Lieutenant Lagerlöf was a man who had a gift for making others happy — his birthday on August 17 became the gayest, most remembered day in the Mårbacka year — but for the practical matter of running a farm and supporting a large family he had no gift at all. As years passed, the inheritance which had once made life so comfortable was dissipated.

The hero of Selma Lagerlöf's first great book, *Gösta Berling*, was a man not unlike her father, joy-giving, impractical; yet, when at thirty Selma was asked to name her favorite qualities in man or woman, she replied, "seriousness and depth." With these words she described not her lovable father but her earnest and purposeful mother.

Her mother's qualities Selma must have had in abundance. As a very young woman, she realized that, if the family's good fortune was to be restored, it was she who must do it. Her resolution taken, she went to Stockholm to study, became a teacher, and began to write.

Her father was dead by now, Mårbacka sold, but the old life was being reborn in her stories. *Gösta Berling*, one of her greatest successes, came first, followed by a procession of other works, some inspired by Värmland memories, some by impressions gained on travels abroad.

Then in 1901 came the famous and fateful request. As all lovers of children's literature know, Selma Lagerlöf was asked to write a geography for the boys and girls of Sweden. In 1906 the first part of *The Wonderful Adventures of Nils* appeared.

The reaction of delight was immediate. One small American girl, introduced to Nils and his goose for the first time many years later, spoke for the generations who have loved the Värmland imp when she cried, "Oh, I've just heard the most *wonderful* story! About such a *bad* little boy and his bird!"

Selma Lagerlöf must have sensed that she had written her masterpiece. Nils would go on furnishing children around the world with joy and herself with an income for life.

In that conviction she returned to Värmland, found the home, for twenty years lost, to be miraculously for sale — and purchased it.

In the years that followed, honors of many kinds came to

her, the Nobel Prize and membership in the Swedish Academy among others. But the story of her personal life is the story of her books and of Mårbacka.

On August 17, 1922 — Lieutenant Lagerlöf's birthday — carpenters began to raise the roof timbers at Mårbacka. So commenced a reconstruction which was to transform the simple red farm dwelling, with its modest porch and gallery, like so many others in the Värmland valleys, into a handsome manor house.

So Mårbacka stands today, twenty years after the death of its owner. The fabulous peacock spreads his tail in the great cage beside the drive. The poplars shimmer, the well-tended gardens grow lushly in Värmland sun and rain.

Selma Lagerlöf once wrote, "I live in a great solitude. I must choose between living alone and writing or being together with other people and not being able to compose a word. It is a renunciation I must bow to."

Mårbacka's solitude is now ended. Every year tens of thousands of people come down the winding country road.

There is an air of reverence about the place — guided tours, medals and honors painstakingly displayed, solemn busts and paintings less of a woman than of a world-famous author. There is a touch of commercialism, too, in the sale of post cards, mementos, and soft drinks! But neither reverence nor commercialism destroy the sense of abiding life.

The long, narrow rooms of the manor house are filled with light. The walls are white and cream-tapestried and pale, soft gray. The fine old furniture is in natural woods and white-enameled. The stoves are of white tile, gaily decorated. Like a trellis of brilliantly blossoming flowers, tiered shelves of Japanese china climb the dining room walls. In the kitchen with its giant stove and polished copper vessels one can almost imagine the rich fragrance of country cooking.

And everywhere, in every corner of the house, are reminders of Nils Holgersson. In murals upon the walls. In figurines large and small. In the exquisite glass vase presented to Selma Lagerlöf by the school children of Sweden.

Far beyond Mårbacka's walls Nils is, of course, remembered — remembered in such ventures as the Swedish State Railway's

"Nils Holgersson Tour," remembered, too, in a way which would surely have delighted his creator more — by the Nils Holgersson Award. First presented on Selma Lagerlöf's birthday in November 1950, a decade after her death, the Award is given annually to a Swedish children's author.

The wings of a wild goose of Värmland are strong and will fly far. Farther still fly the wings of an imagination so sensitive, so gifted that the thought of a peacock's beauty could move a small cripple's legs.

From The *Horn Book* for December, 1961

A PRESENT FOR ALICE

By Margaret Reardon

ONE SUMMER DAY a hundred years ago, three little girls set out on a picnic. They were Lorina, Alice, and Edith Liddell, daughters of Dean Liddell of Christ Church, Oxford. All three wore white cotton dresses with hoop skirts, open lace socks, and black slippers. Broad-brimmed hats tied under their chins were to shield them from the blazing sun on the river, for this was to be a trip up the Isis from Folly Bridge to Godstow, some three miles from Oxford.

The day was July 4, 1862, during the Long Vacation when, in the words of one Victorian, "Oxford was a city of dreams ... of bells ... of fragrant air." In complete harmony with this was the laughter of the little girls on the path through Christ Church meadow to the river.

There were five in the picnic party that day — the Liddell sisters and two young dons from Christ Church College. Of these five, two were to become famous. The tall young man who carried a large tea basket was Charles Lutwidge Dodgson, teacher and lecturer in mathematics. Still unknown and untouched by fame he was to become Lewis Carroll, author of the immortal story *Alice in Wonderland*. The other member of the party who was to become famous was a child — Alice Liddell, for whom the story was written.

On that memorable trip to Godstow, Charles Dodgson had brought with him Robinson Duckworth, a friend and fellow teacher at Christ Church. Several times before he had helped with the rowing on these river excursions. Next to Mr. Dodgson, Robinson Duckworth was a great favorite with the Liddell sisters. He had pleasing manners, a sense of humor, and a very fine voice. On the homeward trip in the long English twilight he invariably led the girls in singing such old favorites as "Star of the Evening, Beautiful Star."

Had one of Mr. Dodgson's students met him that day on the river path he would have been greatly astonished by the change in appearance and demeanor of the very conservative teacher of mathematics. Brilliant but precise to the point of dullness, Charles Dodgson never drew from his students at Christ Church any really friendly response, nor did he ever seem to show any interest in those same students except in a purely academic way.

Yet anyone seeing him that day would have said that he was being very responsive with the three little girls and enjoying their company a great deal. For this picnic he had doffed the black clothes that he always wore in the classroom and had put on white flannel trousers and a hard straw hat tilted at a somewhat careless angle.

Moreover his demeanor was greatly changed. As he walked with rapid strides toward the river, followed by the three little girls, he appeared to be quite happy — a state of mind that no student had ever observed in Mr. Dodgson. He was generally considered to be a strange and lonely young man.

That memorable trip when the story of *Alice in Wonderland* was told for the first time began in an ordinary way. On arriving at the river, Mr. Dodgson selected a boat that would be safe enough and large enough to accommodate the three little girls in hoop skirts. Seating them in the stern, he placed at their feet the large picnic basket that contained a kettle to boil water for tea when they arrived at Godstow. It also contained a generous supply of cakes.

Soon they were off with Mr. Dodgson and Robinson Duckworth manning the oars. Alice was always a little afraid of one swan that thrust his long neck and big bill into the boat, but the joys of the trip more than compensated for this. Sometimes they rowed in midstream; sometimes they passed close to lovely banks and under willow trees that bent over the river. But the best part of the trip for Alice came when Mr. Dodgson began a story.

In 1887, many years after that day, Lewis Carroll in writing a piece called "Alice on the Stage" for *The Theatre* recalls that summer long passed:

> Many a day had we rowed together on the quiet stream — the three little maidens and I — and many a fairy tale had been extemporized for their benefit... yet none of these many got written down: they lived and died, like summer midges, each in its own golden afternoon, until there came a day when it chanced one of my little listeners (Alice) petitioned that the tale might be written out for her.

In 1899, after the death of Charles Dodgson, Robinson Duckworth (then Canon Duckworth) wrote:

> I rowed stroke and he (Dodgson) rowed bow in the famous Long Vacation voyage to Godstow when the three Miss Liddells were our passengers, and the story was actually composed and spoken over my shoulder for the benefit of Alice Liddell... I remember turning around and saying, "Dodgson, is this an extempore romance of yours?" And he replied, "Yes, I'm inventing as we go along."

That day Alice must have looked very much as she did in the small oval photograph on the last page of the original book manuscript. This picture, which was taken by Charles Dodgson himself, shows a dear child with an oval face, dark hair cut in bangs, and lovely eyes.

We do not know at what time during the voyage that Alice begged for a story as she sat in the stern of the boat with her two sisters. We know that the little party had tea in the shade of a haystack in a field near Godstow and returned to Oxford in the early evening. Robinson Duckworth remembered that when they left the children at the door of the Deanery, Alice Liddell said:

"Oh, Mr. Dodgson, I wish you would write out Alice's adventures for me."

Charles Dodgson said that he would try, and with that the little company parted. As the children entered the door of the Deanery they must have left behind them some of the carefree spirit of the day in order to greet their parents with proper decorum. In a short time the little girls went upstairs to bed, tired but happy.

However they were not too tired to play a bedtime game that had been invented by the imaginative Alice. On the posts of the stairway and along the gallery that led to their bedroom there were carved wooden lions copied from figures in the crest of the aristocratic Liddell family. Every night the children pretended that the lions jumped down from the posts and chased them, so the girls would race down the dark corridor to their bedroom.

Tired from their day on the river, the sisters were asleep when the big bell in Tom Tower measured out one hundred and one strokes in memory of the first students at Christ Church. On the last stroke, at five minutes after nine, the gates of every college in Oxford were closed for the night.

After that there was silence. But a light burned in a window across the Quad from the Deanery as Charles Dodgson began to write out in his finest library script the story that he had told that day on the river. Only the scratch of a pen was heard in the quiet room as he began to sketch those first crude pictures that illustrated the story. He worked all night on this book that he was doing for a little girl fast asleep in the Deanery. Dawn was creeping into Tom Quad before he put aside his work.

Many, many nights when Big Tom measured out those solemn strokes, Charles Dodgson was at his task.

The book was of small dimensions, measuring about six by four and a half inches and when finished consisted of ninety pages with thirty-seven pen-and-ink drawings. At the bottom of the last page Charles Dodgson pasted the photograph of Alice that he had taken when she was seven years old. On the title page were these words:

> *To a Dear Child at Christmas in Memory of a Summer Day.*

This manuscript book has the original title, *Alice's Adventures Underground*. It was given to the little daughter of Dean Liddell on Christmas Day, 1864.

The years passed bringing with them the inevitable changes. On September 15, 1880, Alice Liddell was married in Westminster Abbey to Reginald Hargreaves and left Oxford, carrying with her the precious little manuscript book. It was in her possession for almost fifty years.

In the meantime, the world had discovered the genius, Lewis Carroll, author of *Alice in Wonderland*. But Lewis Carroll's other self, plain Mr. Dodgson, was a reluctant celebrity and tried his best to preserve the peaceful life that he had always lived at Oxford.

Very rarely in the long years did he see the "real Alice." As Mrs. Reginald Hargreaves, with a life of her own and three sons to raise, she lived in a world apart from Oxford and the friend of her childhood.

Fame brought multitudes of people into the life of Charles Dodgson and many of these were famous men of that time. But at heart the genius of Christ Church was a solitary person, living always in retrospect. So he kept the memory of the child Alice and the "golden afternoon," perhaps as a symbol of his own happiness in childhood and youth.

In the epilogue to *Through the Looking Glass* he refers to the little picnic party that went up the Isis July 4, 1862.

> Long has paled that summer sky;
> Echoes fade and memories die;
> Autumn frosts have slain July,
> Still she haunts me phantomwise
> Alice moving under skies
> Never seen by mortal eyes.

From *The Horn Book* for June, 1962

VII

FAMILY READING AND STORYTELLING

A mother can have a great deal to say about what goes into the basic character of her children. Richly varied firsthand experience, reinforced and broadened by reading, is the best education children can have. Such experience does not require great wealth or even highly educated parents. It does require parents willing to take the time and able to get to the nearest public library. Certainly one of the chief ingredients in the education of our children is the books we are enjoying together.

From "The Peace of Great Books"
by Edith F. Hunter

Articles

"THE PEACE OF GREAT BOOKS" *by Edith F. Hunter*

READING WITH MY DAUGHTER *by Calvin T. Ryan*

THREE BOYS AND THEIR WORLD OF BOOKS *by Ellen Wilson*

RHYTHM OF THE NIGHT, REFLECTIONS ON READING ALOUD TO CHILDREN *by William Jay Smith*

THEODORE ROOSEVELT AND CHILDREN'S BOOKS
by Peggy Sullivan

THE PLEASANT LAND OF COUNTERPANE *by Claudia Lewis*

STORYTELLING IN THE FAMILY *by Hilda van Stockum*

MORE THOUGHTS ON READING ALOUD TO CHILDREN,
by Ruth Hill Viguers

"THE PEACE OF GREAT BOOKS"

By Edith F. Hunter

CHARLES AND I were sitting on the living-room couch. We were going through our after-the-school-bus-goes week-day morning routine. I was having my second cup of coffee and reading him a story. Only after this ritual are we ever ready for our first round of housework.

The book that morning was *Song of the Swallows* by Leo Politi. Charles is only three and a half, a little young to grasp all of the detail in the story, but he loves what he does get. The story is about the colony of swallows that live in the old mission at Capistrano. Year after year they leave in the fall and faithfully return on St. Joseph's Day in March.

During the long winter months when the swallows are away the mud nests stand empty. Juan, the little boy around whom the story centers, often looks at the nests and thinks about his swallow friends. He misses them, and so he sings a song that he has been taught in the mission school. I was singing the song to Charles and had come to the last two lines:

> Once more I'll hear them calling to one another
> —my lovely swallows will return again.

I have been reading this story to someone in our family for twelve years now and must confess that my mind was not one hundred per cent on the words as I sang.

But Charles' mind was! I heard a funny little intake of breath and looked over to see one tear rolling down his still baby-round cheek.

A little embarrassed to be caught in such a moment of weakness he hastily explained, "That used to make me sad — when I was little. *Used* to," he reiterated as if to make certain I realized that he had outgrown such a childish reaction. Having made his point, he wiped away the offending tear with the back of a small hand.

As Sara Teasdale urges, I slipped the coin of that experience into my heart's treasury, along with the hundreds of others that have fallen into my possession in the seventeen years that I have been reading to our four children.

It is the nature of human nature to want to share with those we love the things we really enjoy. If I were musical, I suppose I would have spent a good many hours sharing my love of music with the children. But literature happens to be the art form in which I am most at home, and so I have spent hundreds of hours reading to them.

Growing a family is a long slow process. Man's ingenuity has produced such wonders as instant coffee, instant potatoes, and instant soup; but there are, as yet, no instant children. They take time, lots of it! I believe that women should be made sharply aware of the opportunity and challenge that lies in spending time raising a family.

A mother can have a great deal to say about what goes into the basic character of her children. Richly varied firsthand experience, reinforced and broadened by reading, is the best education that children can have. Such experience does not require great wealth or even highly educated parents. It does require parents willing to take time and able to get to the nearest public library. Certainly one of the chief ingredients in the education of our children is the books we are enjoying together.

> The peace of great books be for you,
> Stains of pressed clover leaves on pages,
> Bleach of the light of years held in leather.*

I begin "reading" to our children as soon as they are born: songs, nursery rhymes, and poetry flow right along with the milk. By six months any mother can see her child's delighted response to rhythm as he bounces and sways to music and poetry. As soon as it is clear to me that the child really sees something "out there," I begin talking about the objects in the song and picture books.

In spite of the thousands and thousands of books now produced for the youngest children, I have found very, very few

---

*Lines from "For You" by Carl Sandburg in *Harvest Poems*.

that were really completely satisfying to our children between one and two. Either the pictures are inadequate (*to me*, for there is nothing more subjective than evaluations of picture-book illustrations) or the pictures are just right and the words impossible. Since my children have all loved books by a year and a half, I just use those that are almost just right and edit freely.

One book that often appears on suggested reading lists, *Where's the Bunny?* by Ruth Carroll, is an exception. The pictures and the text are a delight to use with a two-year-old. Another that I have never happened to see on a list, but that my two-and-a-half-year-olds always love is Dorothy Marino's *Edward and the Boxes*. For months at a time we have boxes scattered around the house for dramatizing this story.

The urge to dramatize whatever stories are read is a fascinating one to me. It reaches a really dizzy peak by three and a half, in our children at least. I am sure that playing out a story is the child's most satisfying way of understanding and enjoying it.

Right now, *Make Way for Ducklings* is having a veritable Broadway run on the off-Broadway stage of my bedroom. Every morning, as I do my half-hour stint of daily ironing there, Charles puts on a production. As well as being director he plays an astonishing series of roles, changing character in a twinkling of an eye as the need arises.

First he is Mr. Mallard pointing out possible nesting sites to me, Mrs. Mallard. I reject them all for fear of foxes, snapping turtles, and other natural hazards. A few moments later we have a run-in with a bicycle in the Public Garden and push on to our final choice along the Charles River.

Immediately Charles becomes policeman Michael, putting on a pair of his father's enormous shoes, handily located nearby, and in this role he generously feeds me peanuts. Moments later, having kicked off the shoes, he lies curled on the floor, the first of the eight eggs about to hatch into downy little ducklings. After emerging as number eight — I having made appropriate warm quacking sounds throughout — he again becomes Mr. Mallard, making the typically male announcement that he is about to leave for an extended trip exploring the Charles River. He promises to meet me in the Public Garden when I have finished educating the children.

On go his father's shoes again, and he assumes the role of Michael. As he clumps away to the guest room (telephone booth) I am ordered to play Clancy at police headquarters.

"There's a family of ducks —"

"Of WHAT???" I shout.

"Of DUCKS!!!" comes the delighted reply from across the hall.

Charles has made only one improvement in the text. Because I have made some rather bitter remarks about husbands who go off on exploring trips just after the children are born, in Charles' version, when the family reunion occurs on the island in the Public Garden, father Mallard arrives with a variety of foods for his large family. I allow this to pacify me, somewhat.

Of course, since we live fairly near Boston, we have visited all of the real-life locations mentioned in the story and have ridden the swan boats a good many times. Thus real-life and storybook experiences reinforce each other. Also, since we live on a farm, we have had the firsthand experience of losing a whole family of baby banty chicks to a fox or some other barnyard intruder, so Charles knows that Mrs. Mallard's caution about a nesting site is wise.

When the children are between three and six one of the high points of our reading is the old *Peter and Polly* books. These four books, one each for spring, summer, fall, and winter, were written by Rose Lucia as second-grade reading books for children in Vermont where she was a school principal. They are now out of print, but represent the kind of reading I like best: books that open children's eyes to the miracles in the commonplace. In these stories they see a little boy and girl just like them finding fun, wonder, satisfaction in the simplest things: snow, puddles, backyard holes, a daisy, a buttercup, kittens, a loose tooth, a birthday, a thunderstorm, a kite, and a hundred other ordinary things.

Walt Whitman wrote: "To me every hour of the light and dark is a miracle,/ Every cubic inch of space is a miracle...." And to me. I hope that it will be so with my children and their children also. I find myself very much in the minority at this particular period when it comes to evaluating what is "outstanding" in children's books. The fantasy and whimsey in so many of the highly recommended books seem to me thin and irrelevant compared with the textures of reality when it is intimately experienced. I would rather read my children one simple but real story from *Peter and Polly* or their more modern counterpart, the *Martin and Judy* books, than all the Dr. Seuss books put together. Few people agree with me.

Because I like books grounded in reality, several friends have suggested that my children will be lacking in imagination. I often wish such critics could spend an hour with Charles and me during one of his dramatic productions. A child's imagination will go to work on whatever material is made available. People differ as to what the best material is.

When listening to poetry a child has a wonderful opportunity to use his imagination; and we read a great many poems. Parents have told me that they find it difficult to read poetry to their children. Their problem, I believe, is that they begin to read it when the children are eight or nine. Instead, we should realize that the nursery rhymes we read to our babies are poetry; the secret lies in never stopping this kind of reading.

In my experience the poetry of Dorothy Aldis is an excellent follow-up to nursery rhymes. Her collection, *All Together*, containing the favorites from her earlier volumes, is a good one to own. Our other basic poetry books, all anthologies, are *For a Child, Poems to Grow On*, and when a child no longer needs a picture to indicate which poem he wants, *Time for Poetry* and *Home Book of Verse for Young Folks*. It is as natural for an eight-year-old to enjoy poetry as it is for an eight-month-old to enjoy bouncing. All we need to do is to keep the rhythm going over the years.

As children emerge from the here-and-now of their own particular time and place, the wealth of good books available to reinforce and extend their new awareness is overwhelming: stories, biography, history, myths, legends all await us. In just the last winter William, who is nearly nine, and I read: *Little Men, Tom Sawyer, Treasure Island, Kidnapped, Understood Betsy, Rebecca of Sunnybrook Farm, Boy with a Pack,* and half of *David Copperfield*. As William said the other day, eying *Johnny Tremain* waiting for us on the shelf, "Oh, Mother, there are so many good ones!"

Probably the two "series" that our family has enjoyed most are the "Little House" books and Ralph Moody's boyhood recollections in *Little Britches* and the companion volumes. These I have already read aloud three times to the children and expect that I will make it through again twice more, at least. Mrs. Wilder, in particular, had such a fine sense of humor and good sense of values that her books make a wonderful family reading experience.

Just which of all the good books we finally manage to fit in depends on many factors. One year, when we were going on a trip to California, we steeped ourselves in books relevant to the coming journey. We read books on the gold rush, the building of the transcontinental railroad, the Pony Express, the Lewis and Clark expedition, and so on; to climax the whole experience, en route we read *On to Oregon!* by Honoré Willsie Morrow. We have woven books and experience together again and again.

Children are curious, of course, not only about the past of their own country and people, but of all times and all peoples. They are curious about the history of ideas, too. They ask the same penetrating questions that all growing children have asked about birth, life, sickness, and death. They ask about the beginning and the meaning of life. The book *Beginnings: Earth, Sky, Life, Death* offers a variety of myths about beginnings; and the collection *From Long Ago and Many Lands* presents in story form the ethical insights of peoples all over the world. My children repeatedly ask for stories from these collections.

Perhaps because religion and ethics are among my major interests, I have been particularly aware of the number of times that our reading has led naturally into philosophical and ethical discussions. For example, when Will and I were reading *Treasure Island*, we had an extended discussion of capital punishment. "Did people really hang pirates?" He was a little shocked to discover that they not only *did*, but that hanging is still the form that capital punishment takes in several states, including our own.

While reading *Kidnapped* William discovered that drinking liquor made one character kind and friendly, but that another character became ugly and beast-like under the influence of strong drink. "Could liquor then sometimes be good?" We discussed this at some length, and Will decided he would think about it some more when he is older. Reading *David Copperfield* has prompted the first conversations about the phenomenon of prostitution as well as about socialism and child labor. What better place to help a child first wrestle with some of our most persistent social problems than the home?

As a parent I have found the medium of books a far more satisfactory basis for discussion than television, because we can suspend our reading whenever we want to. But you just can't stop a television program to thrash something out. Also, when dealing with a great book, you can know ahead of time the values in the book, while an evening spent with television may prove to be a complete waste of time.

That an experience can be repeated is another dividend offered by books. Our older children are seventeen and fifteen now, and the nine- and the three-year-old love to hear that this story was Graham's favorite, that one was Elizabeth's. More often than not, if the older children are within hearing and I am reading to the younger ones, they join the listening group in order to hear their old favorites. In a day when it is not easy for families to have permanent geographic roots, roots in great books are important. The stories we have read together I know have strengthened the fabric of our life as a family. I like to hope that many of these stories our children will read to their children, too.

Elizabeth and Graham are deeply immersed now in the reading of wholly adult material. I feel sure that the ease with which my husband and I give them reading suggestions results from our many years of sharing books. When a new author is introduced in school, they are glad to have our suggestion of a good title by him. Reading together has kept the doors of communication open between us and our children.

Not long ago I sprained my ankle and had to stay in bed for

a day or two. I felt that bread cast upon the water had indeed come back when William, armed with a book, came into my room and announced, "I've got a good book to read you. I'll have time for one chapter before I have to help Dad."

"Thanks," I said.

From *The Horn Book* for December, 1964

READING WITH MY DAUGHTER
By Calvin T. Ryan

THE most delightful recollections of the childhood of my daughter are of those years from three to six when, just before she went "hippity hop to bed," she would climb on my desk and hand me her *Peter Patter Book*. The routine required that I should read it from:

> "Jingle, jingle Jack,
> A copper down a crack."
> to
> "Twenty thieves from Albion
> All with butcher knives,
> Coming on the dead run,
> Fighting for their lives."

Of course, later years had new duties, but they always included books, stories, poems, and songs. She grew up in a bookish atmosphere, but one in no sense lacking in reality. Books can serve so many useful purposes; they can afford both fun and guidance. Children need help in understanding the world around them, and books are splendid helps. Even Munro Leaf's *Boo* can be both fun and useful. It can serve as a better antidote for the child who "used to be scared of the dark," or who is still afraid, than will most Sunday school stories.

The father who doesn't have time, or who doesn't take time, to relive the storybook world of *Peter Rabbit, Little Black Sambo,* and the dozens of other classics, and relive them through the eyes and minds of his own children, is missing a great deal of fun. I used to read the old favorites some years after my daughter could read them for herself. I suspect I was a bit selfish in doing the reading! I seemed to catch part of the thrill as I watched the response in my child's eyes and her facial expressions. I wondered what I was missing that she saw.

I have watched her stop in her "work" and just sit and have wondered what she was thinking, for children live in at least two worlds, and to them both are equally real. They live in what you and I call the "real world," and in one that exists only in their imaginations. They need imagination as a kind of fortress into which they retire for reenforcements.

Why LeRoy Jackson's *Peter Patter Book* preceded Mother Goose in the book world of my daughter, I do not recall. I think Mother and Dad trusted to their own memories for Mother Goose. But the *Peter Patter Book* did come first, and it was not discarded when the leaves began to drop out. When Zelda Jeanne used to come running into my study, saying, "Hello, you great big hippodoodles!" I knew we were on very intimate terms. Of course Mother Goose did in time have a place on her bookshelves, but more because of Daddy's fondness for different editions. Christopher Robin entered with *When We Were Very Young,* and became another very welcome member of our family. Book characters become so real in a home atmosphere where they are always treated as friends.

On Christmas Eve we had an added ritual in the bedtime ceremony. Zelda Jeanne would hang up her stockings, put on her pajamas, find her rather flimsy, highly colored edition of *'Twas the Night Before Christmas,* and climb up in my lap in the big chair. And as I read the story year after year, Mother made a flash picture of us. Strange how pictures bring back such pleasant, or pleasantly-sad memories! But there we are — each year showing some change in my hairline; each year showing that Zelda Jeanne has grown longer and broader as she covers more and more of me!

One day a copy of *Poppy Seed Cakes* came through the mail. It was on Saturday, my day at home; so before night I had read the book three times, and those "exstornry" names of the characters were tripping off the tongues of the three of us.

I have noticed often that one book will remain a favorite for days, perhaps weeks, and then another will come to replace it. Children, like adults, have their whims and moods, and if they are given the chance will express both in their favorite books. Nature has its own way of working, and we parents can't do very much to change it, but we can do much to play havoc with it, and cause the child to suffer as a result. The book may be all right — just right for Zelda Jeanne, according to the established age-grade placements found on the dust jacket, but if she is not ready, or isn't "all right" for the book at that time, I have learned to wait until she is.

The child of six or even of twelve may not be ready to read and understand Dorothy Macardle's *Children of Europe*, but we have many books to use as stepping stones. One day I read some stories of children in China and other foreign lands, and after I finished, Zelda Jeanne looked at me and said, "Daddy, those little boys and girls are just like us, aren't they?" Well, they certainly are, for children are much alike the world around. If we can use books to help our children understand such "alikeness," then we can do something about teaching tolerance. I do not think it a sign of an immature mind when I say that the stories of children in other lands which I read to my daughter prepared me definitely for a better response to Miss Macardle's book.

Strickland Gillilan's *The Reading Mother* pays a high tribute to the mother who read to him, but I wonder why no one has done as much for the fathers. Can it be that our children will never think of us in that intimacy bred only among book lovers? If so, it is a sad commentary on fathers. Perhaps we need a monument, erected by little children's pennies: To The Unknown Father! The money I put into books for my child, often money I could not well afford, bore immediate dividends in the fun and the thrill I had in reading to her.

The Story of Dr. Dolittle! That book became part of our trip to the mountains each summer. Day after day we had to read it.

Then in later years we reveled in *Silver Chief* and *Silver Chief to the Rescue*. Those books have what it takes to please boys and girls — and Dads who remember a thing or two of their own boyhood.

I used to invite my Children's Literature Class to come to my home. We put Zelda Jeanne's books out in groups according to age level and content. It gave the class a chance to see books in the normal setting of a home with a child who loved them and who knew how to act among them.

I often took members of the class out to demonstrate children's books before parent groups, even before Rotary and Kiwanis Clubs. We always "borrowed" about two hundred of my daughter's books to take with us for demonstration and she was always happy when we told her about other little boys and girls who enjoyed them. At the parent demonstrations we insisted on having the children up front, and after our program my students would show the books to the children and answer the innumerable questions the parents would ask.

On one occasion we spoke in a school where the rooms were small, so that when time came for refreshments, the president explained that we would have to divide the audience in order to serve all present. He suggested that the children go first, and then the adults. But the children revolted. They chose to stay and see the books! The president commented that it was the first time in his presidency that children preferred books to eats!

The early years of our children go all too rapidly. We have so much we want to accomplish for them, so many things we want them to learn, we hardly know how to manage everything. We know they should be given a sense of security. We know they should develop the basis for religious instruction. Then there are emotional security, aesthetic responses, and, perhaps, even more important, something about vocations.

Guidance has become an accepted part of the child's home and school experiences. But guidance should not be confined to helping the young find the right occupations. It is just as important to guide the child in the right attitudes toward his work, or toward life as he makes his living. Parents can use books for the basis of this attitude.

Zelda Jeanne was never deprived of fairy stories. She has been deprived only of *certain* stories. I think her acceptance of the world of fact has never been interfered with by her rather broad knowledge of the land of phantasy. I was gratified to read A. A. Milne's statement, "In Fairyland honesty is not the *best* policy; it is the *only* policy." Do you recall a single fairy story in which the characters failed to keep their word? I doubt that you will find in Fairyland any "guilt by association." In getting Zelda Jeanne ready to understand real life,

I did not hesitate to saturate her with the unreal. There is a residue in folk stories after the froth has blown away that is sound morally. Fairies, gnomes, ogres, giants, elves — all the denizens of the unseen world have marched about and played together in my daughter's imagination. What matter if we call them angels, or fairies, or Unseen Forces? The child well acquainted with fairies will not be abashed in the presence of the idea of angels. When the Psalmist prayed, "O Lord, create in me a clean heart," he meant only what we would mean should we pray, "O Lord, create in me a clean imagination!"

The story is the oldest form of pedagogy. The child sings before he talks. Through story and song we can introduce our children to the world of pretend and give them clean imaginations and a sense of security — all ready for the everyday world. Our children need courage, and they need kindliness. The children of Europe who saw the worst features of the recent World War are suspicious of all adults. They endured so much treachery from some that they became fearful of all. If we could reach those children through books, before they grow into adulthood and begin to take vengeance on the world, we might go a long way toward preventing a third World War.

A story like Marguerite De Angeli's *Door in the Wall* is a lesson in courage and kindliness, and will leave with a child the realization that if he looks long enough, he will always find doors in the walls which seem so impregnable. Books form one of those doors. Such mirth-provoking stories as Kenneth Grahame gave us in his *The Wind in the Willows*, with its "inner significance" of the "warm friendliness of the animals," and friends that stick together, please and help both young and old.

I can recall the night Zelda Jeanne looked out of the car window and saw one of those gorgeous full moons we have in Nebraska and said, "Daddy, is that the moon the cow jumped over?" So from Mother Goose to Nature, and if you please, to God. Anything can happen in the child's imagination. Keep it filled with clean, wholesome ideas and you prepare the child to meet the world about him. It is true that we can't think *low* and live *high*, and how we live depends much upon how we think.

Children do not always know how to phrase their questions about life. Books often tell them what is wrong with them, and what to do about it. One day I was talking before an adult group about knowing children and knowing books, and bringing the two together on friendly terms, and happened to be stressing the early adolescent stage. After class, a woman came to my desk and said, "You have been talking about my daughter! She is having all those troubles you just mentioned. Won't you tell me what books I can get to help her?" I thought of *A Bend in the Road* and *Calico Bush*. Sometimes I find that parents, yes, particularly fathers, need to read something revealing of the childhood they seem to have forgotten. The trouble with children is often their parents, and I recommend bibliotherapy for parents just as freely as I do for children.

Booth Tarkington once said that we are made by the kind of fathers and mothers and grandfathers and grandmothers we have — "and by the people we meet and the friends we make, and by our reading. So if a lot of our reading isn't poetry, and if we don't learn some poems by heart, it's safe to say we are not going to be as well equipped for living as we could be." Tarkington may not have had fathers especially in mind, but his dictum is applicable. I thought so, at least, for I wanted my child "well equipped for living." Furthermore, I knew that implications are that children saturated with poetry are not likely to become cynical in the world of adulthood or to spend their last days in psychopathic wards. Books make the inner world of man, just as clothes make the outer one; and poetry makes the very soul come alive. It has been one of our great pleasures.

Mothers are not ruled out when fathers come in on the fun of working with children and books. It is not the work of one: it is the work — and fun — of both.

From *The Horn Book* for April, 1952

THREE BOYS
AND THEIR WORLD OF BOOKS

By Ellen Wilson

WHEN I worked in the children's section of a lively bookstore in Rhode Island, I used to play a game with myself. The game was to see whether I could, in the course of a day or a week or even a month, find one customer who would say simply and naturally, "My son and daughter are average readers. They like what most children their ages like. What good books do you recommend for perfectly normal eight-year-olds and twelve-year-olds?"

It was a losing game. Always it was, "My child is eight, but she is way ahead in her reading." Or "My child is twelve, but he is way behind most twelve-year-olds." Each time the statement was made with a sort of pride in the difference, the uniqueness of the child. I began to lose faith in the average child. Apparently he did not exist.

But of course he did exist; he always will. And when he himself came into the bookstore, even with those same parents who, often in his presence, claimed that he was "way ahead" or "way behind," he usually settled the matter by choosing for himself the sort of good book that attracted most of his friends and contemporaries.

Now that we have three boys of our own, I rejoice in the fact that they are average boys, for I have great respect for the reading tastes of the average child. Of course I began to read to them when they were very small and often thought I should work out a long-range plan for this reading. Instead, our reading has been haphazard and has gone off in all directions. Perhaps I was scared away from any sort of "master plan" when a friend in my presence resolved that her children were not going to be allowed to read any sort of nonsense. "Nothing but books of hard facts for them," she said, "since they are going to have to face a world of hard facts."

How grim to face a grim world without the nourishment and refreshment of nonsense and tall tales! How much poorer our boys would be if they did not make the acquaintance of that elephantine gentleman of the exquisite manners, Babar; or that staunch lad, Wee Gillis, who developed such wonderful lungs he could blow up the largest bagpipes in all Scotland. And so we did become friendly with them and dozens of other carefree spirits like Paul Bunyan's "Dumb Cookee" who "couldn't read a line, but he didn't want anyone to hear what his girl wrote to him, so he always put his hands over Red Charley's ears when he was reading her letters to him."

How much poorer our whole family would be if we had not chortled together over the things we saw on Mulberry Street; over the amazing Doughnut Machine in *Homer Price;* over the making of "Stone Soup"; and the antics of Uncle Benny in *Ginger Pye.*

Like most mothers, I did have the hope that our boys would enjoy the same books I liked as a child. I find that sometimes these books are a success and just as often they are not. Certainly I know better than to inflict upon the boys any of the long series of girls' books that used to absorb me when I wore pigtails — the "Little Colonel" books, for instance. Perhaps it is just as well I have no daughter to tempt me into testing the permanence of the charms of those romantic Southern belles.

One of the few girls of my long-ago acquaintance whom the boys will accept is Heidi. And there I suspect it is not Heidi herself who is the attraction so much as the mountains, the goats, and the food. Somehow it pleases me that our boys drool over those epic feasts of home-baked bread, cheese and goat's milk just as I did.

Alice, of course, was accepted by our boys. Why not? No hero ever had more exciting upside-down adventures than this demure looking heroine with the long hair and the prim pinafore. When I started reading *Alice in Wonderland* to them, it never occurred to the boys not to pop down the large rabbit hole after her, even if she was a girl. After all, the girl was after a rabbit, wasn't she?

But as for Meg, Beth, Jo and Amy, the boys say, "No thank

you," making me wish I had at least one daughter with whom to share *Little Women.*

Of course the boys tolerate Becky, not because I like her, but because Tom Sawyer liked her. When our oldest son was six and had a cast on a broken leg all summer, Tom and Becky and Huck were our constant companions. Neighbors going by on the sidewalk pitied the lad who couldn't go off to the beach, this son of ours who was anchored in the side yard. They couldn't know that day after day we went floating down the Mississippi River in fine, carefree company. When my husband found us both in tears one afternoon, he was alarmed at the effect our confinement in the yard was having on us until he learned it wasn't our own plight that moved us to tears; it was the far more serious plight of Tom and Becky lost in the cave.

As for the animals I had liked in books when I was a child, I was sure that they wouldn't have changed a hair. Our boys did take to their hearts Kipling's animals and Ernest Thompson Seton's, among others. But something had happened to *Black Beauty* and *Beautiful Joe.* Perhaps it wasn't the horse and the dog who had changed — they were still the noble creatures of my childhood; but we had changed, and the people in the books were no longer real. Since cruelty to animals has largely been done away with, poor Black Beauty and Beautiful Joe had become figures in a battle that was almost incomprehensible to my boys.

McLennan McMeekin's *First Book of Horses* proved far more satisfactory. Besides, dozens of people like Marguerite Henry, Paul Brown and Jim Kjelgaard were producing animal books so far superior to most of those in my own childhood that I finally tossed my nostalgia back on the shelf with my old books. Now it was more fun to make the acquaintance of *Misty, Merrylegs,* and *Big Red* with those enthusiastic fans, my sons.

It worries me that I have done so little in reading poetry with our boys. My own father knew every verse written by Eugene Field, and said them all to me as a child, over and over. Our boys have liked most of Eugene Field and Stevenson, and some of Riley. It may be heresy, but it is true that they are embarrassed to have anyone read them "The Raggedy Man," for instance, with what they call its baby talk.

As country boys, they understand Robert Frost; and as seagoing lads, they like Masefield. But it is sadly true that they don't ever pick up poetry to read just for fun. I am sorry about this, and feel that I should have read them more poetry when they were younger. Perhaps this is their age of prose. When they are older, they may turn to poetry, too.

I was impressed one rainy afternoon when the twins, settling with their after-school gang in the living room, unexpectedly proposed to play for them our recording of Edith Sitwell's *Façade*. I was baffled as well as impressed by this show of interest. But when Edith Sitwell's incredible voice rolled out into the room, all the boys were at first baffled and then convulsed. They rolled on the floor in their glee. Finding her such a success, the twins often produce her for entertainment. They themselves go round quoting sonorously such lines as,

> "Do not take a bath in Jordan,
> Gordon,
> On the holy Sabbath on the peaceful day."

I have decided it doesn't matter that they like *Façade* for all the wrong reasons. Some day when they are in college, solemnly studying twentieth-century English poets, they will be startled to find that, long before, they had made the rollicking acquaintance with at least one of the Sitwells.

While reading Bible stories to the boys, I rediscovered what I had almost forgotten — that they are as exciting to children as any secular tale. It has always seemed to me important that they hear these stories in the incomparable language of the King James version rather than in any watered-down prose.

When, later, I realized that my boys, grandsons of a Methodist minister, knew little of their Protestant heritage, I looked about for a book that would present the story of Methodism with dignity and effectiveness. Fortunately May McNeer and Lynd Ward, themselves products of a parsonage childhood, have pooled their talents in a superb book, *John Wesley*. To me, the most moving chapter is the one called "Birthday," where the five-year-old John, with eagerness and dread, faces the test given in turn to all the Wesley children. "Today he was to learn to read. A fifth birthday in the Wesley house was not a day for candles and cake. It was the day when a child made his parents proud or ashamed of him."

For my children, the vivid account of that day was one of high suspense. For me, it was a personal revelation. Until I read that, I had never realized that my mother must consciously have been following the excellent Susanna Wesley's example when, on my own fifth birthday, she had me follow her to what we called "the reading bench," and there and then began to teach me the alphabet. I suspect that, unlike the diligent John, I did not learn all my letters by mid-afternoon. And I am certain that it was a day in our family for candles and cake. But it touched me to learn, so many years later, of the spiritual kinship between those two women who felt deeply the importance of teaching their own children how to read.

It seems right and necessary to me that our children learn of their own religious heritage. But it seems equally right and necessary that they learn of the religious heritage of others. I know of no book so helpful in this as Florence Mary Fitch's *One God and the Ways We Worship Him*. Here in handsome photographs and in sympathetic text, the boys and I found the clearest descriptions of "The Jewish Way," "The Catholic Way" and "The Protestant Way." Now when the boys' friends observe their different religious ceremonies and holidays, we all have a deeper appreciation of the traditional meanings involved. And the words of Malachi have become significant: "Have we not all one Father?"

Their concept of "one world" I am sure our three boys have gained unconsciously. Having played with exiled English children in their cousins' home during the war, they listened with special delight to my reading of Alice Dalgliesh's *Three from Greenways*. How funny, how poignant, and how true that book is, with its account of the adjustments that had to be made by both the English guests and their American hosts.

Perhaps one of the best ways to understand children of other countries is to read books written in those countries, by their own authors for their own young countrymen. In that way our children are transported, not as observers or tourists, but as participants in the daily life of that country. What might otherwise seem quaint or bizarre ceases to be different and becomes simply the natural and the accepted.

The wonderfully imaginative books by the Englishwoman, E. Nesbit, do this for our children. All one summer our twins clamored for bedtime reading from *Five Children and It* and the companion volumes. I often yielded to the boys' plea for "just one more chapter, *please*," for I was as eager as they were to see what happened next.

Another and amusing kind of touchstone to international understanding was handed to our boys one time when they were given a copy of *Peter Rabbit* in French. Our two younger boys know no French whatever, but they do know their *Peter Rabbit*. What fun to learn that French children call him "Pierre Lapin," but that he hasn't changed a bit! How reassuring that he gets into the same trouble, even if this time it is "au jardin de Mr. MacGregor"; and how consoling that he gets out of trouble as always, even though, "Hélas! Pierre fut malade." It is gratifying to know that he is as much at home in France as he is in England or America.

When I was a girl and read biographies, I seldom felt that the men or women I read about were friends of mine. I longed to be on intimate terms with them, but I did not dare. Our boys, on the other hand, feel close to the men and women of history — really close.

Take Abraham Lincoln, for instance. What could be a more perfect introduction to the child Abe than the friendly one the D'Aulaires give with their wonderful pictures and simple text: "Abe is solemn like a little papoose," said the kinfolk who came to look at him. "He grows so fast I can't keep him in shirts," said his father.

What could better make our boys believe that Abe was a boy just like themselves, than our reading together of Genevieve Foster's "Oh, Abe was strong, no doubt of that . . . but he was lazy. He could husk corn, chop down trees, split rails faster than two men, if he took a notion, but he'd rather read than work."

How could our boys help thinking of Lincoln as a very

human sort of man, when we read in Jeannette Nolan's *The Little Giant* that after Lincoln lost to Douglas at the polls, Abe said, "It hurts too much to laugh and I'm too big to cry"?

And finally, how could our boys resist the Abe they know best of all in *Abe Lincoln of Pigeon Creek?* Here is an Abe who gets into fights, who has to do the chores about the place, an Abe who has a special girl, an Abe who eats three meals a day but whose mother despairs of ever filling him up. Here is an Abe who, like themselves, grew tall in Indiana. This Abe is a friend they will always have, and to whom they would always feel close even if it hadn't been their own father who wrote the book and gave them a copy.

With this book our boys began making occasional raids on the world of adult books. Our oldest boy has just entered college. The twins are in junior high. From now on I may not read to them so much as I used to, but this new period brings its own satisfactions.

When *Caine Mutiny* found its way into our house recently, our oldest boy, his father and I did not read it aloud together; but one of us snatched it up as soon as another put it down; so that we had the fun of sharing as adults the pleasure of reading and talking about a book that interested the three of us.

In the public library last week for the first time the twins wandered out of the young people's room back into the mysterious regions of the stacks. Later they emerged, bringing in triumph what they had gone to look for — two Forester books about their friend, Captain Hornblower.

But it will be a long time before the twins desert the world of children's books — that world they still feel is theirs. And I hope it will be a long time before they give up coming to me as they did recently, saying, "There is a new movie about Ivanhoe and we want you to read us the book." And so we opened to the magic of that first sentence, "In that pleasant district of merry England which is watered by the Don, there extended in ancient times a large forest. . . ."

As I look back over all our good times of reading together, I can't see that we followed any system or any long-range plan. I am afraid it has all been very haphazard and helter-skelter. And yet, somehow, a kind of pattern has emerged.

Part of this pattern is something we had not foreseen. That is an awareness in our boys that books are written by people. In our own house there has always been the sound of the typewriter up in their father's study — a sound as familiar to the boys as the whir of the washing machine. I don't know just when it dawned upon them that this sound was directly connected with the appearance on their bookshelves of such books as *Big Knife,* the story of George Rogers Clark, and *Shooting Star,* the story of Tecumseh. But after that it couldn't have been long before they became aware that behind every book there must be a person, a person who in some house somewhere had spent days on end, going clackety-clack on another typewriter. And so authors became important to them, just as important as policemen and teachers and grocers.

That is why I was enormously relieved and pleased when the twins looked up after reading the proof of Nan Agle's and my first book, *Three Boys and a Lighthouse,* and said, "Why, Mother, it's just as good as a real book by real writers." I knew then that all was well; we were accepted by the most important critics I know.

From *The Horn Book* for April, 1953

RHYTHM OF THE NIGHT

Reflections on reading aloud to children

By *William Jay Smith*

RECENTLY in a lecture entitled "In Quest of Folklore," Padraic Colum, speaking of the disappearance of folk tales in Ireland, referred to what he called one of the basic requirements for their creation — the "rhythm of the night." Night, he said, has its own rhythm utterly unlike that of day; it is acquiescent rather than compulsive: in the old Irish countryside, when all the harsh daytime farm noises had subsided, the country folk would gather round the hearth with its soft-glowing peat fire, and then to the subdued sounds of evening, the storyteller would begin. Night has, throughout history, called forth the dark voices of the unconscious in all peoples; and stories have been told and retold around the campfire and before the hearth. But Ireland has been one of the last places to lose the "rhythm of the night": in most parts of the world the gentle night sounds — the murmur of roosting chickens, the chirping of crickets, the hooting of owls, the hiss and crackle of the open fire — all of which formed the natural background to the rising and falling of the storyteller's voice — have long since given way to urban cacophony. The "rhythm of the night" has come to mean for us the hiss of ricocheting bullets on television, the gurgle and gargle of announcers, the incessant idiot burble of singing commercials: how, under these conditions, can we listen to the storyteller's voice; how indeed can we hear any normal human voice?

There is still, however, a means of restoring something of the rhythm of the night wherever we happen to live; and that is by reading aloud to our children. In a dark room when a child is ready for bed, with the lamplight full on the pages of a book and his mind concentrated on a single voice, that of mother or father reading aloud from the great stories of the past, the child, on the edge of sleep, becomes again the unconscious recipient of the great imaginative currents of history. No new myths are created, but at least the great myths are kept alive. And the sensibility of the child is trained to cope with life's problems; he finds defenses against tragedy and words with which to express joy; his ear is developed to appreciate the subtleties of language and the mystery and power of words.

As any parent, teacher, or librarian knows, there is no richer experience than to see children's faces light up at the suspense of a new tale or the surprise of a new poem. The uninhibited joy with which they listen is surely akin to that of adult audiences of old around campfire and hearth. I have felt at times with groups of children that I was really being what every poet would like to be — a bard in the old sense.

While I have read publicly to thousands of children in the course of the past three or four years, my thoughts about reading aloud must inevitably center on my experience with my own two boys. As a family, we value first the spoken, and then the written, word. A Southerner by birth, I was brought up in a tradition in which talk was constant, varied, and lively; my earliest childhood memories are of stories told by my parents, aunts and uncles, family friends; and as the son of a regular Army man, I was constantly exposed to stories of Army life, brought back from all parts of the world. I suppose that one of the reasons that I have become a writer of children's books is that I had so few of my own: from an early age, they existed in my head, memories of what I had heard. My wife's experience was different but in a strange way similar: brought up in a suburb of Boston, she lived surrounded by books. Her mother read to her regularly every evening; and I have before me as I write a notebook containing a list of all the books that were read to her daily between the ages of six and sixteen. It is an amazing document, and if she had had no other education, simply hearing these books would have been enough to make her a writer.

Because my wife (Barbara Howes) and I are both poets, our sons, David, now eleven, and Gregory, six, have heard poetry read and talked about to such an extent that it seems to both of them a perfectly natural means of expression. (Only now when David hears it talked about in school, perhaps inevitably but certainly unfortunately in the wrong way, does he consider it anything else.) It has always been a favorite pastime of ours to compose verses on long trips: the limerick is the preferred form, and this is a family sport in which we all participate, even Gregory, long before he knew what a "rhyming word" was. The composition of nonsense verses has been, as it was for Victorian writers, a natural release for me as well as for the children. I think it was David who began one day with:

>There was an Old Lady named Crockett

and I went on with it:

>Who went to put a plug in a socket;
> But her hands were so wet
> She flew up like a jet
>And came roaring back down like a rocket.

And so it appears in *Typewriter Town*, with a picture of Mrs. Crockett that I drew to try to convey some of the fun we had had at her expense.

It may be easier to catch children, especially boys, like this on the wing than to get them to settle down to listen for any extended period of time to a poem or story. Everything in American life encourages them to action rather than meditation; and I often wonder that we have been able to get our two to sit still for anything. But when I asked them to supply the names of books they remembered enjoying listening to, we went round the shelves, and the list was long. Of the earliest volumes there was naturally Mother Goose. I have read to them frequently from the *Oxford Nursery Rhyme Book* of Iona and Peter Opie, but that I keep on my own shelf; on Gregory's are the Tenggren and the Kate Greenaway *Mother Goose*, both dog-eared. My wife and I have read all the Beatrix Potter books again and again, a delight for us all. Johnny Crow was also a favorite:

>And the Cockatoo
>Said "Comment vous portez-vous?"
>And the Gander
>Didn't understand her. . . .

One doesn't have to *understand* words like these that fall so nicely on the ear.

"I like animals more than people," Greg said the other day, every child's feeling surely; and I wonder if it wasn't Kenneth Grahame's. Mr. Toad is larger than life and more a person than any person because he is simply and literally a toad — *the* toad — the essence of the funny-looking, sad, wretched, hopeless, helpless creature that every boy has at some time held captive. I read *The Wind in the Willows* aloud to David when he was nearly six, an early age it might seem for that book, but he had to hear it right through again. That same summer I read him *Alice in Wonderland,* and he had to have that repeated, every word of it, and that astonished me. I had not liked *Alice* when I was young, having discovered it for myself and having been put off by the Tenniel illustrations, which still seem to me, as apparently they did to the author, weighty and somewhat too frightening for the text. Reading the book aloud twice through, I discovered it for the first time myself as it should be — a wonderful wild tale filled with terror certainly but also with fun. Edward Lear we read many times that same summer and often since, so often that both boys are half convinced that I wrote the limericks and drew the pictures myself.

Babar was an early animal favorite; we have read aloud every *Babar* book that exists. Other early, and less well known, favorites were *In the Forest* by Marie Hall Ets, which has a subtle off-beat rhythm delicately fitted to its subject, and *The Sailor Dog* by Margaret Wise Brown. The latter begins: "Born at sea in the teeth of a gale, the sailor was a dog. Scuppers was his name." And what better beginning for a small boy could there be? Another book by Margaret Wise Brown that has delighted the boys is one not nearly as widely read as it deserves to be, *David's Little Indian,* evoking in a deceptively simple way the changing of the seasons and the beauty of living things and wonderfully illustrated by Remy Charlip. We have read all the books of Bemelmans; in the *Madeline* verses he is a master of understatement, and, as Marianne Moore points out, of anti-climax:

> They smiled at the good
> and frowned at the bad
> and sometimes they were very sad.

I could go on at length; but I do not wish to give the impression that I have done all the reading to my sons myself; it is much more often their mother who has done so. At the moment, she has involved them to their great delight in *The Seven Champions of Christendom,* edited by F. J. Harvey Darton. She herself enjoyed immensely when young hearing the Dr. Dolittle books; and all these she has rediscovered with David. She also read him every one of the Andrew Lang fairy books, as well as countless other fairy tale collections, the Padraic Colum books, and *The Peterkin Papers.* I can take credit for having got both boys interested in Uncle Remus; I have read many times from *The Complete Tales,* and pride myself on reading them with the proper accent and rhythm. The favorite is "A Ghost Story," one of the best ghost stories ever told. (Mark Twain had a very similar one, the locale shifted to the North, that he told with great gusto on the platform, and which I heard Hal Holbrook tell last year with great brilliance in his impersonation, "Mark Twain Tonight.") The dialect of these stories sometimes spoils them for children, but only when not read aloud or when read aloud poorly by someone unfamiliar with Southern speech. I can understand the objections of modern Negroes to some of the more unfortunate aspects of Uncle Remus's character, but these may be eliminated by proper selection; and it would be sad indeed for modern children to miss hearing these great stories as they were originally told rather than in the frightful Walt Disney adulterations. I can take credit also for having read to both boys a great variety of poems and verses — Stevenson, de la Mare, A. A. Milne, Elizabeth Madox Roberts, Lewis Carroll, James Whitcomb Riley, Dr. Seuss (in small doses), Hilaire Belloc, Edgar Allen Poe (wonderful, if only for the vowel sounds).

Recently David and Gregory flew with me by jet from New York to Los Angeles; when we left our Vermont farm that morning and drove to Albany it was snowing; that afternoon, when we arrived in Los Angeles, the sun was shining and the thermometer stood at eighty degrees. I felt very much the proud parent when a number of passengers remarked on my unusually well-behaved sons; I had read to them aloud as we crossed the continent the adventures of Tintin — *Red Rackham's Treasure, The Secret of the Unicorn, The Crab with the Golden Claws,* and *Destination Moon,* and they had scarcely moved a muscle. While our fellow jet-travelers had got only as far as Los Angeles, we had, in the company of Tintin, reached the moon. As I gazed out at the bright sunlight on the palm trees ("those funny *pine* trees," Greg said), I felt that we had flown beyond time, and in this mad world had, for a moment and surely by the most unlikely modern means, recaptured a bit of the "rhythm of the night."

From *The Horn Book* for December, 1960

THEODORE ROOSEVELT AND CHILDREN'S BOOKS

By Peggy Sullivan

THERE is much talk these days of the lack of leisure in American life and fear of a corresponding lack of shared reading in the family. Yet fifty years ago, one of our most active and versatile presidents was an enthusiastic proponent of family reading. For Theodore Roosevelt, his own pleasure in books grew as he shared it with his family. His letters to his sons when they were away at school were filled with accounts of daily life at home, including the reading time with Archie and Quentin, "the little boys." Shortly before Christmas in 1904, he mentioned that he had finished reading *The Last of the Mohicans* to them and characteristically added, "They are as cunning as ever, and this reading to them in the evening gives me a chance to see them that I would not otherwise have, although sometimes it is rather hard to get time." This was a president who had just won an election for his program of active interest in relations among nations in the western hemisphere and who was earning for himself the prestige and reputation for integrity which were to assure his successful mediation of the Russo-Japanese war and his receiving the Nobel Prize for Peace.

Roosevelt chose Cooper for reading-aloud sessions, and the sturdy nationalism and action must have appealed to his taste, but he also delighted in the gay nonsense verses which he shared with the boys. He read some of Laura E. Richards' poems to them, including "How Does the President Take His

Quotations are from *Theodore Roosevelt's Letters to His Children* by Joseph Bucklin Bishop, Charles Scribner's Sons, 1919.

Tea?" Archie and Quentin immediately christened themselves Punkey Doodle and Jollapin, from the chorus — and another bit of family folklore was added. It is natural that parental enthusiasm would have awakened responses in the children, and these were a delight to Roosevelt. He undoubtedly flattered his sons by assuming they were familiar with his allusions, as when he wrote to Kermit: "You remember Kenneth Grahame's account of how Harold went to the circus and sang the great spheral song of the circus? Well, yesterday Mother leaned out of her window and heard Archie, swinging under a magnolia tree, singing away to himself, 'I'm going to Sagamore, to Sagamore, to Sagamore. I'm going to Sagamore, oh, to Sagamore!' It was his spheral song of joy and thanksgiving."

Roosevelt's allusions to shared reading were frequent, so the fun of books must have been enjoyed by all the family. To his sister-in-law, the President wrote to describe an Oyster Bay picnic which was attended by the German ambassador, Count Speck von Sternberg, "looking more like Hans Christian Andersen's little tin soldier than ever." In the same letter, he relished his son Ted's description of a luncheon to which he had taken the younger boys who "had been altogether too much like a March Hare tea-party, as Archie, Nicholas and Oliver were not alive to the dignity of the occasion." Even young Kermit delighted his father by remembering what he had read. As Roosevelt told it in a letter, Kermit and Ethel were having a Bible lesson and wondering why Joseph had told his dreams to his brothers, when Kermit decided, "Well, I guess he was simple, like Jane in the Gollywogs."

The Theodore Roosevelt House in New York commemorates another bit of the family lore growing from shared reading. In the case with a figurine of a cat is a note from the President's widow, telling how he had called Mrs. Ralph Cross Johnson, a prominent Washingtonian, "Aunt Jobiska," referring to Edward Lear's delightful nonsense poem, "The Pobble Who Has No Toes." Mrs. Roosevelt said she herself had seen the figurine of the "runcible cat" in a shop and "brought it home to send as a joke." The cat figures in the third stanza of the poem:

>   The Pobble swam fast and well,
>   And when boats or ships came near him,
>   He tinkledy-blinkledy-winkled a bell
>   So that all the world could hear him.
>   And all the Sailors and Admirals cried,
>   When they saw him nearing the further side,—
>   "He has gone to fish, for his Aunt Jobiska's
>   Runcible Cat with crimson whiskers.

Roosevelt's own childhood reading had centered around some sternly moralistic stories like "Cast Away in the Cold" and "Grandfather's Struggle for a Homestead" from *Our Young Folks* magazine. He characterized them as "good healthy stories . . . teaching manliness, decency and good conduct." He did not lose interest in the moralistic aspects of literature but fortunately his ebullient sense of humor tempered his taste. To his children, he expressed interest in their independent reading and shared his views with his sons when they wrote home from school about reading the classics. He had a prejudice against Dickens, although he admitted the universality of some of his characters. He compared Dickens to Bunyan and Thackeray, and concluded that "one fundamental difference between Thackeray and Dickens is that Thackeray was a gentleman and Dickens was not. But a man might do some mighty good work and not be a gentleman in any sense."

He was concerned with selecting the right books for his children, and wrote to ask Ted whether he was ready yet for a good history of the American Revolution, suggesting Trevelyan's which he considered the best. He said he might send his own copy, but warned Ted to "be very careful of it, because he sent it to me himself."

For a president who received many gifts of value, he was especially appreciative when Joel Chandler Harris sent one of his books to Ethel, and thanked him by saying, "It is worth while being President when one's small daughter receives that kind of an autograph gift." He recalled his own pleasure as a child in hearing some of the Brer Rabbit stories, but commended Harris even more as "an addition to the forces that tell for decency, and above all for the blotting out of sectional antagonism." Nevertheless, the animal stories had made a lasting impression on him, for he once wrote to Quentin about seeing a Brer Terrapin and Brer Rabbit when he was out riding, but "Brer Rabbit went lippity lippity lippity off into the bushes and Brer Terrapin drew in his head and legs till I passed." Perhaps he had his rabbits a bit confused, though, for wouldn't it be Peter going "lippity lippity lippity" off into the bushes?

What we know of Roosevelt's interest in his children's reading comes mostly from his letters. It would indeed have been more of a joy to have heard this great man reading aloud, leaving to his children a heritage of service to his country and of greatness, but an important heritage of remembered pleasures in shared reading as well.

From *The Horn Book,* February, 1959

THE PLEASANT LAND OF COUNTERPANE

By Claudia Lewis

RECENTLY I CAME UPON a badly torn storybook I had greatly loved in my childhood. It had been my mother's when she was a child — "a reward for having a tooth pulled by the dentist" she had written on the flyleaf. The stories in *Goody Two Shoes and Other Stories*, compiled by Clara Doty Bates and Mary E. Wilkins, had been read aloud over and over to me and my brothers and sister — "Rumpelstiltskin," "Wee Willie Winkie," "The Fox and the Goslings," "The Three Little Kittens," and others.

Curious to know what I would think of them now in the light of the values I hold as both a teacher of children's literature and a writer for children, I began to read the stories. I had not remembered that they were in verse, and surely had not realized that the versification was undistinguished and the style more appropriate for adults than for children. "Of course, of course," I said to myself, "it was my mother's presence and her wonderful storytelling way and her own enjoyment that made these stories so beloved."

I turned to "The Three Little Kittens," one of the tales most fondly remembered. Suddenly in the midst of the pleasantly chattering lines I came upon these four that referred to the mother cat:

> Again she settles herself and sleeps;
> This time she dreams that she crouches and creeps,
> A great gray tiger along the grass,
> While herds of soft-eyed antelopes pass, . . .

"Herds of soft-eyed antelopes." Something stirred in me: a half-recognition of what I had felt, guessed at, wondered at as a child when I had heard this line. No doubt about it, the words were still alive for me. Great poetry? Perhaps not; yet more felicitous than what had gone before, and to me as a child *not quite understood*. Antelopes were creatures I had never seen and knew little about. And where were those herds going? Why did the antelopes with their soft eyes pass by while the tiger crouched in the grass? I never knew; but I must have tried to sense the implication.

I recall a somewhat similar encounter with Robert Louis Stevenson's "The Land of Counterpane" — a poem far more magical for me than Stevenson would ever have guessed it could be for a child. And why? Simply because of that bewildering word counterpane. Yes, of course, my mother explained to me what it meant, and in some rational part of my mind I knew very clearly what it meant. Yet it was not a word current in the everyday speech of the people around me; and it suggested a baffling combination of windowpane and kitchen counter. At the same time, what a splendid-sounding word it was! I must have closed off that rational corner of mine and let my thoughts go romping off with whatever textural images and associations the word called up, and fortunately for me, my mother did not drill in the meaning. I was left to enjoy the poem, and enjoy it I did, in my own way. It would be difficult for me to describe just what "the pleasant land of counterpane" was to me (and still is). This is a case of the quality of a particular word spilling over and giving color to a whole poem, or rather, to the poem one reconstructs inwardly in heightened imaginative dimensions.

Let me say, also, something about my childhood experience with George Macdonald's *At the Back of the North Wind*. Here again I was exposed to words and concepts that were not fully understood. Yet they had the power to generate vortexes of feeling that swirled up through my life and are not yet completely extinguished. I think my mother did not read the whole book aloud to me: I have no memory of any parts of it except the boy Diamond's discovery of the wind in the knothole, his rides in the night, bound in the hair of the great, sweeping creature, and his eerie walk through the ice image to the land that lay at the North Wind's back — in short, the episodes embodying the book's major symbolisms. Certainly they were far too much for me to grasp, but they intrigued me endlessly. Through the author's extraordinary imagination, I entered a realm existing beyond everyday reality and possibility. Perhaps it was the impact of this discovery — that one could walk through the pages of a book into strange, undreamed-of, and wondrous worlds — that lay at the base of the compelling attraction the book held for me. I know that when I returned to the story in my adult years, it was with trepidation. Would I find it a paltry thing, after all? No, it was not paltry, yet it was not as evocative as the book I remembered. I closed it and left it, and let my childhood reactions slip back into their rightful place. After all, Macdonald wrote the book for children, not for adults, and my receptivity as a child was the co-creator of the book's power. Nor should I underestimate the importance of the fact that my story-loving mother, who chose the book for me in the first place, conveyed to me her own responsiveness to the story's strange allure.

I mention these childhood reactions because they seem pertinent to a concern many of us have about an emphasis today on the paring down of story materials until supposedly they are accessible even to the "disadvantaged" child, who should have what he knows, start where he is, and find his own world in his books. I am the last person to raise objections to the effort to improve reading ability and to open up the pleasures of reading to all children. But let us remember, as we assess where children *are* and what their worlds are, that all children can find their bearings in two worlds, the one realistic, the other symbolic. For all of us — even the disadvantaged — are symbol-making creatures and lovers of words. And if anyone doubts this, listen to the way a group of "deprived" six- to eight-year-olds, many of them woefully inarticulate in English, found their way into vivid metaphorical expression, with the encouragement of their teacher, on one of the first warm days last spring:

How did the day feel? Like china cups, like balloons, like your heart is warming up, like a deer feels, like your head is too heavy today, like spring mixed up with the sun. . . .

How did the day smell? Like peppermint, like flowers are going to grow where you're standing, like the trees are having leaves. . . .

How did the day taste? Like ice cream, like French fries, like cherry soda, like clouds, like if you took a big bite of the world, you'd have too much air in your stomach and fly away like a balloon. . . .

Children such as these perhaps need only the enthusiasm of a teacher or a librarian or a parent to open up to them excitements in language, excitements in books. Am I saying that I would attempt to read *At the Back of the North Wind* to them, or to children like them who are a little older? No. Such a complex Victorian story would be a poor choice. But Kipling's "The Elephant's Child," read aloud by an adult who loves the "great grey-green, greasy Limpopo River, all set about with fever trees" could have tremendous impact. Or consider E. B. White's fantasy *Stuart Little*. Many teachers know that this modern fairy tale about a jaunty little mouse-boy can hold eight-year-olds spellbound, whether or not they are children who are adept in the use of English and whether or not anyone has ever opened a storybook and read aloud to them before. No wonder. The little mouse-boy always calls upon his ingenuity and comes out on top; and furthermore, though he moves through the everyday world familiar to children, it is the everyday world overlaid with a new dimension of magical possibility, and no child can enter it without the delightful exercise of squeezing himself down until he can look about with Stuart-sized perceptions.

Interestingly enough, a teacher who spoke to me recently about his success in reaching children with *Stuart Little* was a man, and one who obviously enjoyed the story himself (unlike a number of women who frankly admit a certain distaste because of the fact that Stuart is a mouse-child born into a human family). Very well. Let the men teachers read this book, and let the women find other stories that they feel excited about and really want to read aloud to their children — E. B. White's *Charlotte's Web,* perhaps. This is a book of multifold riches, as a good children's book should be, containing themes so meaningful, characterizations so alive, individual, and full of humanity that almost any child can discover something in the book for himself; that is, can bring his own needs, tastes, and wishes to the story and find at least some of them gratified. And certainly many children, having once heard the book read aloud, will go back to it and read it through again and again, their interest helping them master the words they do not know.

Or try Scott O'Dell's *Island of the Blue Dolphins,* if the children in the class are at least ten or eleven years old. If a teacher ever doubts the appropriateness of presenting fully mature language and concepts to children, let her read aloud only one chapter of this beautiful, somber tale of the Indian girl who was caught in a dilemma very like Robinson Crusoe's.

One young woman I know, just begining her first year of teaching, was herself so swept up by this story that she chose it as the first book to read to her fifth-grade public-school class. I confess that I had misgivings when she spoke of her intention, knowing that her children were by no means exceptional in either abilities or experience. But my misgivings were unfounded. The children loved the story, and I am convinced that this teacher's over-all success in all areas of her teaching may have been partly due to the relationship she was establishing with the children through this deeply satisfying reading experience.

Certainly the adult's own excitement over the story chosen for reading aloud is crucial and can help children over what might seem insurmountable difficulties. Howard Pyle's *Merry Adventures of Robin Hood,* for instance, though matchless for its spirited action and sinewy style, is peppered with archaic expressions that might make it seem on first glance to be an unsuitable choice for boys and girls of our time. Yet the story can be very successfully brought to children by an adult who believes in these archaisms, that is, believes in their power to help the listener plunge away from the present and into the past, where he may give himself up freely to the fantasies of aggressive and righteous rebellion evoked by the story's bold themes. Or the adult need only believe in the power of the language to give delight. What if some of the story's phrases do lack clarity in twentieth-century terms? We deprive the child of his need to exercise his own perceptions, reach for meanings, and discover and savor words in his own way if we oversimplify for him; if we tell him, for instance, that Robin Hood's head was ringing like an alarm bell — as one modernized version puts it — instead of letting him hear the suggestive rhythm and sound of Pyle's "By this and by that, my head hummeth like to a hive of bees on a hot June day."

The same is true of the great Greek and Norse myths and legends — that body of story lore so deeply appealing to preadolescent children, who are molding their growing identification with adults and reaching out to find their values and beliefs. In the myths they discover symbolic expression of their own glimpses into the nature of man's powers and man's fate. For them, story versions that retain poetic overtones and create an aura of faraway and long ago are actually much more compelling than those that attempt to bring the settings close to the present. In the story of Pluto's capture of Persephone, for example, there is no need to present Pluto as "a big man" standing in a chariot snapping a whip, when one can open Edith Hamilton's great *Mythology* and discover that Pluto is "the lord of the dark underworld, the king of the multitudinous dead." And there are other good tellings of the myths more specifically written for children, among them Sally Benson's *Stories of the Gods and Heroes* and Anne Terry White's *The Golden Treasury of Myths and Legends*. Both retain vestiges of the roll of an old syntax and, at the same time, bring modern clarity to the prose. What difficulties remain are negligible. The eagerness of children to leap into the seats of the gods carries them over the hurdles and on with the action.

In what I am writing here I am assuming that introducing children to literature and to the whole process of intelligent reading implies reading aloud to them. Certainly children can read without experiencing the privilege of this exposure, but the loss to them is incalculable. For we can bring to them in our reading aloud what most of them cannot find for themselves, since reading level generally lags behind appreciation level through all the elementary grades.

I am almost too far from that time when the story world was opened to me (at home, for it did not happen at school) to track down the full and furious joy of it. But I think the joy has much to do with the fact that a child's ability to visualize people and places, as a story unfolds, may be at its keenest in these early years, when all the senses are sharp and receptive. For the child, the story world takes on an immediate and vivid reality similar to the reality of the world of play. And since his lively emotions are always trigger-poised to take the leap into personified form, he himself becomes the doer, the slayer, the runner, the weeper. In short, as he listens, he is not merely hearing a story; he is living an intensified life spread out for him in new dimensions of time and place.

It is up to us to see that we offer him personification possibilities that are worthy of him: symbols that are flexible and varied enough to serve the whole gamut of his emotions, and style that is arresting enough in the first place to invite him and then to convince him that the world of words is well worth his mastery.

From *The Horn Book* for October, 1966

STORYTELLING IN THE FAMILY

By Hilda van Stockum

MY FATHER, whose study was lined with books from top to bottom, and who could stand for hours reciting his favorite poetry, only stopping now and then with a twinkling glance over his glasses to see if we appreciated it properly, often told us with a chuckle that his mother had to bribe him to read books when he was a boy. My father was one of nine children, and perhaps his mother was too busy to tell him stories when he was young, because I am sure he would have liked books if she had. After all, stories came long before books; and in primitive places stories still prevail. The most wonderful ancient ballads are handed down simply from mouth to ear; it is only recently that people have started to write them down. It would be a pity if the ancient art of storytelling were lost because of our superior skills.

I have sometimes wondered what the fascination is in storytelling. Any story and any teller will do. My brother and I used to tell each other stories by the hour, while lying in our white metal beds in the nursery. I remember the singsong voice my brother used. His stories were very monotonous, but I enjoyed them anyway, and I think he enjoyed mine. How often, around a campfire, does a very inferior story make a great hit. I think it is because something else is added: atmosphere, and the personality of the narrator. Besides, when listening to a story we are being creative ourselves; we are adding to it with our own imagination. For a child, the story is the way to his heart. He has the adult *with* him, which so seldom happens. People think a child doesn't know when his father and mother are only physically present while their thoughts are miles away; but he does know. That's why he always fires off a barrage of questions exactly when you are trying to think of what to serve for dinner. He wants your thoughts *with* him. And, of course, in a story they are. He's got the whole of you — and that's what he wants. He knows very well that in ordinary conversation he has only part of you:

"Mummy, can I have another candy?"

An abstract stare and a vague "Yes, darling." He takes advantage of the fact that you aren't there at all, and he knows very well that you haven't heard a *thing*. The same thing happens when he is telling *you* a story. As he stumbles through the sentences, trying to get the right reaction from you, he notices that you have lost the thread long ago and are only being kind to him. But when *you* are telling *him* a story he's got you. He asks questions, and you give him intelligent answers. He is even able to influence the course of the story by suggestions:

"No, Mummy — the bear *didn't* fall into the pit — he is *much* too smart. . . ." It becomes *his* story, *his* adventure — and he continues it to himself as he falls asleep. As his mother switches from storytelling to reading aloud, he begins to associate this pleasure with books. And then he begins to find it irksome that he can't command it himself.

"Mummy, read out — Mummy, read this out. I want to know what it says. What do the pictures mean?"

"No, dear, I've no time now. Wait till I've done the beds and fixed the lunch."

"But I want to know *now*."

"Well, then, you'd better learn to read, dear."

So he starts to wrestle with the alphabet. At least that's the way it happened to me and to my children. Trying to teach a child to read who doesn't know the magic of stories seems to me like trying to catch a fish with an unbaited hook. Dr. Maria Montessori has proved that children are ripe for reading long before they are six years old. What she calls the "sensitive period" for reading occurs at about four. A Montessori child can read very well at five. We retard our children by underestimating them. Not that they should be pushed, but an intelligent child is ready for intellectual food long before we think he is. I have often wondered whether the Victorians weren't wiser in that respect. In Charlotte Yonge's books you find tots of five doing their Latin as a matter of course. Intellectually speaking, the Victorian age was a rich one, far richer than the present, which has made such material and scientific advances. It seems to me that this age is gravely deficient in the very qualities which a story hour supplies. Stories are born out of experience and they have often a quality of folklore: the accumulated wisdom of ages, and a sense of symbol. Since the eighteenth century the West has become very smart-alecky, very cocksure and know-it-all, with a lack of reverence toward creation as a whole and toward those spiritual and psychological laws of which we still know little. There is too much scorn for the symbols of more primitive peoples, too much superiority toward their ways of life. There is a sad overestimation of our own conquests and virtues. Poetry has been forced to the background, along with all the other arts, while we live the hardheaded existence of "realists." The "Oh yeah?" attitude is poison.

The story hour at an early age is the antidote to all this. I remember it so well from my childhood. The logs burning in the deep fireplace; outside, the wind howling. My father at his post as commander of the seaport in IJmuiden, an arduous position at the time of the First World War. Europe rocking in conflict, and we children sitting cozily (if a little undernourished) by the fire while my mother told stories. And what stories! She told of King Arthur and his Knights, of the Holy Grail, and of Percival's quest and his sins. She also told us of the knight in search of a maiden who would both blush and smile when he kissed her. The maiden who only blushed was too prudish and didn't love him; the maiden who only smiled was too used to kissing; but the maiden who both blushed and smiled was the wife for him! And she told us Selma Lagerlöf's beautiful story of the candleflame: the knight who tried to bring home a sacred candleflame and had to give up everything in order to guard it. She also told us Agnes Günther's story of the poor little German princess who looked for a doll with a soul. They were all tales with a deep significance, and we thrilled to them. Later, when my elder brother volunteered in the Second World War (in which he lost his life) he said he felt so strongly about it because of Mother's tales which had given him the values of chivalry.

My father also told stories, but they were quite different. He loved "Alice in Wonderland" and Kipling's elephant, and his stories were funny and appealed to our sense of logic. We had a cook who was addicted to ballads. She sang them while cleaning the silver. I remember to this day the sad song of the two royal children who loved each other but couldn't reach each other because the water was too deep. All Amalia's songs were sad, and from the reaction of my parents when I imitated her I doubt whether she had a special talent for singing, but I used to wallow in the sentiment that poured from her lips. Once when Mother was ill, a young girl came to help her. She had dark curls and glittering dark eyes, and when there wasn't enough to eat (on account of the British blockade), she'd tell us ghost stories so gruesome that the skin shriveled on our backs and we crept up to bed, our candles shaking in our hands so that the hot wax burned our wrists. It was quite enough to take away any appetite we'd had. When my mother's illness grew worse, we children were sent to relatives to stay for a while, and I stayed with my aunt, Mother's youngest sister. There I discovered the Bible. My father and mother were agnostic at the time and never mentioned religion, but my aunt was a devout Christian, and every Sunday she would give us Bible lessons. She had a wonderful dramatic talent. Her storytelling was quite different from my mother's. When Mother spoke she spun a web, a silvery web in which we hung like hypnotized flies. She had a beautiful voice which went on and on in rhythmic cadences, and she made us share her own reverence for what was noble and good.

My aunt, however, had the gift to make the people she introduced spring to life. I remember how she described poor St. Peter sleeping in his dungeon, big chains on his legs, and the angel waking him up and rescuing him, while all the time St. Peter thought he was still dreaming. There he was, solid and human — just like us. When Mother told a story we knew it had happened a long time ago, but my aunt Catherine's stories happened here and now. You could smell the dust, feel the crowds jostling you, see laden donkeys and waving palm trees, and hear the whining voices of the beggars. Strangely enough, it was my mother's stories which gave me the strongest *religious* sense, although my aunt opened for me the world of the Bible and made it live for me.

I had loved these hours of listening so much that I wanted my children to have the same joy. I felt diffident, knowing I wasn't half as good a storyteller as my aunt or my mother, but I learned that it wasn't a matter of talent. Olga, at three, would literally gobble up the words as they came out of my mouth, and she proved that she understood them very well by turning the tables on me. I had invented Arabella, an impossibly virtuous maiden, for pedagogical purposes. When I displeased Olga once, she pointed an accusing finger at me and cried, "Arabella's mother wouldn't have done that!"

Dr. Montessori has said, "A child is never idle; he is busy all the time building himself into a man." What is to us a moment of relaxation is to the child a means of learning values, increasing his knowledge of good and evil. When parents tell their child a story it may seem a trivial occasion to them, but it isn't. The child intuitively grasps far more than is said. He is sensitive to the least intonation and inflection of his parent's voice. He gathers in with the words his parent's whole philosophy of life. Can television or radio fulfill this need? If parents realized the importance of the early years in furnishing a child's mind with images they would not leave it to commercial sponsors to decide what their children are to hear and look at.

I have often smiled at the glaring discrepancy between the carefully selected material in children's libraries and the sophisticated programs they get on television at home. I wouldn't be surprised if the child began to classify books as "kid stuff" and television as "the real thing." That it is really the other way around he has no way of knowing. Parents often help children to despise their books. Many times someone has come up to me and said, "My Dicky (or Susie) loves your book, and I'm ashamed to say I rather enjoyed it myself." What is disgraceful about liking a children's book? And if that is the parents' attitude, while television is looked at with respect, how can they expect their children to feel differently?

My parents loved children's books. They relished the poetry and wisdom in them, and the humor. I remember my father's delight in *Johnny Crow's Garden,* for instance. But the books had to be good. When my mother didn't like a book, found it vulgar or untrue, she'd fling it from her. "That's twaddle," she'd snort contemptuously. Many people don't seem to realize that good children's books are works of art. They deal with the fundamentals of life. Good children's authors do what my parents did in telling us stories: they give us distilled wisdom, purified memory, an attitude to life, and dearly bought experience. Hans Christian Andersen's fairy tales sprang from his sufferings as pearls grow from an oyster's wound. Louisa May Alcott and Laura Ingalls Wilder gave us their own stories and poured into them all the joys of their childhood and the love they felt for their families. Mark Twain shared with us his adventures on the Mississippi; Robert Louis Stevenson his dreams born from a delicate childhood; Nesbit gave us her understanding of children. And among modern writers, C. S. Lewis and J. R. R. Tolkien have given us all they most deeply believe in — in the form of fairy tales. I could go on with this list, and add to it the pictures: the beautiful illustrations of Randolph Caldecott, Elsa Beskow, Arthur Rackham, Boutet de Monvel, Robert McCloskey, Lauren Ford, Marguerite de Angeli, Robert Lawson, and many others, all sharing with us the delights of the scenes they loved. These are only random names out of a host of great artists and authors who have given the best of their poetry and vision to children. And children understand it, unless they are spoiled. Children are born with innocent, open minds. They are as yet untouched by vulgarity, prejudice, or fashion. They are not in a hurry, they have all the time in the world to savor every detail of what is given them, and they don't mind reading the same book over and over again. They hunger for what is real and what can nourish them deeply — and though they can draw some honey from even inferior material, it is foolishness to give them anything but the best.

From *The Horn Book* for June, 1961

MORE THOUGHTS ON READING TO CHILDREN

> These tales not only stayed in Dick's head, but *lived* there. He not only remembered them, but thought about them; and he sometimes dreamed about them. He not only knew almost by heart what they told, but would please himself by fancying what else had happened to the people in them after the tales were over or before they had begun. He could not only find his way about in a story-book, chapter by chapter, page by page, but if it told only about the inside of a house he would begin to wonder what its garden was like — and in imagination would find his way out into it and then perhaps try to explore even further.
> —From "Dick and the Beanstalk," by Walter de la Mare

ALL CHILDREN should have access to the tales that not only stay in the head but "live" there, but many children need help to find these stories early enough. Nothing has replaced the age-old custom of reading aloud to entice children into the realm of good books.

A recent television series has called attention to the pleasure of reading aloud and sharing good books in families, but the detailed planning and rehearsal required for a television show destroy the naturalness which is the charm of successful family reading. However, it was a valiant effort, and the sponsors — and their advisors — who sought to revive something that should not be lost to children today deserve our thanks.

Whenever there is occasion among adults for childhood reminiscence almost invariably the recollection of listening to stories told or read aloud is recounted with pleasure. But few of these same people, treasuring such memories, consider the value similar experiences could have for children today. These television programs were a reminder.

The absence of the realization of most young parents of the pleasure that family reading aloud can give was brought home to me again when I read of the newspaper editor, his wife, and three young daughters, who contributed to scientific research by living for one week in a bomb shelter. Evidently a bookish family, each member took a few books for individual reading, but the fact that some well chosen books for reading aloud could have given point to each day, and might have made the experience more than a test of endurance — something to be remembered with pleasure — either did not occur to them or was not considered significant enough for the newspaper report.

Blame for the fact that few parents think of reading aloud except to very young children cannot be laid entirely to an obsession with television and the many demands made today on children's time. Perhaps it is because today there are just too many books. It is not surprising if many parents think that, with the vast spread of color and pictures on the children's book tables and shelves of bookshops, children should have no trouble in finding for themselves all the entertainment they could want in books. No longer are treasures concealed in shelves full of dull-looking volumes. Yet in the very belief that children do not need help to find the good books lies the root of the trouble: the complete ignorance of many adults of the field of children's books.

When read aloud — the acid test of good writing — many books disguised by handsome pictures and stunning format are boring and silly. These are enough to discourage any parent and cause him to decide that the tastes of children have changed, and that with all the attractive books available parents do not need to be bothered to help children find reading material. Nothing could be farther from the truth.

One of the services *The Horn Book* has always tried to give is to point up in the Booklist the books which should be read aloud to give the maximum pleasure. Many of these are experiences for special times in children's lives — picture-story books, fantasy, or unusual historical fiction — which may appeal to one child at a time in a family. It is more difficult to find books which have something for every age, that can hold every member of the family — father and mother as well — when they are read aloud. But such books do exist, and new ones are appearing each year. I believe that George Selden's *The Cricket in Times Square* reviewed in October, is one of these, and among last year's books are Margery Sharp's *The Rescuers* and Mary Norton's *The Borrowers Afloat*.

From time to time *Horn Book* readers write us of experiences they have had reading aloud to children. A teacher, sending to the Horn Book League a picture painted by an eight-year-old boy who had lost the sight of an eye, said that probably the two things that did most to bring about the boy's emotional recovery were his art work and his mother reading aloud to him, especially the Dr. Dolittle stories. An Oregon mother has written describing the family's summer on a mountain catching trout, "watching a family of green swallows grow from egg to flight," and enjoying the wild plants and flowers, and concludes with, "At night we read together. *The Secret Garden* was an especially happy choice, and *Kildee House* also held everyone's interest despite the difference in age." It will be a pleasure to pass on to *Horn Book* readers suggestions of good books that other families have enjoyed.

We should like to call attention to a few books not previously reviewed which we believe have qualities that will make them successful for reading aloud to a varied group.

Walter de la Mare's stories can be enjoyed on many levels. Their good plots endear them to the younger children; their atmosphere and mystery enchant the older boys and girls; and the beauty of their style makes them a rich experience for any age. Unavailable in American editions for many years, it is exciting to have six of them in a new book, *A Penny a Day* (illustrated by Paul E. Kennedy). Included are stories from several early collections, some of which have not before been published in the United States. The quotation above is from one of the stories in this book. The others, in addition to the title story, are "The Three Sleeping Boys of Warwickshire," "The Lovely Myfanwy," "The Dutch Cheese," and "The Lord Fish."

In Warren Chappell's *They Say Stories* fourteen short tales have been woven around such old proverbs as "There is only one pretty child in the world and every mother has it," "Cobblers do not judge above the shoe," and "Who hath no courage must have legs." The stories are original and varied, well told, and delightfully illustrated with Mr. Chappell's full-color and black-and-white drawings. It is a book that is both beautiful and fun and could conceivably start listeners making up their own stories around other old proverbs.

Taro Yashima has translated, adapted, and illustrated *The Golden Footprints* by a contemporary Japanese writer, Hatoju Muku. It is the story of a baby fox captured by a farmer, of the boy Shotaro who longed to set the fox free, and the efforts of the parent foxes to rescue it. Sensitively written, it creates with complete reality in very few pages and with skillful understatement, a bit of Japan and a way of life, as well as a memorable story.

Excitement for the younger children and fun for anyone is in Ursula Moray Williams' *Island Mackenzie*. Shipwrecked on a tropical island, the little cat Mackenzie survived the dangers of sharks and crocodiles and found plenty of good food, but almost did not survive the enmity of Miss Mary Pettifer. Mackenzie is a most engaging character who, through experiences exciting, fearsome, and funny, remains a true cat. A book to read aloud to those too young to read for themselves, it is written with the wit and style to captivate any age at all. Edward Ardizzone's pictures are so much at home they would seem to have evolved with the story. R. H. V.

From *The Horn Book* for December, 1960

VIII

NOTES AND COMMENTS

These notes and comments have been gathered for the most part from *Horn Book* booklists and "Hunt Breakfast," and from material the writers have supplied. The object of the section is to answer the questions that might arise in the minds of the readers of the articles. In some instances the writers have contributed comments that reinforce their papers. If one looks upon this book as a symposium, this section serves as an introduction to the participants and adds a few sidelights on the sources from which their reflection and experience derive. An asterisk after a quotation denotes that it comes from a *Horn Book* booklist.

INSPIRATION — HOW IT COMES

This group of articles by writers about their own writing experiences is illuminating because of similarities and differences. The authors speak of inspiration in different terms. To Mabel Leigh Hunt it is "a magical influence, mysterious, exciting, lovely." To Elizabeth Coatsworth it is "a spark inside . . ., like the turning on of a light." Eleanor Estes "picks up the scent" of a book. To Margot Benary-Isbert inspiration comes from singleness of mind, from dedication. To Marjorie Medary and Elisabeth Hamilton Friermood it comes from background, environment, and "roots."

Both Elizabeth Coatsworth and Margot Benary-Isbert write of a *genius loci*. With them creativity may start with a particular house or village or landscape. With Eleanor Estes the source of creativity is more often a happening, a person, or an animal.

There is a difference in the writing tempo of each author. Elizabeth Coatsworth writes flowingly with an assured ease. Often she drifts into poetry. Eleanor Estes writes buoyantly, although she compares the writer to a singer, "striving, pushing, reaching higher for a still higher, and more eloquent note." To Margot Benary-Isbert there is the element of struggle, battle against periods of inability, against words that intrude and do not have potency. All these writers, however, do their work with earnestness, integrity, and the desire to give their best in thought, understanding, and craftmanship.

MABEL LEIGH HUNT has written a great many stories which please children because they ring true. Beginning with *Lucinda,* published in the thirties, she has written of family life with reality, freshness, and charm. A few of her books are *Little Girl with Seven Names, Better Known as Johnny Appleseed, Stars for Cristy, Ladycake Farm, Singing Among Strangers.* She writes:

> I had almost forgotten "Yeast in the Mind". I reread it with close scrutiny and a keen awareness of the contrasts between the pleasant world of 1951, when it was first published, and the tensions and violence of today. In these mid-sixties, the children's writer finds it very difficult to withdraw to a quiet place where she may try to spin her webs of creation into something tangibly and intangibly worthwhile. Yet it is the spirit of childhood, forever inviolate, we hope, in its innocency and gayety, that must blend and collaborate with the writer's projection of her own self into the child world. She cannot produce without this vital and joyous sharing.
>
> The premise, therefore, that inspiration derives from children is undeniably true. Perhaps, in these clouded days, the writer who is doubting and confused needs to give herself fresh assurance of this truth. For the sake of strengthening her own faith and purpose, perhaps she may even shape it into strong and definitive words that she may follow as if commanded, "Thou shalt write them upon the posts of thy house, and upon thy gates."

ELIZABETH COATSWORTH's contribution to children's literature is one of the most remarkable of any writer. From the time she won the Newbery Medal in 1931 for *The Cat Who Went to Heaven,* a legend in the life of Buddha, she has had published more than fifty books: fanciful tales, historical stories, regional stories (many of Maine), stories of other countries, retellings of legends, and poetry. All are written with imagination, style, and beauty. Her more recent books for young children are *The Little Haymakers, Pika and the Roses;* for the middle age are *The Princess and the Lion, The Noble Doll;* for older children, *Jock's Island.*

In MARGOT BENARY-ISBERT's books dealing with the tragedies of World War II and its aftermath, there is a dedication so earnest and deep that it is felt keenly by the reader. *The Ark* and *Rowan Farm* are stories of a refugee family in Germany and tell how they meet the difficult changes in their lives with courage and a new assessment of values. In *The Shooting Star, Blue Mystery,* and *A Time to Love,* following Annegret from the age of nine until her growing-up, we have a picture of the dangers and disillusionment of that dreadful time. There are roots here, roots in grim experience. Mrs. Benary-Isbert makes young people see the cruelty and futility of war but also that there was still the continuing presence of "fundamental goodness, the beauty and wonder of nature, and the strength of love."*

Everyone knows the Moffats — *The Moffats, the Middle Moffat,* and *Rufus M.,* and the 1952 Newbery Medal winner, *Ginger Pye.* Frances Clarke Sayers in writing about ELEANOR ESTES' books in the August 1952 *Horn Book* calls attention to her vitality.

> There is no doubt that the Moffats derive from their author's own remembrance of childhood, but one feels that the source of her inspiration is inexhaustible. The Pye family, for example, whose adventures heighten the pages of *Ginger Pye*, the Newbery Award book, are not a repetition of a story already told. The setting is the same, the town of Cranbury, but a whole new deep-running source of invention, events, pets, people and reactions runs through this first-rate "mystery" which, once again, is filled with the immense vitality of its author's creative gifts.
>
> There is little or no use in discussing the sources of that vitality, since the mere cataloging of them in no way explains them. But there is some small satisfaction in standing beneath a tree and tracing its pattern of trunk and twig and veined leaf that clothes the boughs. To this observer it seems that the vitality of Eleanor Estes derives from the fact that she sees

childhood whole — its zest, its dilemmas, its cruelties and compassion. She never moves outside that understanding, because she never needs to lean upon the crutch of adult concepts or explanations.

Among other books by Eleanor Estes are *Pinky Pye, The Hundred Dresses, The Sleeping Giant and Other Stories, A Little Oven, The Sun and the Wind and Mr. Todd, The Witch Family,* and *The Alley*.

MARJORIE MEDARY has given us the regional story written with authenticity and feeling. Three of her early books, *Daughter in Crinoline, Prairie Anchorage,* and *Prairie Printer,* are stories of action and fine characterization; all are laid in Iowa, her native state, where her roots are deepest.

Miss Medary has this to add: "In writing this article I recall that I was much concerned about the expression of the *regional* spirit.... Roots are a matter of time, and of late the older I grow, the more I am concerned with the rapid changes in American life and a fear that our young people will know nothing at all about their roots."

A young person will find roots in the soil of the United States in many of the stories of Mabel Leigh Hunt and Elizabeth Coatsworth. In discussing regional stories one should also remember the stories Lois Lenski has written of many parts of the United States showing different ways of life and people of different backgrounds. Her *Strawberry Girl,* laid in Florida, won the Newbery Medal in 1946.

ELISABETH HAMILTON FRIERMOOD's first story was *The Wabash Knows a Secret,* a fine example of regional fiction. Mrs. Friermood tells how the idea grew:

> As a children's librarian I often felt the urge to create a book myself and was continually trying to think of a subject. Then suddenly one day I thought of my mother and the many stories she had told to my brother and me of her childhood when she lived in a two-room log house on the banks of the Wabash River. As soon as I could I traveled to my hometown, Marion, Indiana, to spend the weekend with her. I followed her about asking questions. "What was your log house like? Tell me about the murder of your great-grandfather in canal days. Tell about the country store in Richvalley. What about baptizing in the river?

Tell about your school." Mother enjoyed the reminiscing as much as I did.

On the train going home I looked over my notes and began to see along the river bank a girl who loved the Wabash as much as my mother always has. Three weeks later came a package from her. She had filled a notebook with things she remembered. One thing she wrote impressed me deeply: "Years later when distressed about something, I got better if I remembered June along the Wabash; the corn in the field east of our house, all green and growing; garden coming along fine; hens with their broods in the shade of the maples; Snow, our white cow, grazing in a pasture west of the house; redbirds whistling in the sycamores; the smell of baking bread and the good sound of the Wabash trickling over the stones east of the ford.†

Henrietta of *The Wabash Knows a Secret* has the same deep feeling for the river that Mrs. Friermood's mother had. Her latest book, *Focus the Bright Land*, tells how Vicky proves herself as a good photographer. The period is the time of Garfield's inauguration, and the stage of the development of photography a hundred years ago is well described. All Mrs. Friermood's heroines have determination, a sense of responsibility, and a wholesome point of view.

GOALS AND GUIDELINES FOR WRITERS AND ILLUSTRATORS

There is much in Paul Hazard's *Books, Children and Men* that defines what children want to find in their books, that determines certain guidelines and goals. He writes, "Do not fool yourself into believing that children are going to read any kind of stories, and that all you have to do is to impose your taste on them; that is a beautiful illusion." He agrees with other bits of advice such as, "Do not fail to start off with orginality and liveliness;" — "Avoid wordiness, descriptions that only adults endure kindly; do not forget that almost before one round is ended your reader will be all set to ask you what happened next. They are indefatigable. Be brief. Be nimble."

†From "The Hunt Breakfast," *Horn Book*, July-August, 1951.

PHILIPPA PEARCE feels an obligation "to have a view almost from the inside, to recreate — not what childhood looks like now — but what it felt like then." At the same time the "two parts of an author's life should come together: his own childhood experiences and interests recreated fictionally, and his own maturity reflected in the significance he chooses to give them." Mrs. Pearce's *The Minnow Leads to Treasure* is an English adventure-mystery written "with unusual skill in the development of character and atmosphere and with an awareness of little things important to children."* *Tom's Midnight Garden* (which in 1958 won the Carnegie Medal, the English counterpart of our Newbery Medal) has "time" as its theme. "The episodes are made credible by skillfully created atmosphere and logical conditions governing time."* The phrase "awareness of little things important to children" shows that the writer has "a view from the inside."

MARION GARTHWAITE's plea is for toughness in stories for young people — no "watering down of witches". She has had experience as a librarian, a writer, and a lecturer on children's literature and on storytelling. Several of her books are set in her home state of California. *The Mystery of Skullcap Island* depicts young people who possess initiative and courage. *Shaken Days* tells of the 1906 earthquake and how it affected the Dyke children, each one so different in temperament. As a believer in strong fiction, she writes: "I have the old grandmother in *Bright Particular Star* advise Torrey, the young beginning story-teller, to tell fierce stories — stories the children can get their teeth into and remember. Dragons and flaming wheels and witches and hobgoblins. Ghosts too. If ever our children needed stories of courage and valor and steadfastness, they do now."

DAVID C. DAVIS, professor of children's literature and young child education at the University of Wisconsin, is the orginator of the Lewis Carroll Shelf Award, which for ten years has honored distinguished books which deserve "to sit on the shelf with *Alice*." His satirical essay "It's This Way, Kid!" (*Horn Book,* October, 1964) is a reaction to the Newbery Award winner of that year, *It's Like This, Cat*, by Emily Neville.

ANN PETRY tells us that she is fairly certain she became a novelist because of her writing teacher, Mabel Louise Robinson, a member of the Columbia University English Department and author or editor of thirty-one books. In Miss Robinson's creative writing courses, encouragement and understanding were the major teaching tools. In addition, "she left an unmistakable stamp on all of us. Because of her, we are realists, we are good critics, we work very hard at the job at hand, and we are able to set a standard of excellence for ourselves. I hope that we acquired some of her generosity of spirit."

Mrs. Petry's hope is certainly fulfilled. Reviewers speak of her sympathetic insight into the feelings of Harriet Tubman as a slave and a woman, and the simplicity and beauty of her characterization of Tituba. Readers of *Harriet Tubman, Conductor of the Underground Railroad* and *Tituba of Salem Village* discover that these heroic woman slaves are real — sturdy, indestructible, wonderful Americans.

WARREN CHAPPELL is an illustrator whose recent picture-book adaptations of musical and theatrical productions are especially interesting. *Coppélia: The Girl with Enamel Eyes* is the seventh in a series. Mr. Chappell is the adapter-illustrator of *Coppélia* and the musical themes are by Leo Délibes.

In giving permission for the use of his article Mr. Chappell writes:

> Without looking up the "Bench Marks" article, I can recall that I led off with comments about Ernest Shepard. We began corresponding in 1944. Last June I spent the better part of a day with him — he was then past 87. It seemed strange to be meeting after 22 years of letter writing and collaboration. It was most pleasant — and so I can say that I am especially happy that you want to use the old piece I did because it will teach someone — someday — to get to know Ernest better. By the way, I sent him tear sheets on "Bench Marks," and he replied that Abbey was the man who introduced him to *Punch* and began his illustrating career. Shepard has a roomful of *Punch* artists (his dining room) all framed. In the midst of them, there's a small Caldecott in color — a sketch. It seems to have found the right home.

HENRY C. PITZ' article is based on a paper given in 1961 at a conference on the design and illustration of children's books held at Drexel Institute. His *Illustrating Children's Books: History — Technique — Production* was published in 1963.

> This handsome volume surveys the history of children's books from the illustrator's viewpoint, the place of the illustrator in the children's world, the structure and design of the books, methods of reproduction and the preparation of pictures for reproduction, and concludes with suggestions for the aspiring illustrator about handling an assignment and getting work.... His thoughtfulness is evident in a statement concluding a summary of recent picture books: "The legitimate craving for freshness a few decades ago has brought about a determined and contrived pursuit of freshness, which is beginning to defeat its purpose. One gets the feeling that a brilliant age of children's books is becoming the victim of its success and that a new one is forming behind the polychrome of the present facade."*

BARBARA COONEY won the Caldecott Medal in 1959 for *Chanticleer and the Fox*, which she adapted from Chaucer's "The Nun's Priest's Tale." She tells in her acceptance address how she was inspired by coming upon a little barn when she was returning from a walk in the woods. There before her was "a most gorgeous and impractical flock of fancy chickens — gold chickens, rust-colored chickens, black ones, white ones..."; in short such a colorful array that it started the ball rolling toward the Caldecott Medal. Miss Cooney has been the illustrator for more than fifty books.

BETTINA ERLICH is an author-illustrator who has woven her childhood memories of an Adriatic island into picture-stories about Cocolo the donkey. The titles are *Cocolo; Cocolo Comes to America; Cocolo's Home.*

RE-CREATING OTHER TIMES

CYNTHIA HARNETT, who lives in Henley-on-Thames, has studied medieval London so thoroughly that one wonders if she is able to see the modern London about her. The street, alleys, houses, and historical buildings are carefully and vividly described, often with maps, and always with her own line drawings. But so skillfully are the descriptions woven into the story, the reader does not feel that he is being informed but rather that he is being absorbed into the setting as is Bendy, the young apprentice to William Caxton, who runs about London drinking in its beauty. At the end of *Caxton's Challenge* is a postscript:

> Writing a book of this sort is rather like a detective story in reverse. There are clues all the way through it, but they are not put there by the author to help the reader unravel the plot. The clues in this sort of book are bits of history and facts about people and places that really existed. It is the author's job to find them all out and then to knit them together so that a story comes to life.

Miss Harnett was awarded the Carnegie Medal in 1951 for *Nicholas and the Woolpack*. Other books of hers are *The Drawbridge Gate* and *Stars of Fortune*.

MARCHETTE CHUTE is the author of sixteen books, at least half of them for young people. Behind the writing of her historical stories there is careful historical research. In "Progress Report: 1962" (*Horn Book*, 1962) she says: "Having enjoyed living in Chaucer's century, I thought I might enjoy living in Shakespeare's also. This time I disappeared from view in a sea of research, leaving hardly a trace, and reappeared four years later with a book called *Shakespeare of London*."

The Innocent Wayfaring, which is laid in Chaucer's England, was first published in 1943 by Scribner; it was republished in 1955 by Dutton. Anne Carroll Moore in "The Three Owls' Notebook" (*Horn Book*, June 1955) writes, "Now after twelve years, I have read *The Innocent Wayfaring* again. This time with heightened appreciation of the scholarship behind it and admiration for its balanced sense of humor and regard for contemporary intelligence. I think it not only a book of special appeal to girls but one which aspiring writers for a youthful audience of both sexes may do well to read and reflect upon."

The Wonderful Winter is the story of a boy in Shakespeare's troupe, and Queen Elizabeth's London is given in colorful detail: . . . "I was seized by the conviction that I wanted to write about a boy who acted in Shakespeare's company, as a kind of companion piece to *The Innocent Wayfaring*. This time my runaway was a boy in Suffolk instead of a girl in Surrey, so I went back to the Public Library to find out what hour of the morning the cows were milked in Suffolk in the sixteenth century and the precise coloration of a local frog."

How much more Miss Chute has given us than "gadzooks and rapiers and glimpses of Good Queen Bess" when even a frog has to be accurately described. No one writes of Miss Chute's stories without speaking of their humor, which is unusual and most welcome in children's historical fiction.

LEONARD WIBBERLEY is an experienced, versatile writer who has many adult and young people's books to his credit. The volumes of his Treegate series are *John Treegate's Musket, Peter Treegate's War, Sea Captain from Salem,* and *Treegate's Raiders*. They cover different areas of the American Revolution, some of them little touched upon in other stories of the same period — for example, the Scottish Mountaineers in the Appalachians who served in the Continental Army (*Treegate's Raiders*). He has also written stories about the Spanish Main (*Deadman's Cave*) and the English slave trade (*The Secret of the Hawk*). The adjectives used in reviews of his books are *well-knit, fast-moving, vigorous, real.* In the field of biography, which Mr. Wibberley calls "nonfiction fiction," he has written a series on Thomas Jefferson. Objectively and sympathetically, the social, cultural, and political growth of a great man are recorded in *Young Man from Piedmont, A Dawn in the Trees, The Gales of Spring,* and *Time of Harvest.* These are biographies which will bring Thomas Jefferson back into the minds and consciousness of young adults today because, as Mr. Wibberley says:

> The Past is the generous earth out of which the Present grows to produce the fruit of the Future. Not then to live in the Past and with the Past is to fail to understand the society into which we are born, the culture which we have inherited from others and to which we must ourselves make a contribution if we are not to be mere parasites.
>
> Those who insist that only the Present has importance spend their lives in a mental and spiritual cell, existing as I suppose

leaves exist, but not living. Men must have at least three dimensions to have a full life and those dimensions are Past, Present, and Future.

JOHN and PATRICIA BEATTY write books together and separately. As associate professor of history and the humanities at the University of California, Riverside, Mr. Beatty is the author of a college textbook, *Heritage of Western Civilization*. Mrs. Beatty writes fiction for girls, the last, *The Queen's Own Grove*, is a story of a California orange grove in the 1880s.

Through their work together as accurate and exciting storytellers of English history the Beattys are best known. *At the Seven Stars* and *Campion Towers* give the true sense of history to seventeenth and eighteenth century England. How they solve their problems is told in their own words in an article in the April, 1964 *Horn Book*, "I Would Not Coddle the Child." "It is all too easy to 'write around' or avoid or resolve problems by the calculated ambiguity and appropriate vagueness that are the hallmarks of the lazy, the ignorant, or the dishonest historical novelist. We reject such trickery. And though it makes writing more difficult, it also makes the result more satisfying. Our conviction has its own pitfall, however. When one has a lot of accurate information, he has to restrain himself from overburdening, overwhelming the story with the results of research."

EILEEN H. COLWELL, children's librarian, critic, and reviewer of children's books, is now lecturing on children's literature at the School of Librarianship, Loughborough Technical College, Leicestershire, England. Her enthusiasm for Rosemary Sutcliff's historical novels is shared by readers on both sides of the Atlantic. Miss Sutcliff has seriously studied early Britain and made its history vivid and interesting to young readers of today; moreover her range is even wider, for she moves into legend and mythology with equal soundness of scholarship. In "Beginning with Beowulf," an article which appeared in *The Horn Book* in 1953, she speaks of the books her mother read to her when as a small child she was very ill and spent several years "more or less on my back. . . . Her choice of books was unusual; and from the age of five I was reared on Dickens, Thackeray, and Trollope, on Kingsley's *Westward Ho!* and Lord Lytton's *Last Days of Pompeii,* and other strong meats including two fat and fascinating books of Father's: *Myths of Greece and Rome* and *Hero Myths and Legends of the British Race.* And in this last was the story of Beowulf, which I demanded most often and loved better than all beside."

Miss Sutcliff's stories of early Britain are *The Eagle of the Ninth, Outcast, The Shield Ring, The Silver Branch, Warrior Scarlet, The Lantern Bearers,* and *The Mark of the Horse Lord. The Lantern Bearers* was awarded England's Carnegie Medal as the outstanding children's book of 1959. "Rosemary Sutcliff brings extraordinary scholarship to every one of her books and complete integration of setting and story, but it is the re-creation of life — her penetration into the human heart no matter how distant the time — that makes each period live and gives continuity to history."*

ROSEMARY SPRAGUE is professor of English at Longwood College in Farmville, Virginia. Her historical stories present a range of periods: tenth century Norway, England at the time of the Norman Conquest, eighteenth century London. She is a Browning scholar and has written a biography of Browning, *Forever in Joy,* and compiled *Poems of Robert Browning.*

A Kingdom to Win is the story of tenth century Norway, and the hero, the young Viking Olaf Trygvison, also appears as the liberating king of Norway in Longfellow's *Tales of a Wayside Inn.*

CAROLYN HOROVITZ has had library training at the University of California, Los Angeles, and studied children's literature under Frances Clarke Sayers. She has chosen for analysis several books by well-known writers who she thinks have given "depth of time, place, character, and plot" to the period about which they are writing. But even more important, their works have an "emotional vigor" that reaches to the heart of humanity, that does not change in time or place.

THE MATTER OF POETRY

If the writers in this section were to sit down together for discussion, the interchange would be lively. The questions raised would be, How best to introduce poetry to children? What poets would be most likely to awaken their imagination? What kinds of poetry lead to an appreciation of the words, the rhythm, the meaning of a poem? They would all agree that poetry gives a richness and depth to an individual's inner life and that poetry in childhood, as Harry Behn says, "is essential to maturity."

It would be impossible to discuss poetry for children without reference to Walter de la Mare, a poet, anthologist, and storyteller with the greatest sensitivity, wisdom, and understanding of human aspiration. His first poems for children, *Songs of Childhood*, came in 1902, followed by *A Child's Day*, *Peacock Pie*, *Down-Adown-Derry*, and *Bells and Grass*, among others.

The title of his anthology *Come Hither*, which LOUISE SEAMAN BECHTEL reviews here, is an invitation to partake of something which he considers very special. As Mrs. Bechtel points out, his introduction and notes add immeasurably to his selections, for they take one through intriguing byways to secret places in his own mind and heart and in the minds and hearts of the poets whose poems he has chosen because "they are not mere pretty flowers of the fancy, but the tough piercing roots of the tree of life that grew within their minds."

LEONARD CLARK is an English poet and anthologist, and the editor of Longman's Poetry Library, a unique series of small books devoted to a single theme or to the work of one or two of the major poets. He has also edited *The Complete Poems of Walter de la Mare* and has written a monograph, *Walter de la Mare*. *Drums and Trumpets* and *Flutes and Cymbals* are his own anthologies, and *Green Wood* is a collection of his poems. He has written a delightful foreword to the 1961 edition of Walter de la Mare's *Tom Tiddler's Ground, A Book of Poetry for Children*, in which he says, "Walter de la Mare would certainly have regarded the world of poetry as the richest kind of Tom Tiddler's Ground because all the treasures of poetry are free and are there for the taking. They are compounded, too, of the finest gold and silver, since they are the treasures of man's mind and spirit." This anthology has a plan similar to that of *Come Hither* and includes an introduction and notes in which de la Mare has set down many wise comments on poetry and poets.

Mr. Clark has also written for *The Horn Book* "Andrew Young and His Poetry" (June, 1961).

When HARRY BEHN's first book of poetry for children, *The Little Hill* (1949), was to be published by Harcourt, the sales manager was doubtful that Margaret McElderry, the children's editor, could convey to the salesmen and advertising people the excitement and pleasure she felt for the book. Miss McElderry tells this story:

> A day or two before the conference our sales manager went over the list of new titles with me. "There's only one turkey on your list," he said, "that book of poetry." Out of deep conviction, but with an attempt at humor, I replied that he'd live to be proud of *The Little Hill*. At the sales meeting I gave the book the very best send-off I could, then turned to the sales manager and — foolishly — said, "So much for your turkey!" Whereupon he called the salesmen, one by one, in turn. Each stood up and recited a poem by Harry Behn, which he had memorized, leaving me overwhelmed and overjoyed.†

Since 1949, Harcourt has published many of Harry Behn's books of poetry. He has quoted from some of them in his article. *The Golden Hive* was published after this article was written. "Although Mr. Behn is first of all a poet of nature, his poetry collections have variety of form and mood. . . . Like Mr. Behn's other poems those in the new collection will grow in meaning with every reading."*

Mr. Behn is first of all a poet, but he has written an exciting, imaginative story, *The Faraway Lurs*. Heather is the daughter of the chieftain of a forest-dwelling tribe. Her story is one of "intrigue, taboos, and tragedy; but beauty shines all

†From "'A Few Men and Women,' an Editor's Thoughts on Children's Book Publishing," by Margaret McElderry, *Horn Book*, February, 1962.

through. That is what is remembered. Whether or not this is a true picture of the Bronze Age does not matter — who can know for certain? A dead past is of no interest. The genius of a poet here gives it life."*

Other articles Mr. Behn has contributed to *The Horn Book* are "Reading Up to Ten," June, 1952; "The Golden Age," April, 1960; "Worlds of Innocence," February, 1963; "On Haiku," April, 1964.

SAMUEL FRENCH MORSE is a professor of English at Northeastern University, Boston, and is a critic and reviewer for several well-known literary magazines. He has written a collection of verse for children, *All in a Suitcase*, which is an amusing alphabet book with many original tongue-twisters and bits of nonsense. He is very sure that most children have a "lively sense of rhythm and sound effects." He comments further:

> After making allowances for the differences in an audience of children and an audience of adults, I think a poet who writes for children needs to be as exacting about matters of craft and precision and substance as we expect any other sort of poet to be. A poet must always be conscious of these things, including his audience; but if he is too self-conscious about writing just for children, he is almost sure to spoil what he is doing. He will probably please no one, neither the children nor himself. If he writes as well as he can, he is going to run some risks, although they will be risks worth running. Poetry ought to be "genuine," the real thing, whether funny or serious, if it is to win its readers. It will probably be the better if it does not scream, "I am poetry!" And it will be best if it proves itself by making sound and sense inseparable.

MYRA COHN LIVINGSTON has written many poems for children. Among her books of poems are *Whispers and Other Poems, I'm Hiding,* and *The Moon and a Star*. At the time she wrote this article she was teaching classes for children in creative writing at the Dallas Public Library. In these she had an opportunity to observe children's reactions to poetry and to find out how successful certain poems and certain types of poetry are in developing a feeling for this literary form. She is now continuing her teaching in the enrichment program of the Beverly Hills (California) Unified School District.

PATRICK J. GROFF, professor of education at San Diego State College, has written for many educational journals. Another article of his, entitled "The Transformation of a Poet: John Ciardi," appeared in *The Horn Book* for April, 1964. Here he said:

> Seldom, if ever, have students of children's poetry had, first, a complete description by a practicing critic of what a poem should be, followed by several books of his children's poetry. In the same year Ciardi's first volume of poems for children appeared he published *How Does a Poem Mean?* With this coincidence there became possible a unique opportunity: to see if a poet's work is what he says it should be.

So Dr. Groff goes on to "examine a poet's assumptions about poetry through an observation of his practices."

DOROTHY E. AMES teaches primary grades in a rural district of Maine. Before marriage she worked for a time with the Dance Theatre in Washington, D. C., as a verse narrator for performances for children. Asked if she thought the interest in poetry which she had aroused in a second grade class had carried on into the next grade, she wrote:

> As far as the particular group of children involved in my description is concerned, I'm fairly sure that their further experiences with poetry were only those incidental to occasional reading lessons which happened to contain verse. It would be easy to leave the subject there, with a "tut, tut, too bad that the next teacher was not interested." It's not so simple, however. . . . The reason is time and subject matter scheduling. What "Sputnik" did to the school day is a very real change. For better or worse the future will have to tell. I only know that I am attempting to help the youngsters gain some sort of understanding of a science textbook which expects them to digest the molecular theory of matter when many of them can't yet write a simple declarative sentence.

FANTASY, YESTERDAY AND TODAY

This section opens with Jane Douglass's appreciation of George MacDonald, for a hundred years have not brought any lessening of the significance of his writings or any diminishing of his stature as a religious thinker. In fact his teaching may be better understood today than it was in his own day. Though we are here concerned with his fairy tales, these reflect the depth of his experience in many fields — his ministry, his love of friends and family, his knowledge and appreciation of literature, and his concern with the growth of the human spirit. JANE DOUGLASS is a free-lance writer with a special interest in Victorian children's books. She wrote another article for *The Horn Book* for December, 1960, entitled "The Gentle Gift: An Appreciation of Arthur Hughes." Just as Tenniel is forever associated with Lewis Carroll, so Arthur Hughes is thought to be the perfect illustrator for the stories of George MacDonald.

In "Daily Magic," by EDWARD EAGER, we turn to another type of fairy tale, namely, stories of magic, the field in which E. Nesbit reigns supreme. She does not create another world in which wondrous things happen; rather, she brings magic into the everyday world. Her children are inventive, and by their own invention they stumble into magic. Mr. Eager himself has written in a similar vein. His *Half Magic* features a mysterious coin which gives the children all kinds of fun, as a ring does in E. Nesbit's *The Enchanted Castle*. Her magic has a fascination all its own, especially when controlled by such individual creatures as the Phoenix, the Psammead, and the Mouldiwarp. But it is the children of the stories who captivate. They are at their most original and enterprising in *The Treasure Seekers* and *The Wouldbegoods* where the five Bastable children maintain a high standard of excitement and suspense, and delight the reader with their conversation, their unpredictable reactions, and their oh-so-innocent deviltry. Other books by E. Nesbit are *The Five Children and It, The New Treasure Seekers, The Phoenix and the Carpet,* and *The Story of the Amulet.*

It was HELEN DEAN FISH, children's editor for Frederick Stokes & Company, who recognized the appeal of Dr. Dolittle when he came knocking at her door. Here was a book of originality and humor in spite of the fact that it had been dreamed up in the trenches of World War I. It is doubtful whether Hugh Lofting would ever have supposed that his good doctor would appear on a movie screen some forty-five years later, or that he would be condemned in later years for his African characters, King Koko and Prince Bumpo.

Mr. Lofting said on a visit to Boston at the time *The Story of Dr. Dolittle* was published, "In my years in West Africa I saw many things the white man had taken away from the negro but not comparable things he had given in return. One great gift the negro possesses, the white man does not have to give — a capacity for joy."

LILLIAN H. SMITH was for many years head of children's work in the Toronto Public Library and is the author of a book on children's reading, *The Unreluctant Years*. She writes of fantasy:

> There are factors other than imagination which determine the enduring place in literature of any book of fantasy, such as the writer's experience of life and his power of language, among others. But since he has chosen to write a book of fantasy, the degree of creative imagination he possesses must be our first concern. Creative imagination is more than mere invention. It is that power which creates, out of abstractions, life. It goes to the heart of the unseen, and puts that which is so mysteriously hidden from ordinary mortals into the clear light of their understanding, or at least of their partial understanding.

George MacDonald and C. S. Lewis had this creative imagination, and their stories have a depth of spiritual meaning to which children respond.

JAMES E. HIGGINS, while writing his doctoral thesis, *Five Authors of Mystical Fancy for Children*, corresponded with C. S. Lewis, one of the authors he discussed in his dissertation. Now assistant professor of education at the State University of New York at Stony Brook, he was previously an English teacher and school librarian.

The article on Paul Fenimore Cooper's *Tal* places it somewhere between folklore and fantasy. DR. LOUIS C. JONES is a well-known American folklorist. Mr. Cooper published in 1964 another book, *Dindle*, which is similar in conception to *Tal*. "The typical fairy-tale conflict between evil and good is muted to a struggle between scorn and compassion. The ending, therefore, is not triumphant, but it is victorious."* *Tal* has been reprinted since Dr. Jones wrote of it, and is published by Stephen Daye. In Marcia Dalphin's article reprinted in *A Horn Book Sampler*, "I Give You the End of a Golden String," she writes of *Tal*:

> In these fourteen short tales, as well as in the story of the return to Troom, one is conscious all the time of the apparently inexhaustible reserves of fancy and invention upon which this author has to draw. As I read I have over and over again the impulse to exclaim aloud in surprise and delight as the writer's fancy takes some new and unpredictable turn. A charming vein of nonsense runs through it and a homely matter-of-factness.

LLOYD ALEXANDER's mythical Prydain is a land of many kingdoms in which strange beings engage in the struggle between good and evil. *The Book of Three* recounts the adventures of Taran, the young assistant pig-keeper, in his desire to play a hero's part. *The Black Cauldron* and *The Castle of Llyr* carry on Taran's development toward true manhood, as he and his followers overcome the dangers of wicked enchantment.

> The same kind of engagingly fantastic nonsense lightens this story [*The Black Cauldron*] as it did the first one; but the overtones here are more truly heroic. The reader's involvement is intense as the excitement leads up to the climactic meeting of tragedy and triumph. An exalting experience for the fortunate children whose imaginations are ready for great fantasy.*

PEOPLE AND PLACES

Joan H. Bodger's book *How the Heather Looks* is her account of a literary journey which she took with her husband and two children through Great Britain. They visited many places where favorite authors and illustrators had lived and worked. Two excerpts were published in *The Horn Book*, February, 1959 issue; "A Children's Literary Tour of Great Britain" outlined the tour from Mary Poppins' London to the Edinburgh of Robert Louis Stevenson, with Pooh Corner,

Toad Hall, Puddleby-on-the-Marsh, and Hill Top Farm among the places visited in between. The second article, "Caldecott Country", appeared in *The Horn Book* in June, 1961. In Whitchurch, near Liverpool, the Bodgers had a difficult time finding anyone who had ever heard of Randolph Caldecott or knew his *Picture Books*, but the fields and country lanes, the church, the shops, and the old men were the same as those depicted in *The Farmer's Boy*, *The Three Jovial Huntsmen*, and all the other beloved picture books.

The places and people visited in this section will serve to make those of us who have not been fortunate enough to make literary journeys feel that writers are indeed people, that their human qualities and warmth of personality grow from their lack of pretense, and that their environment plays a large part in the development of their genius.

How many Americans have visited Hill Top Farm! ELIZABETH H. STEVENS was most fortunate to have known Beatrix Potter, but there have been countless others who have felt like Tasha Tudor, who wrote in a letter to *The Horn Book* in February, 1959: "The sun was shining when we arrived and walked through Tom Kitten's gate and up the garden path. I'm sure I felt then what the old-time pilgrims felt on visiting a shrine."

HILDA VAN STOCKUM's visit to Patricia Lynch has something of the same delight and enchantment as Patricia Lynch's visit to E. Nesbit ("Remembering E. Nesbit," *Horn Book*, October, 1953): "Between the wars, a few years before her death, I went to see E. Nesbit. I had been rereading her book, *The Magic City*, and when I entered the old house of Well Hall in Kent and saw her standing there I felt as if the gates of that city had opened before me."

Patricia Lynch's stories of Ireland's old, old days are found in *The Turfcutter's Donkey*, *The Donkey Goes Visiting*, *The King of the Tinkers*, *The Turfcutter's Donkey Kicks Up His Heels*, and *The Grey Goose of Kilnevin*.

Other people have written of their visits to Walter de la Mare and Eleanor Farjeon. Anne Carroll Moore wrote in "The

Three Owls' Notebook" in the special issue of *The Horn Book* for Walter de la Mare from which PAMELA BIANCO's article was taken:

> It was on a lovely Sunday in June 1921 — close to Midsummer Eve — that I met Walter de la Mare for the first time at his own home in England, but I recall as vividly as if it had happened yesterday how he looked as he came to the door of his little house in Anerley and the warmth of his welcome.

Ruth Hill Viguers in an editorial, "A Continuing Radiance," writes about her visit to Eleanor Farjeon:

> Not long ago, I too saw her in her cottage in Hampstead. After the visit, as I walked down the cobblestone lane toward the underground, I wondered what it was about the woman I had just seen that caused my extraordinary glow of happiness. It was, of course, the timelessness and endlessness — the extending outward of her thinking, imagining, and love for people that gave her the radiance to make anyone in her company enjoy life on her terms. The sun within her warmed and illumined those about her. Its warmth and light fill her stories, her poems, her essays — none of them comes to an end. The songs keep sounding in the listener's ear, the meanings lead to new meanings in the reader's mind, and the stories go on and on in the imagination. In her "flashing awareness of beauty," others see beauty; in her love of life, others know life's value.

ERNEST H. SHEPARD's account of his visit to Kenneth Grahame and of his afternoon with his sketchbook along the banks of Ratty's river is the second preface of the Willow Leaf edition of *The Wind in the Willows*, copyrighted 1954 by Charles Scribner's Sons, and is reprinted here with their permission.

ARTHUR S. GREGOR's visit to Charles Darwin country was the forerunner of his biography *Charles Darwin*, which has a basis of thorough study and most of all an infectious enthusiasm. He has drawn an unforgettable picture of Charles Darwin from the schoolboy, outwardly "dull and apathetic," to the man whose theories changed scientific thinking for all time. The carefully planned book includes excerpts from Darwin's writings and a Darwin calendar records intimate details and shows Darwin's humor and lack of pretense:

1831, December 27: sails on H.M.S. *Beagle* ("I had run a very serious risk of being rejected because of the shape of my nose.")

In MARGERY EVERNDEN's account of her visit to Mårbacka we find the same kind of reverence for place that Tasha Tudor felt at Hill Top Farm. Mrs. Evernden has written several books for children. Her *Secret of the Porcelain Fish* and *Runaway Apprentice* are stories of Old China. The first is about a young boy apprenticed to a porcelain maker; the latter is about adventures with itinerant shadow players. Both are well told and include fine atmosphere and characterization.

In connection with MARGARET REARDON's story of "Alice" it is interesting to call attention to Greta Lagro Potter's article in *The Horn Book* for December, 1965, *Millions for Wonderland*. It tells about many editions of "Alice," the sale of the original manuscript, and its final resting place in the British Museum.

FAMILY READING AND STORYTELLING

We hope that some of the children who were listeners when these articles were written are now continuing a sharing of stories with their own children and that the mothers and fathers who may now be grandparents are still functioning as "readers aloud." Booklists have been omitted in connection with the articles, but suggestive lists for home reading may be obtained from *The Horn Book*.

EDITH F. HUNTER has written several books: *The Family Finds Out; The Questioning Child and Religion; Child of the Silent Night*, and *The Story of Laura Bridgman*.
Another interesting article by Mrs. Hunter is in *The Horn Book* for June, 1962 — "Why, Walt Disney, Why?" It was written after seeing the Disney television showing of Mary Mapes Dodge's *Hans Brinker*, which she had watched with her eight-year-old William after they had read the book together. The changes made in the story dismayed them:

William went to school on Monday. All the TV addicts had tucked *Hans Brinker* under their belts along with the rest of their steady diet. They had never read the book and for all they know there is no need to now.

"How did they like it?" I asked William at supper.

"Great!" said William in utter disgust, "Just great!" And then he looked me in the eye and said, "Why did Walt Disney do it? Why?"

"Walt Disney Accused", an interview with Frances Clarke Sayers which appeared in *The Horn Book* for December, 1965, is in vigorous agreement with William.

CALVIN T. RYAN was head of the English Department at Nebraska State Teachers College and taught children's literature there for many years. He is now retired.

The "Three Boys" undoubtedly were pleased with the stories by their mother, ELLEN WILSON, and Nan Hayden Agle. In these easy-to-read books they and their dog, John Paul Jones, have amusing and exciting adventures. *Three Boys and a Lighthouse, Three Boys and the Remarkable Cow, Three Boys and a Tugboat* begin the series.

Mrs. Wilson has written three biographies of the childhood of famous Americans. The most recent is *Robert Frost: Boy with Promises to Keep*. She teaches a course in the history of children's literature at Indiana University, and in 1966 she conducted the workshop in writing-for-children at the Rocky Mountain Writers' Conference in Boulder, Colorado.

Among the books of poems for children by WILLIAM JAY SMITH are *Typewriter Town, Laughing Time, Ho for a Hat,* and *Mr. Smith & Other Nonsense*.

The August, 1959 *Horn Book* contains his article "So They Smashed That Old Man . . ., A Note on Edward Lear." Mr. Smith has also written poetry for adults. During 1968-69 he is Consultant in Poetry at the Library of Congress.

PEGGY SULLIVAN reminds us that if a president in the White House found time to read with his children it should not be too difficult for others of us to do the same. She herself had enjoyed as a child hearing her mother read Earl Hooker's *The White House Gang*. *Theodore Roosevelt's Letters to his Children* and *Letters to Kermit from Theodore Roosevelt, 1902-1908*, edited by Will Irwin give us more about Theodore Roosevelt's "sharing" with his children.

CLAUDIA LEWIS teaches children's literature, creative writing, and language arts at Bank Street College of Education in New York City. She has also conducted training sessions for Head Start programs in New York, Mississippi, Louisiana, and West Virginia. She has written for adults and for children. *When I Go to the Moon*, illustrated by Leonard Weisgard, is a poetry-picture book. More recently she published *Poems of Earth and Space*.

HILDA VAN STOCKUM is an author and an illustrator, a mother and a grandmother. She has lived in Holland and Ireland as well as in the United States and Canada. She writes realistically and fancifully using varied backgrounds and appealing to a wide age range. The family life in her books is rich in humor and understanding. There is lightheartedness and there is sadness. Favorites are *A Day on Skates*, *The Cottage at Bantry Bay*, and *Canadian Summer*. *The Winged Watchman* is a fine story of Holland during the German occupation. "There is no dwelling on the inhumanities of the times but there is no overlooking them either. The story has tragedy but it also has humor. The author's genius for capturing the ways of people of all ages in small incidents or bits of conversation helps to make this a living experience which readers are not likely to forget."

The importance of the family reading section is that these articles show how the sharing of books and stories brings the family together. The relationship of the parent to the children takes on a strength that comes from shared reading experiences: weeping together over Becky and Tom lost in the cave; laughing together "over the things we saw on Mulberry Street; over the amazing Doughnut Machine in *Homer Price*; over the making of 'Stone Soup'; and the antics of Uncle Benny in *Ginger Pye*"; dramatizing *Make Way for Ducklings* in which both child and parent participate; and discussing the moral problems raised by events in particular books.

Perhaps there are not many born storytellers in the average family today. In America storytelling has become a professional art. We no longer have the grandmother as a permanent member of the household to whom children turn to hear original stories of "When I was a little girl . . ." or the nurse who brought with her from Ireland the natural gift of storytelling — the spontaneous recounting of personal experience or the passing on by word of mouth stories of a national culture.